THE LAST FURLOUGH

THE LETTERS OF PAUL CLAUDIUS 1943-1944

Jack R. Meister & Erika Wolfe

Wasteland Press
Shelbyville, KY USA
www.wastelandpress.net

The Last Furlough:
The Letters of Paul Claudius 1943-1944
by Jack R. Meister & Erika Wolfe

First Printing—April 2009
ISBN: 978-1-60047-298-5
Front cover photograph by H. Julia Claudius

Printed in the U.S.A.

PROLOGUE FROM A GHOST

My name is Paul Claudius. I was a soldier in the Wehrmacht. I died on the Russian front in 1944. Like so many other soldiers in so many other wars, I did not get to go home. They buried my remains very hastily near a little town in the Ukraine. The Wehrmacht marked the row and gave the grave a number. After our army's retreat, the little cemetery was ravaged by the war and now exists as a memorial sight, set up by funds from the German Volksbund, an organization dedicated to locating the graves of fallen soldiers.

At the time of my death I had a wife and three children. I had a get-away spot called Distelhof with a little cabin I built myself. We spent as much of our free time there as we could, relaxing and working in our garden. I missed my wife and children every second of my service. War is the abomination of humanity. It is the burglar of life, stealing our youth, tearing families apart, exposing the nasty, animalistic side of humanity. Sigmund Freud once said that nothing does more to bring out the beast in us than war. I've never felt that way. Like so many of my young companions, I just wanted the war to be over so I could go home. I prayed that God would protect our Reich and my family.

To you I leave my letters, a testament to my time and my people. I wrote my dear wife over 170 letters. The heartache, the coming home, the leaving, those things so familiar to soldiers, soldiers' wives and families, are all there. I have left them for you that you might gain a better understanding of me and my beloved Germany. These letters, kept by my wife, were handed down to my sweet little daughter, Erika. She lives in America now. We fought against America, but had no hard feelings against that country. That's an ironic thing war does! It makes enemies of

1

friends and friends of enemies. Amazing though it seems, this organized killing has been with the human race forever. The blood of millions and millions has done nothing to stop it. It marches through the history of humanity.

When all the history books have been written, when all the pundits have spoken, when my war has been sifted and analyzed and scholars have tried to unravel the threads of my time and my people, to them my letters will remain a truth, a truth left for you.

Erika

The bones of my father
You bring them to me
one by one.

I have ten
There are 168 more to come

Will the whole of them
take on an earthly form?
a human flesh?
Will there be a face?

I tremble

and am laid bare
at the thought
of staring into his eyes
and finding the wellspring
of my own imperfect nature
revealed in his gaze.

CHAPTER ONE

My Family

I was born, Erika Hertha Johanna Claudius, on Easter Sunday, April 12, 1936. At a little more than six pounds, I was small but not frail and birthed by a mother who I don't think ever weighed more than one hundred pounds until she was in her late 40's. Hertha Julia Gabriele de Veer had married my father, Paul Matthias Claudius, the great, great grandson of the beloved German folk poet and journalist, Matthias Claudius,[1] just a little more than a year earlier, at the age of twenty three. Her father, Gerhard Friedrich Wilhelm, was an engineer, as was her father-in-law, Ludwig Peter Wilhelm Martin, and it was my father's profession as well. Gerhard was a doting father to his only child, born to his wife Auguste Karoline Aloyisa, in the maturity of their quiet, sensible and orderly German life together. My grandfather was thirty-two at the time of my mother's birth; my grandmother was ten years older. In the blush of her own youth, Auguste Karoline had briefly been married to a young, handsome Prussian Cavalry officer who had not survived a military equestrian misadventure.

---

[1] Matthias Claudius – Born August 15, 1740 in Reinfeld Holstein, died January 21, 1815. As a German folk poet and editor of the important journal *Der Wandsbecker Bote (1771-1775)*, his publication was popular not only with the common people, for whose enlightenment it was designed, but also with the most important literary men of the time. Claudius sought to preserve a natural and Christian atmosphere in literature. His poems have a naïve, childlike, devout Christian quality. Among contributors to his journal: Herder, Klopstock and Lessing.

Gerhard was an earnest and exceedingly sensible man, and did not outwardly bless or welcome Hertha Julia Gabriele's marriage to the young upstart engineer, who was simply not an equally yoked life partner for his beautiful, traveled and well-educated daughter. But as stern as he was, the warmth of his love for this brave, gifted and very intelligent young woman never failed to reach out to her in generosity and true fatherly devotion.

My mother attended the Theological Adventist University in Freidensau, Germany, for her first two years of college. Although girls were generally not given to need schooling beyond high school, her sincerely devoted Evangelical father strongly felt, as Luther did, that an education sets a person free from the hard toil of the masses and the ideological doctrines of the Catholic Church. My grandmother did not disagree but insisted that my mother's education be Seventh Day Adventist oriented, as that was her personal religious belief. My mother therefore spent the last two years of her college education studying music and languages at Collonges sous Saleve, a Seventh Day Adventist University located close to the border of Switzerland in the French Alps. Her studies centered around voice and piano, and she became fluent in English and French.

The years between World War I and II were hard times for the young Paul Claudius family. Grandparents did not live close by, and train travel was an expensive luxury. Visits with Oma and Opa were rare occasions. There was a strange restlessness in my father. I don't think he was ever free of it. For awhile he had his own electrical engineering business. It had its successes, but the dreams that were often much larger than life also led to potholes of failure that decidedly strained a marriage that had begun to deeply test my mother's patience and understanding for the man she deeply loved for every day of her life.

After the birth of my brother, Matthias Paul Claudius, in 1938, things picked up for the young couple. Their move from Königsberg to Erfurt, the garden city of Germany, along with family connections, led to employment for my father with the Siemens Schukerwerke.[2] This wonderful turn of events made for

---

[2] Siemens Schukerwerke – Founded by Werner von Siemens in the early 1870's with his first invention of the Pointer Telegraph for which he received a patent,

shared happiness for our daily lives together as a growing family. We moved into a good-sized, two-bedroom, six-unit apartment complex in Hochheim, a very nice suburb of Erfurt. Employment at Siemens, a company destined to become one of the world's largest conglomerate companies, seemed to suit him. Life, for the most part, was comfortable and tranquil. In October of 1941, my youngest brother, Detlef Gerhard, was born, and my family of siblings was complete.

On July 27 of 1943, much to the consternation of my mother, his family, and in-laws, Paul Matthias Claudius enlisted in the German army. Mother Claudius and her husband, Ludwig Peter Wilhelm Martin Claudius, had already sacrificed their oldest and only other child, Otto Gerhard, a Dresden architect. He was one year older than my father. My father's employment as an engineer would have spared him from being drafted, and my mother must surely have done everything in her power to dissuade him from going off to war. The restless, adventure-seeking vagabond in his soul had once again emerged. The song of patriotism in a war-torn Germany and his love of his homeland must have cried out to him deep within the veins of his dissolving youth.

My Mother and the Letters

Hertha Julia Gabriele died of heart failure on the second day of 1994. She would have celebrated her eighty-fourth birthday on July second of that year. She had spent the last two years of her life in the gentle confusion of dementia. The always reserved, stern, overly judgmental and deeply German woman had become sweetly loving, childlike, funny, affectionate and easy to love. My regret at not having made enough of a personal effort to get to really know her much better than I did, is enormous. I was there for her, the countless times she really needed my help, but all too rarely just to listen, talk and share time together. There was an efficiency of emotion between us that haunts me as I now, in my

---

the Siemens Company laid the first transatlantic cable from Ireland to America. The company developed the first electric train, the world's first electric car, developed the X-Ray machine, contributed to the development of television, and built the world's first pacemaker.

own old age, try to reach beyond the pieces of my own personal family for a larger and more composite photograph of my greater ancestral history.

As executer of my mother's earthly possessions, I received a blackish gray box that I knew existed but about which we had never talked. It now became part of my legacy. I knew that it was full of her most personal belongings, old family photos, documents, postcards, letters and mementos from her youth and days in college. She had saved and collected all of them during her days in Germany, packed, stored and given them enough priority to bring them with her from East Germany to be smuggled, along with her children, into West Germany. And from there they made it to the United States of America. A sacred legacy, indeed, most every document had been carefully folded or neatly arranged in a bundle, out of reach or comprehension for me. And as I grew older there was a formidable language barrier, similar to the one I faced when I arrived in America, knowing only German. I had seen and looked at the small, black and white stacks of family photographs, but like pieces in some old and quaint puzzle, I was only vaguely familiar with how their faces fit into my family history. She had made me aware of a small, black leather-bound book of farewell poems, notes and writings at the time of her commencement form Collonges sous Saleve. Even in not being able to decipher most of the carefully penned entries, I marveled at the beautiful small ink sketches and small color drawings that graced so many of the pages, like some old and lost form of art. As if witness to a really good, old-world kind of education, some of the entries were written in English, more of them in German, and the majority in the French language.

There were also legal papers and documents pertaining to the Distelhof [3] property and German bank accounts, accounts by now

---

[3] "Distelhof" – "Estate of Thistles" – in the town of Bishleben, Stedten am Kirchberg, Herman Goering Strasse 13/14. Kreis Erfurt. Property size 1009 Q.M. Street frontage -35-40 meters. My parents bought this piece of property in 1941 for 3,500 reichsmarks, money that my mother inherited after the death of her father in 1940,and her mother, in 1941. My father built the one room wood cabin or "Wohnlaube" in 1942. The main living space was separated from the kitchen and small bathroom space by a single interior wall of three built-in bunk beds.

too old to warrant any serious inspection or consideration. And then there was the faded, dark, bluish-gray manila folder in which my mother had tenderly stacked and clipped the letters that my soldier father had sent her in the almost twelve months that he had been away from her. Most everything in the grayish black, lidded box was interesting and dismissible with regret, everything but the letters, all one hundred seventy plus of them. Each time I handled them they burned in my hands and gnawed at my mind like a fever that I knew would never go away.

They consisted of faded writing papers of all sorts, mostly written in ink and reaching into every inch of space of the material. Here was my father's handwriting, penned in what looked like a strange and unfamiliar combination of old and new German script. I could decipher and painstakingly make out small groupings of words and phrases, but never anything that could ever, in any way, be even the beginning of one small revelation. Was it too private for me to know or too personal for me to unlock? However, hadn't my mother treasured and saved them just so they might someday be brought back to reveal not only the deeply romantic and loving Paulus who had written them, but also the beautiful, brave, hardworking woman for whom he had written them?

I found his War-pass book, some military photos, family birth and death certificates and copy printouts of both of my parents' genealogy. The whole of it mattered! And each year of neglect made it a greater concern for discovery. In the winter of 2004, I had carefully taken the precious folder apart and, assuming as well as I could in terms of a date that this was the last letter received, I slipped each page of writing into a plastic protector sleeve and clipped all of it into a four inch binder. It was a start, but I had no definite plan for further action. In the spring of that same year, I was planning a trip to visit my son and his family in California, and thoughts of dropping in on my youngest sibling brother, Detlef, who lives in the southern part of that state, crossed my mind. The computer had always been second nature to him. Couldn't he, couldn't we e-mail resources and find someone, pay someone here, or in Germany, to decipher and translate these letters for us? He hadn't shown any interest in any of these things in the past, so the idea didn't burn all that brightly, but then, I was the one willing to pay to give it a try. So I got four Xerox copy letters ready to take with me for the project.

I had them in my car during downtown Keokuk[4] errands before my trip and completely on the impulse of chance, stopped at Meister Music Store on Main Street. Word had it that the owner, Jack Meister, could read and write German. It was Saturday morning, and the store was somewhat busy. I waited for my turn with papers in hand. I then explained my mission, holding the full measure of my heart in the tears that uncontrollably fell into my hands upon his direct and simple words, "Sure, I can read this."

I believe in miracles, but this one was extraordinary in every sense of the word. Keokuk, this very small town and this man, a music store owner and repair technician, born and raised here, is more German than any person that I have ever known. German is in his heart and in his soul. He asked for no pay, no remuneration. He painstakingly read studied, deciphered and carefully translated every word of each letter to give them to me, one by one, over a period of twenty-five months. Not wanting to edit or interpret any of the writings, he translated the sentence structure just as it was penned by my father's hand.

One by one, much as my mother might have, I awaited each precious letter and, as my father had, I often carried the cherished communication around with me, waiting for just the right piece of space and quiet in my day to unwrap cargo of such deep meaning and profound personal fulfillment. One by one, I experienced the letters and entered them on the working memory of my computer. Nothing was left out, changed or rearranged other than to bring the sentence structure into better conformity with that of the English language here and there. Finally, everything received an editing in book form with a prologue, historical perspectives and postscripts by Herr Meister.

The first language I learned on this earth was German. Through the research of my father's life and letters, and

---

[4] Keokuk – Small town of some 10,000 – located at the very southeastern tip of the state of Iowa, on the Mississippi River. Famous author Sam Clemens (Mark Twain) and his brothers worked on the first Keokuk City Directory in 1856. Clemens, began his career as a professional writer, receiving pay for articles to the Keokuk Post.

conversational use of German with Herr Meister, much of my lost native language has returned to me.

Between the Lines

You toss me pieces of air and
on tiptoes, I stretch
to catch your secret thoughts.

My basket is empty –
but I am bathed in points of light.

Not from sudden bursts
of memory or recollection,
but from the seamless silence of
somehow knowing

that I was there with you.

CHAPTER TWO

The Letters of Paul Claudius

Letter no. 1[5]
July 29, 1943

My Dear Little Wife, Dear Parents and Children,

Two days of being a soldier lie behind me, and the only thing that I can say is that I am the only college educated guy in the entire outfit and so, because of my training, I have become known to everyone here as, Herr Engineer, a title I won't reject. My sergeant major is a great guy and wants to learn more about my profession. So far I have been lucky, but things are not exactly going as we had thought or hoped. Don't send any more mail to me here. It doesn't get to your Pioneer[6] Claudius. We are on the

---

[5] The first letter was written and sent to Erika's mother and grandparents in Dresden. Her father's departure to the military front was by troop train. The entire family, Erika, her two brothers and mother accompanied him from Erfurt to see him off. After his departure Erika's mother and brothers returned to Erfurt, but Erika stayed behind for a visit with her grandparents in Dresden. Her father was thirty-one years old at the time of his enlistment. Erika was seven. Brother Matthias was five and little brother, Detlef was just a year and a half old.

[6] German Pioneer troops were infantry troops with specialized training. They were often engineer-type troops. Because they were familiar with building construction, they also knew where to place explosives in the demolition of edifices. They were smart and well-trained. As an engineer, Paul Claudius was well-suited to gain an advanced position in the German army.

move and being outfitted for winter. I am writing to you, here, from my bed. I miss you.

Paul

Letter no. 2
July 30, 1943[7]

To my lovely little Wife . . . . To Grandma and Grandpa in Dresden,

Finished lunch a little early today and, as always, thought of home – my beautiful home. I want to give you a short report about what has been going on here in the last three days. A lot of marching around. We did two kilometers on Wednesday and the day after that a one-and-three-quarter kilometer march with full packs. After that we waited around in the barracks and slept on the bare ground with our weapons. The next day we were outfitted from head to toe: 2 raingear, 1 fatigue, 1 winter coat, 1 satchel, 1 rifle, a gas mask and a cartridge belt. Everything must pass inspection at all times, and if it does not, an entire morning must be sacrificed. All clothing and equipment must be kept in top shape.

I went to the barber yesterday. My hair is nearly all cut off. Currently there are 10[8] men in our ranks, older fellows, including farmers, all ranging in age between 30 and 40 years. I am the youngest and yet have come up from the rear to become the senior officer in the barracks. The Engineer seems to have become more useful than when he first got here. Because of my training, I seem to be noticed more and more. The Sergeant talks of an official promotion,[9] but most likely, nothing will come of it, since we expect to be shipped out tomorrow or the day after that.

The food is good, but not as good as the wonderful things of home – home, . . a peaceful, beautiful remembrance of a world lost to me for now. I have some data to record and so must close for

---

[7] In his early letter, Paul Claudius does not disclose the location.
[8] There are 10 older men in the unit. Germany was, at this time, beginning to draw on the older male population to fill ranks, having been at war since 1939.
[9] German solders were often promoted "in the field."

today. Many, many heartfelt greetings to the children and a loving kiss to my dear wife and to all of you.

Paulus

Letter no. 3
August 1, 1943

My Love in Dresden,
My Little Wife and Children—

It is Sunday, and the world is decorated as if with jewels. The sun shines brightly from the sky, but here, in the barracks, everyone is fed up and full of complaints. We were strafed[10] and I don't mind telling you that the sweat rolled down my body in streams. The day after tomorrow we will move on and travel for the next eight days. You can expect more mail once we get settled again. So far, the food in the barracks is good, but not as good as Mom's. I have sewn on buttons, beat rugs and cleaned the barracks—by now all of that is pretty much old hat. The esteemed Engineer got another commendation today. This time it was for being intelligent and having everything in good order.

Love,
Paulus

Letter no. 4
August 4, 1943

My Dear Little, Sweet Hertha!—

The wheels have been rolling for hours. Unimaginable hardships lie behind me and worse are sure to come. We travel 20 kilometers a day and ride in a wagon. I have thought of you so often; you and the children are my solace. I love you with an

---

[10] strafed – An attack on ground position troops and installations with machine gun fire by low-flying aircraft. Fighters based in England ran strafing sorties on German troops as the war progressed.

14

unending love and will endure anything to be able to see you again. It will be a long haul before we will be together again. Tears come when I realize how devoted I am to you, and I thank the dear Lord for giving me you and the children.

Air attacks against us today. I must go.

Love and kisses,

Paulus

Letter no. 5

August 5, 1943

My One and Only Love, the Light of my Life,

Little Goldchen[11]

Dear Wife and Love,

The vehicle grinds on, putting me farther from my Hertha, farther away from the happy life. I wonder when I will be able to return home. Yesterday evening I was sick, had a fever and swollen tonsils. I spent a rough night, but it is behind me. Hopefully I will be able to shake it all off by tomorrow. I get teary when I think about how long I have already been away from you. Early tomorrow morning we should roll on to our destination. No one in our company seems to know exactly how far that is. Your letters are food for my soul and my body. When I think about what I must contend with here, it is crazy madness.

I kiss you all with the fervent wish that all this murdering will find an end.

Love to all,

Paulus

---

[11] Goldchen – little golden one, little gold piece, something like English "Goldie."

Letter no. 6
August 6, 1943

My Dear Sweet Hertha,

The very, very first bit of rest while my glasses are being repaired. I am sure that you often wonder exactly where we are. I cannot give you the exact location, but I am allowed to pass the general area on to you. We are in the Loire Valley, on the southern tip of Treu. As I write, it is 40 degrees Celsius. The city that is nearest to us has five thousand inhabitants. How so often I have though about your stories of France during our travels in this country. Our trip has taken us through Paris, but unfortunately, not through any of the places familiar to you.

The population appears hostile, and if we were not carrying weapons, any one of us would not be alive for very long. Because of their dislike of us, the people of the Alsace region, as well as other locals, immediately began to spy on us. France is exactly as you described it, but you are better with the words. In all likelihood I will get a Christmas furlough, and the thought of that manages to get me through all the misery of being a German foot soldier.

From six o'clock in the morning until twelve noon, yesterday, we had nothing at all to eat. With the officers being too busy with roll call, we were left to unload wagons—dumb that they never caught on that their help was needed. I really miss your abilities in being able to speak the French language. Heaven knows that I have no skills there. The Loire flows "slow and wide" before me, and from what I can tell, seems to be un-navigable.

In the short time that I have been here, I have come to see that the Frenchman lives a splendid life. The German, on the other hand, is a hard worker. To the left of us lie houses with flattened dikes. The houses all have shaded windows and other various ways of regulating the sun. Six Frenchmen are loading two trucks that are standing next to me. They laugh and engage in lively conversation. They seem to be well-fed and have enough wine to drink.

Oh, if only you could come and be with me –
but not here,
and not right at this moment –
I'm too dirty.

Letter no. 7
No date

We are in a rural French city with a population of some five thousand people. The Frenchmen, and especially the French women, live a cozy life; it is the damned German dummy who works all of the time. I will relate more of my impressions to you in greater detail later. Our lodgings are in the school of the city. Our quarters lie on the ground level. The doors and windows don't close well, and everything is pretty dilapidated. Life seems bearable enough for the time being. There is plenty of fruit for sale, but it is expensive and not as yet ripe for the eating. I have, however, already eaten several pounds of it. The French won't eat this fruit, but the hungry Germans devour it.

My sergeant and the other noncoms have praised me for being a thinker, for being quick on my feet. I stand out among the others for that and have had several arguments about technical matters and world politics. The spirited confrontations, however, always end up in my favor. One of my superiors told me today that he could not compete with my intelligence and that, in those matters,[12] I stood head and shoulders above him.

Our trip to France was in a cattle railroad car. Like the first cavemen, we have learned to live on bread, water and wine with some soup and coffee thrown in now and then. We sleep on boards covered with fresh straw and have no bed coverings. The question of a toilette was a catastrophe, as was just about everything else. After three nights of traveling like this, we arrived at our designated location. Evacuation of the railroad cars was our first order of business. The older officers worked us like galley slaves, until we were completely exhausted and extremely hungry.

---

[12] "those matters" here refers to matters concerning science and politics. An engineer would have a very good knowledge of scientific matters.

The crowning point to a very tough day came when we were packed into a very overcrowded truck and transported yet another twenty kilometers.

On nights like these I put my hands together in prayer, clasp your picture in my hands and cover it with kisses. Only this gives me that strength to weather life's hardships. I can write for a short while only. Hopefully the Creator will permit me to return to my home and our love, since, for now all has been thrown into this murderous struggle. We have been loading and unloading the equipment for our Pioneer Company for days. This sort of activity and work is more suited to furniture movers and haulers – but I pitch in until the very end. Two days before our arrival in France, I came down with a fever and swollen tonsils. My longing for home, for you and for the children, was endless. I have managed to overcome this. Like an animal, I stayed in the darkness of the train car with the sliding doors just slightly open. My eye glasses, which were sitting on my nose, cracked in half during an air attack. Conceivably you can picture the misery of this sort of travel in your mind and remember how beautiful it once was, in times now past.

My dear, I must close prematurely because the outgoing mail is being collected. I will immediately begin another letter so I can give you more of an orientation. You, my Goldchen, pray to the Creator that my family will not be destroyed and that this bloodletting will come to a quick end. I want to see my children again. Regrettably, there are not enough words to describe my longing and love for you, my Goldchen. I look into the heavens at night, see the stars overhead and know that you are with me, just as it was on our last night together at the hotel in Dresden.

Paulus

Letter no. 8
France, August 8, 1943

My Dear, Little Sweet Hertha,
My Little Soldier's Wife, Dear Eki, Blond Mattheu and Sweet Little Dettos,

Today is Sunday, the second Sunday in my life as a soldier, and I feel so far away from home. Although I have a few shirts and some underwear to wash, I want, first of all, to write to the owner of my life and the love of my heart. Today, I'll fill you in on what has happened up to this point. Remembering my departure from Erfurt, on July28th, will no doubt bring painful memories back for you. After several kilometers, our railroad car was hooked to other cars that were filled with troops from the West German region. In Rudolstadt [13] each soldier took his handbag, and we all marched to the barracks.

We spent our first night sleeping on a bare floor with nothing more than a blanket. A sincerely hearty reception! The next morning we were mustered out, and, after standing around for an hour or so, we were divided into groups and led to our quarters. In the meantime, our military clothing and equipment was being passed out to us. That's when the strain began. A noncom greeted me with Oooh, the engineer!, . . .and so forth. Turns out I am the only educated person, the only intellectual in the entire company of 60 to 100 soldiers, and that news got around fast.

Further orders consisted of cleaning and organizing our rooms. The steps and entrance floor area had to be scrubbed. We were senselessly ordered around in a relentless manner, but as noncoms we never uttered a word of complaint. By the end of our first week in Rudolstadt we had scarcely been given time to eat, wash up, shave, or even catch our breath. They drilled us on the barrack grounds until the sweat poured out of every hole in our heads. But that wasn't all. To top it off, the entire company was called out for a forced march, carrying seventy-five pound packs. The heat made it a murderous test of endurance for everyone. The stinging sweat rolled off the end of my nose. After that, we practiced with our rifles. It was intense to the point that we honestly felt that we were engaged in a battle against our enemy. We were repeatedly instructed and tested. We were supposed to sight in at close range, but my eye glasses were in such poor shape that no matter how I adjusted them, I could not sight in properly.

---

[13] Rudolstadt – The city in Thuringia, Germany, used as a preliminary staging area for the gathering and dispersing of German soldiers to various training assignments and to war fronts.

The company doctor asked me about my posture and unusual way of bending and stooping. He ended giving me a thorough examination, only to tell me that I was an intellectual fellow. By chance, I ran into him again yesterday while I was waiting to have a new pair of glasses made in Orleans. After the fitting and lens grinding we did some quick shopping. That left us very little time to write home to our loved ones.

A man is no more than an object in this time and place.

Letter no. 9
France, August 8, 1943

My Dearest Goldchen, Little Soldier's Wife,

So, I must ask how you have been during the days since our separation. I know that you took at trip. Is Eki still with my folks in Dresden? I always have so much to tell you in my letters that I have somehow neglected to ask about you. Who sleeps next to you in our beautiful little bed? Tell me about home. I don't have a photo of Detti and would be really happy to have one. Did all go well in regard to the insurance? Although things are very expensive in France, I am able to make ends meet with the money I get. One kilogram of fruit costs one reichsmark. One French Frank is equal to five reichsmarks. I haven't yet had any of the French wine. It's too expensive, but even at that, some of the soldiers seem to drink up most of their pay. Hopefully I will be able to save some of mine.

I have a terrible craving for something sweet and sincerely regret having carelessly left that box of marmalade at home. Our rations consist only of army bread, butter and tins of meat when we are marching. Nothing much on taste, but it does manage to fill us up. After a few days, though, we begin to suffer from stomach problems, and the stomachaches result in our not being able to perform up to snuff. How are we to fight an enemy with these concerns?

Because of my broken eyeglasses I will be going to Paris tomorrow. With my lack of abilities with the language, it won't be an easy matter. You will naturally laugh about the whole thing and want to go along. For the poor, untraveled home guy, though, this world-class city is an intimidating place. Because I know that you are interested, I will let you know how it all went.

Have any money matters come up that need my attention? Please do let me know, so I can discuss them with you. There will certainly be a host of concerns that you will now have to face alone. What I would not give to be home with all of you and to be able to sit at my family's hearth. I cannot write more without beginning to cry out loud. How are things going with our daughter? Give her my love.

I close in the hope of soon receiving a letter from you. It is dark, and my thoughts hurry out to you in rushing waves.

All my love,
Paulus

Letter no. 10
France, August 10/11, 1943

My Dear Little Goldchen, My Beloved Protector of Our Three Children!

We'll just have to see whether or not the few moments that I have are enough time to send a few lines out to you. Oh, how long I've already been away from home. To me, it seems like years, and still no mail has reached me – but it might be just a few days away.

Today we were ordered to do a short march through the dirt and mud. The sweat rolled, but all of us were able to keep up with the eighteen-year-olds. The officers see themselves in me. Bombers fly overhead or change directions while I lie in the grass. Rabbits scurry in the dirt as we make our way through the meadow with a quick prayer and a strong sense of gratefulness.

How are things at home? Every evening, while lying in my bed, I climb up the stairs of the Wachsenburgweg.[14] I enter our

---

[14] Wachsenburgweg no. 7 was the address of Paul Claudius's apartment home in Hochheim. Hochheim was at that time an up-and-coming suburb just outside of the city of Erfurt. Erfurt was known as the "Garden City of Germany."

little home, and I count each step until I surprise you, my Love, and then . . . .! Little Detti looks at me in wonder, and, with that, I sadly realize that my abilities at picturing him are somewhat failing.

I went to Paris yesterday. It is a powerful city, and oh, my, how well the French know how to enjoy their life. I won't go into it now – we'll chat about that when we're together again. It is Tuesday once more – 14 evenings with no letters. This business of waiting around for the mail is a frustrating, pace-around thing. My sleeping space partner is a thirty-seven year old. He's a great guy, and we get along quite well. They do go a little easier on the two of us older guys.

Well, my Love, I must close. I am brain sick about you and live every day for the children who currently have no father. Do they ask about me? I'm sure that a letter from home is on the way to this poor fellow.

Many, many heartfelt kisses from your
Pioneer Paulus

Letter no. 11
France, August 12, 1943

Dear Parents in the Fatherland,
Dear Mother and Father,

If you consider Otto's education, you can see good reason for my concern. Otto was still young while here; I am among the oldest. Life of a recruit is very hard, and while never easy for anyone, it is even more difficult for an educated person.

I haven't done anything that would be considered outstanding, but I expect to stay the course. I am in good health, just tired, exhausted, and worn out. My longing for you and for my home is so very strong. The food is good, even if it takes some getting used to. So, any marmalade, cookies, or dumplings that are mailed will be greatly appreciated.

Wachsenburgweg consisted of six, spacious apartment units. Paul Claudius's apartment was located on the third floor of the building.

How are things with you? Is Erika all right?[15] Give little Eki a loving kiss from her Papi. Hope that she is being good. Yes, I really miss my children and wonder what it will be like when I get back home once more.

You can write to me at Field Post Office no. 59345 (Soldier Claudius).

I have received no mail as of yet and eagerly await some sign of life from home. This poor guy is so desperate for attention that he will gladly accept any small token that might come his way. Because of problems with my eyeglasses, I had the chance to be in Paris again, just a few days ago. How splendidly the French live, and how encumbered the Germans are under the yoke of war.

Please write to me. A letter from home would be my greatest fortune. Perhaps something will arrive for me when I go to send off my mail. Otto[16] had become such an enthusiastic soldier and, moreover, as a first lieutenant, a damned high price to pay.

Well, dear parents, do write me soon and let me hear from you.

'til then, a thousand greetings from your son,

Paulus

---

[15] Erika had stayed with her grand parents in Dresden after her father's departure by troop train for the army. Her mother and two brothers had returned to Erfurt.

[16] Otto Gerhard Claudius -- Paul Claudius's brother. He was fifteen months older than Paul. He and his wife, Eva, lived in Dresden, where he was employed as an architect. He was promoted in the field, as was the policy of the German military, and killed in action.

Letter no. 12
France, August 12, 1943

My Heart's Love, My Sweet Goldchen,

Just a few words before the battle begins in a few minutes, just a small chat with you to make everything better. Last night, I was with you at Distelhof.[17] The moon shone brightly above the mountain. The fountain trickled gently, and I could hear the soft sleeping of my three children. We sat in an embrace, outside, on the terrace. I knew that I was about to leave you, and I became afraid, very afraid. You, my Love, how does one make a connection? For me it is from soul to soul.

The troops are on the move again. Our orders call for helmets, sidearm, carbines and grenades. There is always some kind of a commotion, and with that I must bring this little note to a close. How are things at home? I still don't know anything. How are you managing with the money? You, my little Lover, are now also a soldier's wife, and I am just a poor, dismayed and ordinary fellow. Well, a long tender kiss on your sweet lips. Then, after that, all thoughts are hard for me to continue.

Heartfelt greetings to the three,
Your Paulus

---

[17] Distelhof – means Estate of Thistles. It was the name that Paul Claudius and his wife gave to the piece of property that they owned some distance out of town. Family transportation to and from was always by bicycle, with children on back seats and a two-wheel wagon towed behind one of the bikes. Paul had built a small weekend cabin on the piece of land. It consisted of a living room with a modest stone fireplace, a small kitchen area that included an interior wall of built-in bunk bed space for two children.

Letter no. 13
France, August 15, 1943

To Goldchen,
My Darling,

Day and night my longing for you is renewed in my writing. I long to talk to you and talk of furlough. Today is Sunday, the sun laughs in the sky, but the beams do not fall into my yearning heart, where everything hurts with a desire to return to you, my Goldchen, and my children and my home.

I got mail from my folks yesterday and also today. I know that all of you returned to Erfurt on August 6th. I am counting on a letter from you and know about your concerns and need for clarifications over the life insurance. More about that later.

Unfortunately, my free afternoon has been ruined by another trip to Paris, and I will have to spend the night in Orleans. What's a poor, ordinary fellow like me doing in a large cosmopolitan French city? It was there that I clearly came to see how splendidly we could live if we Germans were free to do so.

Things have changed for me here in Rudolstadt.[18] I am no longer in with the older, country farmer guys. I have been promoted to group number 1 and am now expected to keep up with the eighteen and nineteen-year-olds. As second oldest in the group, I have a terrible time trying to keep my old body, step by step, in line with theirs. My poor feet are swollen and covered with blisters from marching in those boots. You cannot imagine the pain. Even my elbows and my knees ache from the up and down, and my leg muscles are strained from the march, march, march! But I am holding up and hanging in there with my head held high at all times, and I know that they are aware of the strain that all this has on me.

It's another story when it comes to my morale. Everyone in the company knows that I am a smart hyena, and all of the soldiers and noncoms come to me for advice in matters on how to get all kinds of things done. During general instructions the company leaders often turn to me on matters requiring complicated concepts.

---

[18] "Rudolstadt" is used here instead of the word "training."

It's "Ahaah, . . . the engineer!" that I get to hear over and over again as they leave the explaining up to me. Our Lieutenant recently called me over and asked me to explain projective resistance. This resulted in an interesting technical discussion of physics, leaving me the undisputed scholar on the subject. These are subject matters with which I am familiar and often asked to explain. Hopefully this kind of knowledge will keep me out of the regular service, but I know that will probably take months.

Since I would really rather not leave this city, I will write to you in more detail from Orleans. My longing for you is boundless, and my only wish is to get a letter from you very soon. I must go. My ride is waiting. This evening, my Goldchen, I will be reunited with you. I kiss you on your sweet mouth and think of Distelhof.

Greetings to the sweet little ones,

Your Paulus

Letter no. 14
France, August 16, 1943

My One and Only Goldchen,

Finally, I got mail!

The train travels through the plains of southern France, and the sun burns incessantly on the French fields of wine and grain. Small towns and villages roll by, and I watch with a painful feeling as the kilometers roll on and on. I don't show it outwardly, but in my heart I think only of you and our three children! The quiet land and peaceful French houses bring out a desire and need for rest and relaxation in me. The reality of the situation looks bad, though. The Tommies went to work with their bombers today, and for a while, bombs fell everywhere. And up ahead, there was a derailment. Our D-Train was delayed for quite some time. I am hungry and thirsty, and the relentless heat drains me. Out of uniform, and in evening wear, life is totally different – like running around the Distelhof half naked. Yes, yes, a man is a man, but to get out of this hell hole I would run all the way back to Erfurt, . . .

just to be back home again. But then I would be AWOL,[19] and that carries a sentence of death.

Now, I want to tell you about Paris. I didn't get to spend all that much time there, and one has to keep a map handy if one doesn't want to get lost in this gigantic city of magnificent wide streets, splendid boulevards, memorials, liquor stores and inviting cafes. The carefree life of the French is visible everywhere. The women are all well-dressed, as are the little children, who no longer have to worry about their fathers being taken away to be shot at. The men stand elegantly by at a distance.

There is a lot that is still for sale and to be bought in Paris, but the prices are shamelessly high. Elastic band material for clothing costs one reichsmark; a pair of silk stockings, 8 marks; a simple, small hand mirror, 3.50; a handkerchief, made from cheap material, 12 marks; a simple outfit is 30 marks, and so on. There are carts with all kinds of junk imaginable, piled high in a Jewish manner. An atmosphere like that takes your breath away, and Jews on every street corner – a strange feeling of discomfort. The 15 reichsmarks that I have on me won't buy much, and I want to save my money. Maybe I could bring you some pretty underwear in your size?

Paris is expensive – an evening meal costs 2.50 RM; a piece of cake, 1 RM; one kilo of fruit, 1 RM. A poor fellow like me can't afford that, but I honestly don't regret it because the French products that are available to the German soldiers are usually defective. The French keep the good stuff for themselves. In our (German) soldier hostels we have a canteen. There goods are inexpensive, and they work. Anyway, that's about the way it is for this, my short report on my impressions of Paris. It is a proud city, and, for a German, high and mighty.

Well, my Dear, I've given you more than enough of German thoroughness and detail and must close. I'm starting to get writers cramp. My frequent letter writing has made the other soldiers think that I have been married only for a short time.

Be well, and I will continue to talk to you in my dreams.

Love to you and the children.

Kisses to you and the children. Paulus.

---

[19] AWOL – Absent without leave.

Letter no. 15
France, August 16, 1943

My Dear Sweet Golchen!

The D train is so packed that I have had to stand up for hours. Still, I write to you because I know that you are worried. As far as Grandpa has told me, the money for the lawyer has been forwarded in order to clear up the matter of life insurance, but he is of the opinion that the payments, of 50 marks, are too high for us to be able to afford. If my pay remains as you have checked it out to be with the military government, then I have no qualms about going ahead with it. If Germany loses the war, then we are all broke. The crux of the issue, for what it's worth, is that you, my Love, and the children are worth more than 20,000 reichmarks.

We have been bombed and are taking cover. The news out of Hamburg is disturbing. Hope that everything is all right with you.

My thoughts are with you, day and night. I remember your story collages about the French. A happy people, who coined the saying . . . "to live like God in France!"[20] This expression hardly applies to us. Meat is scarce, and the fruit is expensive and hard to find. I don't like eggs for lunch; my stomach is just not used to it, and we have to work a lot harder than the French. Writing to you every day is my only escape from this misery. Kiss the little ones for me.

Tears well in my eyes as I write.

When will I see you again?

Your Paulus

---

[20] Translation of the German idiomatice expression equivalent to the English "living the life of Riley."

Letter no. 16
France, August 17, 1943

My Beloved, My Goldchen,

Hooray! Hooray!

The first letter form my Sweetheart, from home, has arrived, and from noon until this evening I have carried it in my pocket to read, over and over again. I have taken a few minutes before our night duties begin to be alone with you and to thank you.

Oh my Dear one, tears fill my eyes when you write to me about home. I am so happy about the success at Distelhof. Our heartaches and hard work were not in vain.

My Love, You, Beloved, I will hold on to this letter from you like a talisman of good fortune. At the same time, I ask for a photo of you and the children. Because of my night duties, I wasn't able to answer all of your loving questions. Should I request a permit? I am in agreement with you regarding the insurance in the amount of 5,000 reichsmarks. At any rate, the amount should be increased after the relationships are clarified.

That Etzel is not as popular as he once was, is not completely new to me. That he has as many enemies as he does, is a surprise. At any rate, I have no desire to wish Mr. E. any bad fortune. If I can find a precious minute, I will write to the Doeges tomorrow. As for you, my dear Goldchen, I want to be sure to answer your letter as thoroughly as I can. And since I cannot do that as lovingly and accurately today as I want to, I will get to the work of that in the next several days to come.

Today was our first day to check out and fire the machine gun carbines. In five shooting sessions, at 100 meters, I had 46 successful target hits. Nevertheless, I really have to work at it. Your Paulus does have to work hard to keep up, but I am certainly far from being the worst.

In relation to the location of our garrison, you are completely correct. I made a mistake in reference to Orleans. We are situated on a beautiful, short expanse of flatland, just a stone's throw to the west. My Love, your letter is a joy in the many dark hours, and I will be strong. You are my happiness, and I thank you. I will write to you as often as I can, my Goldchen. The whistle blows for night duties. You, my Love . . . . kisses for you and the children.

Paulus

(Continuation of Letter 16 at a later time.)

My thoughts often turn to Detti, [21] the neat little blond guy. It's really a sad thing for him not to have his Dad. As you wrote in your last letter, our last little Claudius is a dandy. He looked so much like a small little urchin at the time of my departure, and it all happened so quickly. Tell me about it. He has probably been told that his father is a soldier, but most likely can't understand why I have already been gone for such a long time. Erika, I know, will be very well-behaved at Laubegast,[22] and will always be Grandma's pride and joy. They wrote me a beautiful letter about our oldest. Things will soon get serious in the life of our little guy – but I know that Erika will make it. She has your fortitude and can handle things, and being in the position that I am, I'm especially thankful for that and thank God for the mate who is as beautiful as you.

Unlike you, back at home in the civilized world, we poor country boys, we foot soldiers do not own a radio, and therefore cannot listen to evening concerts. The division is much too macho to care about artistic or cultural matters. I have already said my Amen to the concerns of the life insurance and am strongly in favor of any support that you may finally be able to get.

The hot weather here in France causes me to suffer from nosebleeds. The inside of my nose is covered with scabs, and I have a torn muscle in my left shoulder from the constant up and down of carrying a full backpack. Toward evening, it gets a little better. Write to me and tell me about home. You know how much faster the heart beats for this troubled and worried protector of the Reich when he gets a letter in the noon mail-call. Tomorrow I will

---

[21] Detti – Detlef, the youngest child in the Claudius family of three children. At the time Paul Claudius enlisted in the army he was a little more than a year and a half old. Erika was barely six, and the middle brother, Matthias, was four years of age.

[22] Laubegast – A town just outside of Dresden where Paul Clauidius's parents lived. Erika stayed there for two weeks after her father's departure for the army.

send a few lines to those (friends) in Hamburg. With everything that is happening there now, the poor people in Hamburg are hard-pressed. My hunger for the homeland hearth is strong. Here it is eternal company soup and the eternal army bread with runny butter and horsemeat sausage. Everything tastes better if there is marmalade sent from home to go with the food. Many of my buddies have gotten sick from eating too much of the local fruit.

I am sending you a group photo of my unit buddies. A nice guy stands next to me. He's also the one in the single photo. Write to him if you like. It makes non-intellectuals feel proud to get mail from educated people. Bed fever prevails in our quarters, and I am working the broom.

I am happy to have been able to get something off to you today.

Till tomorrow, I kiss you tenderly.

Last night, during night duty, I saw a shooting star above the Loire.

Letter no. 17
France, August 18, 1943

My Dear Little Goldchen,
Dear sweet Matti and blond Detto.

After a short, hot night and a strenuous day of service duty in 50 degree[23] weather, we finally have some free time.

We are all tired and wiped out. Even at night there is no substantial cooling down. We, the July recruits, have had nothing but bad luck with the weather situation. It takes all of one's strength to get around in our thick cloth uniforms with gas masks, cartridge belts, rifles and other necessities. Since I will only get into more political crap, I won't even say anything about the constant piracy that goes on around here.

Back to your letter – I kept it with me at all times and finally got enough time today to be able to read the entire letter over again. So far, we have had eight days of leave, excluding

---

[23] 50 degrees Celcius – over 100 degrees Fahrenheit!

weekends. The eternal polishing of our weapons in preparation for combat against our enemy makes free time into a time of restlessness. Sunday is party time. So far, I haven't participated, but in order to be friendly with my buddies I will. I want to try some of the wine. There is good drinking wine and then there is just ordinary wine and liquor. I will try to bring some good wine when I get a long leave to come home. I want to get to know this country and write you lengthy accounts of my initial experiences here, so I can discuss them with you later.

Because the French see us as the enemy, we are always armed. With the summer heat, the women tend to smell of sweat and body odor and are covered with powder. The young women don't appeal to me, even though they are all very slender. Your news about the first harvest celebration at Distelhof made me happy and proud. You should write a Distelhof journal to keep track of the great adventure. Our first cucumbers turned out to be a first-class batch, the pole beans also. I would really have liked the tomatoes. We set them out in such nice neat rows. Again, all our trouble and hard work have paid off, and it is a joy to see the Distelhof mature so well. You know, Goldchen, in spirit I am often up there with you, my Love. Continue to let me know what is happening there. I have written a nice little letter to the Doeges to let the two of them know that they need not be jealous. Dr. Mann will also receive a few lines from me. The clever old man is a fine fellow.

What a great joy to have had my name called out during mail call today. I carried the letter around with me all afternoon, and not until early evening did I finally have the chance to read the sacred contents. You, my heart's love, ignite tears of happiness and a boundless longing for home in me as I look at the photos and read the lines. You are the source of the flame in my heart that fuels my thoughts. You are the one that I love so very, very much. My heart would otherwise not be heavy. Be brave, Little One. God will protect our Reich and our family. We will not remain separated. Except at the start, when I had so many things to do that I didn't even have time for even a few lines, I have written to you almost every day now.

Tomorrow we will be out marching with full packs. So, my poor Sweetheart, I must now make good use of the time that I still have. I did get the package, and it was wonderfully received. The pictures of Distelhof are outstanding. You look wonderful! I cannot get enough of the photos. We look so wonderful together. The picture of the children is truly a masterpiece of photography. The little ones look so good. It just shows that they are of good stock and name. Matthias has good posture and such an intelligent face. He is probably a Claudius dreamer and perhaps not of Erika's temperament. The picture of the entire Distelhof, taken out on the terrace, is the most beautiful. I have never seen a photo so clear and lifelike. I am very thankful to you for sending them to me. They do my heart good and lift me up during the tough hours. I dare not let myself go, lest I be dealt with by the military. While doing some heavy work on a tank this afternoon, all of us jumped, buck-naked into the Loire River. Boy was that a refreshing treat for our hot, sweating bodies!

My friend, Klute, was very surprised to see that we owned such a nice place, and I won't tell you what he said about you – you just might get to feeling overly self-conscious without your Paulus around to do that for you.

My buddy is 46 years old and somewhat battle-worn to the advantage that he does not have to participate in some of the more physical activities. He is a great and upstanding guy with a heart of gold, a large family and a love for all of them. We two are the white sheep of the recruits.

Tomorrow, Sweetheart, when our forced march is finished, I will continue to write to you because it is in writing that I am able to close myself off in my love for you.

Kisses for the children and a long one for you.

Your Paulus

Letter no. 18
France, August 19, 1943

My Only Treasure, You My Goldchen,
and Dear Little Children

I left off my previous writing by telling you that we were about to complete a march with full back packs. Picture this! We set out with full gear . . . . tents, mess kits, and rifles. We began to march down several sun drenched streets, heading in a southern direction in lousy conditions for marching. After a time, things changed. We left the streets and marched into the fields. A five kilometer march-tempo pace was set, draining us of most any strength we had left. As we sat there in the searing heat, in our helmets and gas masks, one of the commanders yelled "Gas!" Then, to wear us out even more, we were ordered to march, in step, on up to the next bridge. Completely exhausted, we arrived at the river only to find that the bridge had already been blown up. No problem! An ordered march of ten kilometers, at the same insane tempo, and on we went to the next bridge. That too had been destroyed. Still, every man was ordered to wade, chest-deep, into the river until water poured out of every pocket and all of our food got wet. All kinds of crap ended up getting into my boots. This bridge march in a 50 degree Celsius[24] sun was led by officers uniformed in light clothing and carrying no personal weapons.

Because of my education, I am hopeful to eventually succeed in getting to do what I want. A recruit really has no opinion of his own. Everything depends on his superior officer. So far, I have earned respect for what I have had to say, and my intelligence has allowed me to resolve some conflicts through verbal problem solving. I will follow up on your advice in future matters of this sort.[25]

---

[24] 50 degrees Celsius – this is the second reference to the heat in France during the summer of 1943. A direct conversion of the 50 degree Celsius mark would be 122 degrees Fahrenheit. However, this figure may have been an estimate in an attempt to indicate the intensity of the heat.

[25] Soldier Claudiius's wife was a great believer in decorum and diplomacy and obviously advised him to use diplomacy in settling arguments.

Your wonderful package has given my stomach reasons to celebrate. There were two packages, and I really miss your cooking. The meals served here are not light enough. My solution is to reach for rations of fruit and such. French cooking is sinfully expensive and not to my taste. The corn bread is not too bad. I will bring some when I get to come home for leave. Toppings are scarce, especially marmalade and such. The midday meal is adequate.

Your lengthy question regarding the army tank division duties deserved an answer. As Pioneers, our first and foremost duty is the destruction of enemy tanks and fortifications. We have successfully practiced and completed the techniques of demolition for which my calculations were used. My duties couldn't be any more dangerous.

Well, Love, I have managed to pass lots of news on to you, and I hope my letters are reaching a safe and sound you. In the evening, my thoughts fly to you. When it is dark, my buddies can't see my tears.

Tomorrow I will write again.

Kisses for you, my Love, as I silently cry out for a momentary reunion with you.

The children are always in my thoughts.

When the stars arise, it is then that I fly to my home, . . . to my only happiness, my Goldchen. I love you so much and long for you so, ... you, my Goldchen, and you, my dear children.[26]

Letter no. 19
France, August 21, 1943

You, My Goldchen
Love of my Heart,

Today is Sunday, and duty beckons . . . and two letters flutter on my table, greetings from home – from my loved ones, from my

---

[26] When the stars arise, etc. – was written upside down at the top of letter no. 18.

Goldchen and from my children. The first was dated August 8th, and the second one August 16th. Your lines, my Darling, destroyed all of the defenses that I had built up against my homesickness. My tears flowed, and my heart is exceedingly full.

I have so much to tell you and so much for which to thank you. All of the photos, there are eleven, lie before me – How beautiful life is! Most of all, I was impressed with how good you look. Such beautiful pictures. I could not have longed for anything better. Hopefully, Mr. Vollhaber will be able to make more prints. The picture of you on the sofa should be enlarged. It is so splendid. You look so lovely and life-like in the photo of you with the children at home. Matthias looks so serious and distinguished. You, my Loved Ones at home, a letter, a greeting, ... this is the highlight of my day. I must thank you, my Goldchen, for these children, so lovely and bigger than life in the photos that you sent me.

And so my Sunday, distinguished as it was, was made much better by these greetings sent from home. At the times of my most extreme exertion, when I feel down and out of breath, one reach for the envelopes and my courage grows, I feel restored and am proud to be able to accomplish something. You, my Goldchen, are the great power that binds us together, and our children are the keys to that union. You could say that your love for God has also been passed on to me.

I knew about your visit to Dresden. Father sent me a few lines. I immediately wrote to him to let him know that I had complete confidence in you and have no reason for any concerns in regard to your handling of all money matters. I don't want to spend precious time on this subject since the wonderful way that my parents have conducted themselves has come to my attention. My mother is stone-stubborn and, unfortunately, succeeds in getting my father to go along with her.

Your letter of August 7th fueled my greatest desires to return to you and our homeland – soon. Our life must go on. We need to be together.

Paulus

Letter no. 20
France, August 23, 1943
Sunday

My dear little Goldchen, Love of my Heart,

This is the third letter that I have written to you today. Over and over again, I look at the photos and pictures and the past comes back to me, . . . visions so precious in spirit that they make my heart ache. I should go drinking with the others, but it's not my way to spend time. I also know that you, my Goldchen, have concerns, concerns about money. I also know that you are sad because I am no longer there to talk things over with you. From early morning 'til late in the evening, my single-most desire is to be there with you.

Our quarters here are pretty much empty. The young guys are gone, and only a few of the old ones remain. The atmosphere in here isn't good. Hope is not abundant, and everyone is concerned about his family at home. Only the young, the 18 year olds who have nothing to lose want to experience more of the war. Life in the military is a waiting game and tough on anyone who is used to being in charge of his own life. But, because I have become an active part of the war machine, we don't discuss these concerns among ourselves.

Writing to you and communicating with you has become my one and only world. To know that you, my Love, are my wife and that our children are protected relieves me of a heavy burden. I also worry and wonder about what will happen to me once this period of training is over. May these letters speed their way to you so you will always know now much I love you and the children. In all of my thoughts and deeds I will forever be thinking of you. Maybe for that, God will reward me by keeping me alive to come back home to you. Together, we would be able to endure anything, even if the Fatherland should fail to win a victory.

What did you do during all of this Sunday? The little ones are probably there with you. It is a comfort for me to know that you are all together. When I have finished writing these lines to you, I will smoke another cigar, look at the photos from home, and dream. Yesterday I had no idea that I would be getting two great letters from home, much less these beautiful photos of you and the children, my Dear. I literally lived off of your last letter. It felt so nice to have it in my pocket. Its contents made me feel so good. The room is filling up again with whistling, singing, and bragging about how much wine was consumed. How little use I have for this sort of thing. I want only to think about our wonderful hours at Distelhof and deeply re-experience our last night together up there. The moon was so beautiful as it glistened on the lawn and the terrace. Yes, Dear, memory is a precious thing, especially in my circumstance of being so far away from home, so far from my greatest spiritual love.

I get so much out of the photos when I look at them in the evening. Beloved, you are everything in the world to me. Tell little Erika, who will soon be going back to school again, that her Papi thinks about her often. She should be diligent so that we can both be proud of her mental accomplishments. Matthias, as a representative of his Papi, will have his challenges. Hopefully they will not be affected by the bitter reality of our times. May the Creator see to it that our children do not have to grow up without a father and that I come home again. Sunday will soon be gone, and duty begins at 5:25 AM. I will write again tomorrow evening – and I look forward to it, Goldchen, my Love.

I love you so much that it hurts.

Your Paulus

Letter no. 21
France, August 22, 1943

I just tossed my Sunday letter to you into the mail bag – and I forgot the stamp! I will immediately grab a pen and attempt to duplicate it to mail off right away. I took a walk this afternoon – beautiful fields of wine grapes on one side of the road and fruit of all types hanging from trees on the other side. What a magnificent sight! When I came to a blackberry bush near the street, I stopped and ate some of these magnificent berries. They were ripe, easy to pick and very juicy. I think I ate nearly a pound of them.

The shops here are open on Sundays. People of all types, big and small, sit in the cafes. The men play billiards, and the women keep them company – even if it doesn't look all that friendly. Everything that is available to us is so expensive and has no taste. I plan to sample my first glass of wine this evening – I will most certainly sit on the banks of the Loire River and look at the photos. There, I can let my feelings go unchecked. Sweet Love, it is so hard to live without the hope of seeing you soon. It must end sometime. We don't get much news here. I will be happy to get a furlough, even if the weather will be hot.

My Love, keep well, 'til tomorrow.

Your Paulus

Letter no. 22
France, August 26, 1943[27]

My One and Only Goldchen and Dear Children,

The 26th of August, 1943 – I am at a loss for words to tell you how I literally tremble at the thought. First, a lovely package from Erika, Matthias and Detti, and a large package from my Goldchen arrived just yesterday. God how my heart beat! Yesterday, I just walked around the package; this afternoon I opened it. Sweetheart, if you only knew what a powerful feeling of joy and longing the gifts in the package brought forth in me. Despite my feeling of loneliness at being in the military, I feel very fortunate. How shall I ever thank you for your love, my Goldchen. The cakes are undoubtedly made with real butter and that does my heart good.

The children will receive a letter because they have minded their Mommy. I will write these letters next Sunday, and you will, of course, get one too. My health at the moment is not good. I have some rheumatism in my back. It drives me crazy at night, and I wake up exhausted in the morning. I have already been to the doctor in Orleans and had two daily massages without any positive results. I am afraid of fall asleep. At the moment, I also have diarrhea from the lousy food. I will not walk away – I love you and the children too much for that. I will write in more details

---

[27] Paul Claudius's 31st birthday.

on Sunday evening. My Goldchen, You, my Love, 1000 kisses for you.

Letter no. 23
France, August 26, 1943

You, my One and Only Love above All
Goldchen, Mother of your Children,

It is deep in the night, the alarm clock sits in front of me, ticking softly as it measures away my time. The identification tag, number 5777, lies before me – it has two parts. If I am every unable to continue out in the field, half of it will be broken away. One other thing lies on the table top, and outshines everything else –my Birthday letter. Just a few minutes ago I read it again, and for the entire day I have lived and dreamed of the contents. With that letter everything was made better for me. No one saw the hot tears that fell upon the luminous lines of the paper. It was like a religious experience for me – you and I talking intimately across the thousands of kilometers. A lost world was resurrected, and you, my Love, held my trembling, longing heart in your little hand. What power love has in me, and what courage it gives me when I am allowed the time to look at the letters, at the stars, or commune with the pictures. Communicating with you like that inspires me for the entire day, and I always feel blessed because of it.

Yesterday, August 26th, all throughout my duties my thoughts were of you – lost in memories of home, the children and my future with you. At times like those, my self-conviction that everything is all right is so overpowering that it is hard for me to bear. Yes, my Goldchen, even though I must spend my birthday as a soldier, far from home, a great joy has come of it. You understood and sent it to your soldier with your own hands, and that means everything to me. Streams of happiness flow from your precious package into my aching heart. For me, your lovely lines are the altar from which I draw my strength to serve, and I will remain strong for you, my Goldchen, and for your dear children.

At four or five o'clock in the morning, the entire company will go on a march with full packs. You can have no doubt as to the source of my strength. Your letters, my Love, and the photos, will inspire me to keep on going. In a few minutes my watch will be over. Then, I will sleep for two hours before the march begins. I sent my father a 100 gram package of cigars. I gave the same to my superiors and some to my buddies – a great present. Today, August 26th, I also received a fairly cold-hearted letter, one that I want to throw away. It is from my father and contains, as you can see for yourself, the first handwritten words from my mother. This is not as I would have imagined.

Once again, I will march with my thoughts of you, as you, my dear Goldchen, have brought your thoughts of the children to me. Many kisses accompany these lines along with my longing for you.

Your Paulus and Papi

Letter no. 24
France, August 27, 1943

My Heart's Love, My Dear, Sweet, Little Mother – Goldchen

It is late, my Love, but I am certain that you will be happy to know how things are going with me. You know that it pleases me to write to you – and so I will proceed. At around 4 o'clock this morning we set out with full march packs and full food sacks. It was still dark when we crossed the Loire suspension bridge. We sang as we marched down the roads into the French flatland.[28] In a forest we received instructions concerning surprise attacks, camouflage and night action maneuvers. It was beautiful, marching together with my young buddies at the break of morning. Most certainly my thoughts were there with you at Distelhof and on how we spent our last night there, together – on the beautiful twilight of a summer evening. I carried these thought and was uplifted. I carried all of your letters in my pockets. Every morning when I wake up, I think of you, Sweetheart, and of little Erika who

---

[28] German troops sang as they marched. Their songs were Romantic ballads, songs of nature, of the forest, of pretty farm girls, of heroism. The songs helped to bring them together as a unit.

has to get up early to go to school. And I know you are busy. For breakfast we knocked down apples and grapes in a French village, and I dug into the sausage and felt happy and satisfied, in spite of my plight. Toward eleven o'clock we marched to a spot where we establish camp. I was tired, and even with blisters on my feet I was able to stand firm with the march.

The foot ointment you sent is really excellent, and I still have a can of it. I know, Sweetheart, that you do not want me to be sad or in pain.

I am so plagued by longing that I have to be alone when I read your letters. I needed the inspiration of your latest letter so much that I have not read it yet. My entire afternoon was aglow with the thought of having a lovely letter from my Goldchen at home in my pocket.

My Darling, I hope that you feel as happy as I do when you get a letter from me. I still have about a third of the splendidly rich butter cookies with so much butter in them that I could eat them with a spoon. Before I clean up today and go to sleep, I will put everything that you sent me out on my bed. Sweetheart, I have a package ready to send to you, but I need for you to send me some 20 Reichs-Pfennig stamps. Your brave Pioneer, Paulus, wants to make his Goldchen happy. Tomorrow is Saturday, and you will receive another long letter from me . . . .

With kisses. The children will also get a package – hope they will like it.

Letter no. 25
France, August 29, 1943

My Goldchen,
You, my One and Only Heart's Love,

Your lovely letter of August 20th lies before me as a clear confession of your love for me and the children and is to be treasured above all other things considered of earthly importance. You are so brave, you, my little soldier's wife. I have received a lot of mail from you lately, my Heart's Desire. Something was always there for your Pioneer. Today, I carry your letter from

Distelhof around with me and reread it with an even greater happiness than your last one.

Unfortunately my Sunday has been ruined. I have just received orders to complete a set of calculations for a company on bridges and water vehicles.

Bread is rather expensive here. I will keep track of that sort of thing, just as you have written. In other words, France is a beautiful and splendid country, if you can somehow forget about being a German. I could tell you a lot more about that this afternoon.

As to whether or not you could come here – and that would really be great – I will keep you informed. When I come home, I may just be able to speak a little broken French. My back is still a problem. Toward morning, it hurts so much that I have to get up and go outside. Even shaving causes me pain, and I am fearful about going to bed at night. I will go to bed and read your letter right away. Then, my Love, there in the dark, I am with you, my Goldchen.

1000 kisses from Paulus

Goldchen, what you wrote about me today – those were beautiful words.[29]

Letter no. 26
France, August 30, 1943

My Dear Little Sweet Wife!
You, My Goldchen,

Yesterday, I read the dear letter you wrote from Distelhof. I was so very happy to hear that you are pleased with the fruits of our labor and how well it has all paid off. Your description of the sun-filled fields on which the garden is located, full of vegetables and fruits, reminded me of our parting, ... you and I, on our peaceful evening walks, passing through the fruit-laden fields and blooming neighboring gardens. It reminded me of our crossing the little bridge, covered with moonlight, on our way back to our

---

[29] This sentence written on the side of the letter.

place. These thoughts live in my memory. Yes, love releases so much from within the chambers of my memory of our time together, of you and of the children. You say that my flowers have grown, and I have not been there to see them.

You can't imagine my joy at hearing about the tea plants in our test plot. Who is taking care of the meadow by the terrace? Uncle Kleineman wrote me a fantastic letter about you and your last trip up there and also about the bad storm. Are you all well? Little Detti was probably all worked up. It is really nice of the Doegeses to have stood by me the way they have.

Early this morning I received your letter dated August 26th. I will read it after my duty, when I can answer it. In regard to the money, you can send me 36 reichsmarks every month – but I beg you, do not do this if you have any reservations about it. France is expensive, but I would like to buy a few things. I have mentioned this to you and hope to be able to make you especially happy. I am going to rest a little now. All of the pictures and letters will lie down with me, held tightly in my hand – there you will rest with me, my Dear. My back becomes more painful from night to night. I kiss you and the children and love you so, so very much.

In answer to you question – I have a buddy who is 46 years old and an honorable father who is very concerned about home. He says "hello." He is a farmer and knows a lot about Distelhof.[30]

Letter no. 27
France, August 31, 1943

My Heart's Desire, You!

It is deep in the night, and yet it is beginning to dawn in the forests along the banks of the Loire. Soon they will blow reveille. In the first few lines, I send my longing thoughts to you. You brought me so much joy with your letter of August 26th. I really am fortunate, Sweetheart, and I want you to always know that. Your letters and your spirit go with me when my duties begin, and

---

[30] These sentences were written at the top of the letter.

everything around me takes on a beautiful glow of colors. My close buddies toss around like monkeys in their beds at night. Unfortunately, my rheumatism won't let me get any sleep. Hope the damned doctors here find the right medicine for me. The pain is horrible.

I get better and better news from Distelhof. Did the roof withstand the storms? That must have been a severe storm. Even uncle Kleineman wrote me about it. Your handwritten letter is my good like charm, Goldchen. In it you have opened your soul to me

A long kiss for you from your Paulus

Letter no. 28
August 31, 1943

To all the Distelhofers, Big and Small
Especially to the Female Distelhofer, Goldchen,

The August 28th letter lies before me, . . a genuine Goldchen letter wherein I can recognize the logical, illogical, and also very unceremonious me. You are doing a very authoritative job in regard to Germany and our home. What you have written about Distelhof fills me with a great deal of joy. It is too bad that I couldn't have been there to see the two ladies on bikes with my own eyes. When I get some leave, you will have to give me a full recount of the whole event. I can imagine that must have been quite something. You have such a talent for describing all sorts of things in such great detail. You should write a book, and then we'll have it made as far as our income goes.

I would think that writings about homeland settings would make for real tearjerker reading material for all of the young maidens. I am currently involved with a company that is responsible for everything that is possible and impossible in regard to the subject of all of the water transports and bridges in the area. Yes, the engineer is developing a good use for his knowledge. I have also become a specialist in regard to truck lights and did a fantastic job with that assignment. Writing paper and utensils are hard to find in France – think about sending me pens, paper, etc. We will have battle planning and practice with live ammo and camouflage this evening, along with simulated confusion everywhere. I often have to laugh to myself and tend to think that survival depends on something more than just a foxhole. Just what the future has in store for me is pretty uncertain.

Today, know how much I love you, my Love – so much that I think of you every free hour. I'll be writing to you.

My Love,
Your Paulus

Letter no. 29
France, August 31, 1943

My Dear Little Erika

And now, because I think of you so very often and enjoyed the letter that you sent from Dresden, a few greetings from your soldier Papi who is so far away   Please ask your Mommy to read this letter to you. You are now back at home again with Matti and Detti. School has begun, and you must be diligent so that your Mommy can write good things to your Papi. Tell Detti to do the same. Be good, my little Erika, and your Papi will surely come home on leave, soon. Since you are the oldest, I ask you to say hello to your brothers Matti and Detti for me today and tell them that you got a real field mail letter from me.

Please tell your Mommy that Papi loves her very much and that he feels so lucky to have such a well-cared-for home and that he thanks God again and again for the gift of his wife and dear children.

Kisses to you, Erika, live well and be happy. Your Papi would be happy to get another letter from you. Take care of your Mom. 'til I see you again.

Your Papi

Letter no. 30
France, September 1, 1943

My Dear Little Wife
And to the Children Growing Up!

And so, this is how it is with your soldier Papi after he educated himself and went on a buying spree. In the next package you will receive some small cooking utensils and other things. After some relentless hours of shopping I have, hopefully, succeeded in finding some useful things to send to you. At any rate, I am proud of myself and happy to be writing these lines because I know how special it is to be lovingly cared for by someone.

I am feeling pretty well. I'm always hungry, especially when I run out of butter cookies. Oh Sweetheart, do send me some.

The trees are beginning to become more colorful and lose some of their leaves. The tomatoes here in the fields are not yet ripe. In my letters, my Darling, I show you so much of my longing, and I want so very much to talk to you face to face. I am in hopes that the war will be over within the coming year. That is what the Sergeant told my colleague, Boris. Rebellion against us has been predicted. It is then, my Love, that the hour of truth will come.

I washed my underwear during duty hours today, and when I put them on again, my Love, I am home. The oak cabinet is another matter. Did you attend to all of the details yourself? God will protect you and me for our children, my Love, and your Papi will be there for you.

And so, this is the way it is. The younger guys rely on me during maneuvers – the older guys know what to do. It is when it comes time to march, march, that we must all run just as fast as the younger guys. There is always a lot to do. During the short free times that we have, our guns need to be cleaned, the mess must be scrubbed, and in the course of all this, we also have to clean our uniforms. Then, there is the matter of the classroom, getting instructional materials together, exchanging money and other details, and that leaves very little time free for personal clean up. I write my letters by working them in on my weekdays ...but then, it would be impossible for me to abstain from writing to you. I always manage to find the time to write a letter.

We have been to the movies, and it was a great experience to have such a thing in the field. They start at 5:45 and run until 7:30. For those on night duty they naturally run it later. I have gotten used to everything and do my shift of duty in fatigues. In visiting the company commander, I have always received preferential treatment and so have no reason for any complaints. By means of having done some small favors, I have succeeded in gaining some small privileges in the way of company life. Mr. Claudius is well known and respected. I am naturally very happy about that. If I were not performing well, there would certainly be no praise. Well, Goldchen, there you have a little insight into my daily life. In spite of all of this, I would gladly run home barefoot, if I could.

My Love, it is 10 AM, and something probably needs to be attended to. It's great for me to be able to write to you, but I do not know what the coming hours of the day will bring. I do know that you are so very good for me and that everything in your care will be in good order. It is such a comfort for me to know that, and this feeling of being closely bound to you makes me happy and proud. I think of you constantly

Sweetheart, say hello to everyone at home from Pioneer Claudius.

And for you, a long kiss on your lovely mouth. Goldchen, my dear, God will stand by us.

Your Paulus

Letter no. 31
France, September 3, 1943

My Little Goldchen – You!

I received your little package with the cigars and the foot powder yesterday. Your lovely lines, however, were the most important thing. Goldchen, I am ever so grateful for your loving concern about me. It is good to be so cared for, especially by as pretty and slender a girl as you.

I received a 100 gram package from my parents. Contents: 5 cakes, which I instantly and literally inhaled. Father wrote a witty note on the outside of the package: Attention: – Do Not Get Sick! I am so proud that all of you care for this soldier so much.

My buddy seems to have developed a sensitivity and fortitude to go along with his competence and believes in letting his superiors know when an injustice has been committed. The worst penalty that could befall him would be kitchen duty. As a person, he is the best. On our solitary walks together we have discussed home, the children, and Distelhof. As a farmer, all this is of great interest to him. I get white bread, bacon and marmalade from him, since, along with his military rations, he gets a lot sent to him from home. I profit from this arrangement and give him my cigarettes. As far as I can tell from his conversations, everything is going well for his family back home. We need to visit him later. He owns a small inn. Right now, the morale in this unit is not the best. The young guys like to stir things up and think that the older guys should do penance when the officers order us to march, hit the dirt, on your stomach, and so on.

As a special note, I must tell you that we have been on alert since last evening. At about midnight, we had an alarm – with full packs. We are battle-ready, and since we could be dispatched at any moment, there is no regular duty today. Do not be alarmed however, my Dear. It is better to have the alarm sounded too often and be safe, than too little. Something must be happening though.

I promised to tell you about my buddies. We are seventeen men and housed in two rooms. Two thirds of them are eighteen years old or younger. Among them are a lot of "Rowdies." Most of the older guys range from 31 to 37, and we sort of hang out together. The younger guys are not as close or as well-educated, but they do not object to being led by the older members. I have a good education, and the younger soldiers know that they can learn something from me. Our team comes from every part of Germany. Like me, some of them were shipped out on July 28th. One of them had to take on the role of the acting train leader. He is a great guy and a buddy without faults. He is a miller and hails from near Erfurt. We have become good friends and have talked about our homeland, children, and our respective homes. Some of the men here are from Hessen, Frankfurt am Main, Kassel, and an area near

Thüringen. Although he traveled on another train, there is even a guy here who is from my own beloved home city and, yes, together we have talked a lot about home.

One of my good friends is Paul Klute, a 46 year old Bavarian farmer. He is so attached to his home and family that he has become seriously sick. He is one of the older guys in the military who is not really suited to be a soldier and so gets moved around a lot. He is afraid and, unfortunately, does not have the gumption or courage to be able to pull himself together and look into the future with clear eyes.

Fruit grows and ripens in the eternal sunshine of this mild climate –an exclusive gift of the French style of life. Traveling along the outskirts of the city, I can see new fields and large orchards. The owners however, are making the mistake of not taking good care of their orchards. Almost all of the pears and apples are juicy and sweet. I always carry pocketfuls of pears and eat the fruit fresh off of the stem. As soldiers, we are permitted to get wine from the French people. Unfortunately the young comrades often take a little too much advantage of this situation, and then there is such a thing as just stealing. The peaches here have a wonderful taste, and I will have to send you some. It makes me feel guilty to be eating this beautiful fruit while you, back at home, must do without. Everything is available in Paris – but one must have a coupon for it. I have found Paris to be quite pleasant. If I had more time, I would tell you more about all of the beautiful things. I know that you would love it.

I know that everything is in order and that the little ones are sleeping. Soldier Papi is with them. On Sunday, I will take my camera and take a picture of my friend Klute with the countryside as a background. I have saved some bread, and we will try to buy some butter and some eggs. The entire company is still on alert. As far as I know, the Americans have landed in beautiful Italy.

I take your hand, Love, and, in spirit, wander through the harvested fields at Distelhof. You must surely feel the longing that I have for you. Just before I left, you and I spent such an emotional time up there together. At that time, I had no idea just how strong my memories of you and Distelhof would end up to be. I thank God that it is so.

I kiss you, Goldchen, ... Your Paulus

Letter no. 32
France, 3 AM on the night of September 3 - 4, 1943

My Dear Sweet Goldchen
My Little Soldier's Mommy

I've taken over the watch. The clouds are dreary, dark, and heavy, and even in spite of that, the stars twinkle through. Autumn is everywhere, in the fields and in the forests. During the day, the sun has only a warming effect and is no longer oppressive. The grapes in the fields are thick and plump and beginning to taste sweeter than ever. During a few peaceful hours yesterday, I drank my first two glasses of wine in a French wine room at the edge of the city. Yesterday, five years ago, the war began and with that, the greatest plague of murder on the planet.

Sweetheart, your letter about the countryside really moved me to want to look deeper into the life of the French people – and I have found a lot of things that are beautiful. Their houses are almost always built with an earth berm around them and windows that reach down to the earth's surface. The characteristic shutters protect the rooms and halls from the heavy intrusion of the sun. The halls are tastefully done and hung with good works of art. A semidarkness pervades and leads to the inevitable garden area. This plot of earth is especially noteworthy in that it is full of patches of flowers with trees providing areas of shade. Artfully laid out pea-gravel walkways lead past fountains and statues to an open space in the middle. There the French sit on comfortable low-slung chairs and large loungers. Newspapers lie next to fruit-filled baskets. What peace is to be found in a little garden such as this! Yesterday, I was in the house of an aristocrat. All of the rooms were filled with magnificent furniture, and heavy-woven carpets lay in the hallway entrance of the first floor. Most of the homes do not have a second story floor. What a fine style of life these houses and gardens represent. The French way of life is in knowing how to live a fairy tale and certainly not like the painful sense of order that permeates every German dwelling.

One of my buddies paid a very high price for a suit that he could not wear – the Frenchman took him for a ride.[31]

Letter no. 33
France, September 5, 1943

To my Goldchen
My longing and Lovely little Soldier's Mommy!

Today is Sunday, and it is to be a very beautiful one. The autumn sun shines in the blue sky. I want to talk to you, Sweetheart, ...listen. This afternoon, my buddies and I will walk up the Loire River. We will take our bread with us and have our supper in a little village nearby.

Your letter of August 28th arrived this afternoon. I plan to read it when I am alone with nature. That will be most beautiful. How can I thank you for this letter which brought with it refreshed thoughts of you and of home. When I feel the letter in my pocket, happiness, love, and hope fill my heart, and I want to write to you when I am alone with nature.

First, I want to quickly tell you about a recent experience. We had four hours of instruction at our headquarters concerning bridges and watercraft travel. The Lieutenant read the papers that I had written to the troops along with all of my calculations. Only two to three percent of the men probably understood what he was reading. I, however, am now famous!

In the meantime, the alarm has sounded, and we hurried to where we now are. The French have pulled off a few acts of sabotage in the past few days. As a result, we only travel armed. An all-alert roll call was set in motion this Sunday morning. Roll call is a hard-line command to clean up, brush up, and cut loose, with good intentions behind it. Everything from a locker to a bin was turned out. Any missing buttons were sewn on. Boots were polished, and so on. You should have seen me. I took great pains to clean up my clothes, do the sewing, and have everything in tip-

---

[31] "One of my buddies . . . ." This sentence was written on the side of the letter.

top shape. I washed my pockets. After that, I needed to clean my caps and gas masks. In any case, I will show you later where in the closet areas the officers found dirt, and dirt they do find, at least when they want to. We bit our nails during the inspection – many were cited. I was not and was very proud of that, primarily because I did not want to ruin my first beautiful, free Sunday and secondly, I simply did not want to be called out. In the end, I knew that they would avoid citing me because they know that I am one of their best instructors. The personal matter of home and most importantly you were on my mind. You will be glad to know that I met a Lance Corporal who has studied foreign affairs; he's a lively guy and a fine fellow. His father is a pastor. He has heard from him and filled me in. We have had some lively discussions. He loves his wife, who lives in Gotha, and has a child. He expressed the wish that you two should meet.

I will write more about my 46 year old companion, about him and the other intellectuals. It is our nature – we take pen and paper with us so that we can write to our dear wives about the natural world around us and of people who live here. I am so happy to have found a person that is a lot like me, and I'm sure that you are also. Yes? We went to the theater in our fatigues yesterday, and I was probably alone in my understanding of the tragedy between the Catholic Church and the politics of the people. The actors were good, and it was highly interesting. It included long and lively dialogs which led to deep thoughts. Despite all that, it is difficult to relate the play to contemporary times. We will consider the issues this afternoon. You, my Love, would really have liked it. The theme would have struck a note with you. I am so proud of you and happy to be allowed to be your life's partner. That is why I try to be a good soldier. The kids should know that their Papa can be pretty snappy and trained in using a rifle and dagger.

To our great joy, I can tell you that I have spoken for a pair of women's or men's leather shoes, and even a pair of children's shoes. I await a decision from you and some money. You could certainly use a pair and, Eki, also. Please send me a paper pattern of your feet, or sizes, so that I can compare them to the sizing here.

Sweetheart, I want to protect you and the sweet children against all domination because I love you so much – I'll write again. Your Paulus (I leave in an hour)

Letter no. 34
France, September 5, 1943

My One and Only You
My Love!

I have just read your lovely, oh so lovely letter. I sit in the evening sunshine near to the Loire River. It is beautiful here, and I have spent any spare time that I had with my friend, Schorsch. We talked about you. He has a lovely little wife, like you, and she is also very devoted to him. I prize his friendship and being able to talk to him as we share our longings with each other. Paul Klute was also with us, but he didn't say much – he is not as talkative. Sweetheart, you were in my thoughts each minute, and it was a shame that you were not in the midst of us. Schorsch really enjoys his kids, and his wife is in her ninth month. He has a fervent wish for the two of you to meet, and it would be great for both of us to know that you are chatting about us while we are here in the field.

I am writing to you out here in the open. Your lovely letter has made my Sunday a golden one because of the way that you described the children. You celebrated my birthday, there, at home. In regard to me here, it wasn't anything that was noticed by anyone. That's just the way it is with a bunch of thoughtless chaps.

In the meantime, you have probably received several letters from me that have answered some of your questions. I am very happy to get your package with the marmalade since that is something that I miss over and over again. We took our bread and some splendid butter along with us on our walk and ate in the sunshine. Earlier, I had managed to procure a briefcase. We collected fruit from two fields and ate until we were full. On the way back we enjoyed some conversation, along with our haul of fruit, to complete the most beautiful day that I have spent in the service. Today felt like my birthday, and your letters were the living ray of hope and sunshine in my heart. Sweetheart, you know how much I long for home. Your letters are the beat of my heart. Again and again, I thank the Creator for giving you to me as a lifetime companion.

The rays of the sun throw long shadows on me. Schorsch is painting a watercolor picture, and both of the Paulus images are writing letters home. The water of the Loire is silvery and flows silently through the body of the countryside. Earlier this evening, we waded stark-naked in the water. I found a pearl in the water, and I will send it to the children at the first opportunity. Everything in France is robust, and the fruit is heavy and ripe. We need only to help ourselves. When I look upriver, I see a haze above the grass, between the Fargeau Bridge and the St. Denis Hotel. In between are broad fields of the most magnificent blue and gray grapes. When October comes they will be very ripe and tasty. My gaze falls down around my naked feet and the pictures are spread around me, my eternal companions. They become ever more beautiful each time I look at them, and a great feeling of pride and joy comes over me. . . . You, my Dear and special little wife, and three wonderful children! All of us brought our photos out and talked about them; it was so very satisfying. All three of us have a great longing for home. If not, our eyes would not have become so moist.

My boots are up on the dike. My feet are covered with blisters. Had it not been for the foot powder you sent me, I would not feel this spry. A heart-felt thanks to you at home. We are going to need to leave soon because we have to be in bed by 10 o'clock and are looking forward to making a leisurely evening pilgrimage back. I will always be there for you, my Love, – hopefully the war will end soon, and I won't have to be away from the dear children – and we, you and I, will have a wonderful reunion.

Your longing soldier

Kisses to you, Goldchen,

What you wrote about the Strefals was great – The state could have cleared him long ago – Yes, that's fun.

Letter no. 35
France, September 6, 1943

My Dear, dear, Goldchen
My Everything,

Although I have a hot day behind me and my joints feel like they are filled with lead, I want to say good night to you, my Sweetheart. I have just read your longing lines of August 28. I am so moved and sad. If only you knew how much your lines, your thoughts, mean to me here, so far away – but then, you don't need to hear it from me. Goldchen, everything in me yearns for you and for home – especially when I don't want to see things go on the way they are. However, Sweetheart, I am healthy and in good shape.

At 4 o'clock, we are to fall out for shooting practice, anti tank maneuvers, and so on. Our troops in France are kept continually on alert. Just now, one hundred tanks rolled by in a cloud of dust. Sweetheart, as soon as I have completed these few lines, at the end of this day, I will climb into bed and look at the photos of you. I feel so happy then – You are so good to me.

Your Paulus

Letter no. 36

My Dear Little Goldchen
You, my dear, dear Children,

I just came out of church, and although I begin night maneuvers in just two hours, I want to chat with you and the children a little. There I sat in the church of our city with my buddies and listened to the masculine voice of a spirit-filled preacher. The church was very beautiful, a small work of art, and yet I have never seen so much dust. The preacher spoke of war, comradeship and, just think, ...He also spoke of the great sacrifice that the soldier on the front is making in leaving his wife and children behind. It was gripping to hear him talk about the children growing up – he himself has children, otherwise it would not have been so easy to detect the warmth of his words. I don't need to tell you how it moved me. There I sat, in the French house of God and yet, as far, far away as I was, my thoughts were of you back home. Do you know what that means? Home – infinite sweetness lies in this one word.

It is a great blessing for me because I have such a deep longing for it. I prayed, as only a husband and a father who loves his family as much as I do, could.

Goldchen, I was deeply locked into my longing when I got your precious package along with your lovely lines. So now I feel renewed and go back to the package, again and again. It tastes so good, like your lovely hands. In the air that came out of the box when I first opened it, I could hear the words that you spoke as you packed it. Goldchen, I thank you for this greeting from your hands. It has made me extremely happy – not to mention that the marmalade will become a pressing issue at breakfast time. I received the cookies, but . . . .promise not to be angry, I became possessed and devoured them all in an instant. In the afternoon, when rationing is applied, we have very little butter left to put on to our bread. I am enclosing a voucher. The second one I sent to Dresden. The others ought, also, to go out.

In the meantime you will probably have received the first package from me. Hopefully it made you and the children happy and held their interest. I will take care of the other detail in the coming days.

Please write to me if you are involved with certain details. Maybe you need some organization. How are things going at home? I hope that Detti doesn't get sick. I really like it when you have nice things to say about the little one. My longing for the children grows more intense. I often find myself thinking of him when I see a French child. These little fellows don't go to school. They are escorted around and, for the most part, stay at home.

At dawn yesterday morning, we had shooting practice with our LMG[32] and carbines. I succeeded in making the grade of sharpshooter with the carbine, in both maneuvers. The test consisted of 25 targets at a distance of 150 meters, as they appeared in the morning fog. I was happy to make it because the

---

[32] Machine gun.

greater part of the unit did not shoot well. Our assignments have become more diversified – more infantry – less pioneer! That is, for example, battling tanks in the fog, placing mines into mine fields, all kinds of work with explosives and bridge construction with pontoons. It's a lot to have to remember.

When it comes to carrying heavy mines and large beams, that is another matter. For me it's vigorous work. At any rate, I have gotten to the point where hopelessness is no longer an issue and has grown into a gladness to serve. The officers talk about the fact that the standstill in Russia will end and that the decision to move forward will be made sometime during this month. Things, here with me, have essentially become less peaceful. Yesterday, there was a huge attempt of sabotage against our furlough train. It had to do with the tracks and, thank God, the train had already passed by.

How are you, my Sweetheart? I'm sure that the beautiful autumn evenings fill you with a sense of sadness and longing – but Darling, it is often as painful for me during those same nights. I silently get out of my own bed to set my nerves and yearning free in the form of tears.

My back is still giving me grief. All attempts at healing have failed, and every night is torture for me. I know how you would heal me. In such moments I would like to turn up missing. Sweetheart, always remember that I love you very much – that you are everything in the world to me. I kiss you, my Love. When the children ask about me, make sure that they don't forget me.

Your Paulus
France, September 8, 1943

Letter no. 37
France September 8, 1943

My Goldchen and Love of my Heart,

We just got the news that Italy signed a capitulation with the allies on September 2nd, which included an agreement that they should continue to fight, in appearance only, in order that the German soldiers could be identified. In the meantime, the enemy has allowed our landing troops to march past – with orders to cordon off our troops. I do not know to what extent they will succeed. So, the great battle is now on. Some of our people were shipped to Italy this evening. At any rate, the posture of the French has changed. How it will all come out remains to be seen. Our training was immediately interrupted, and we have received firm instructions on use of gas. I need to know if you have gas masks for the children. Sooo many heartfelt greetings.

A note to Detti – My little Detti, your father has something for you.

For Mom – yet another writing has been taken care of and a package is on its way to you.

1000 greetings from your Papi

Letter no. 38
France, September 9, 1943

My dear Little Goldchen,

We already have something on the docket for today, and everything is at high pitch. The only one who is not, is me. This evening, at 18 hundred hours, we had a dress roll-call, and let me tell you, . . . First I had to stuff my socks so that I could patch them. I had some misgivings about the socks because the foot cream had made them a bit stiff. Then, we had the misfortune to have the company commander pay us a surprise visit to inspect our coats and socks at just about the time that we were getting out of our clothes. Concerning this matter, many were caught unprepared. I was lucky to have everything in order. Caps, jackets, shirts and pants had to be turned inside-out along with a "show all buttons." Footlockers were also inspected. Field lockers were another matter, and many were difficult to close and were not fastened. As they fell open, soldiers were written up. Again, I had all in order – same went for my rifle. I have always avoided attracting that kind of attention. It is the older guys, for the most part, who keep their socks in good shape. Unfortunately, we all suffer when the younger guys get caught.

Yes, you know me and the way that I take care of things. We older fellows report for duty on a regular basis because the younger guys either fail to complete tasks correctly or manage to get them only half done. I try to keep things pristine, and believe me, it doesn't go unnoticed by the noncoms. I have tried to make things easier for the 18 year olds when I can. They just sounded the alarm – I must interrupt.

Many hours lie between the last lines and these. It is now 3:30 AM, and I am on watch. Because of the Italian capitulation, our entire unit, tanks and all, is march- ready, and all of our equipment is packed. In the meantime, we have news that the Italian capitulation is not valid and the battle continues under German leadership and that all measures are being taken to shore up Badoglio and the surrounding area.

The world is being turned upside down, and we are living in a time that is rich with upheaval and conflict. With this extraordinary unrest, we will remain under alarm status. In night flights, the capabilities of the enemy are increasing to the point of a hurricane level where we don't even know from which direction they are coming. I'm sure that you will get a completely different story concerning this situation in Italy.

This afternoon we have received company instructions, and I assume that we will be given the real story about Italy at that time. I will then update you since I know that you will be interested. Today, even more than yesterday, we were given further instructions on gas. We learned that there are three types of gasses. Two are Nitrogen, and LEDIT, which destroys the lungs.[33] The other chemical weapon that is spread by the enemy as a dust gets on one's clothes and skin or feet and causes terrible pain and can lead to death. With our home being located where it is, you are in a less dangerous position, According to theoretical instruction, things will happen in the following manner: A portion of the terrain will be poisoned and a unit of gas-detection troops

---

[33] Gases listed: Possibly Mustard gas, Nitrogen gas and Lewisite. Mustard gas, Bis2-choroethyl sulfide burned the skin and lungs. It took weeks to die from exposure to Mustard gas. Combinations of gases were used in WWI, and by WWII all countries involved had stockpiles. Lewisite, named after the US chemist Winford Lewis, 1878-1943, was often mixed with Mustard gas. It had similar devastating effects on troops. Judging from Paul Claudius's description, the powder mentioned in the letter was undoubtedly a mixture of the caustic chemicals developed after WWI.

will seek out the area. I volunteered to serve with one of these patrols and have even become a unit leader. For that, we put on a special airtight suit. A gas mask is fastened under a steel helmet, all of which makes one look pretty ominous. And so we set out with guns, ammo and decontamination material. In case something happens, a tear in the clothing or such, I carry a small tin in my shirt that contains a powder that has the ability to turn blood red in color if it comes in contact with any enemy chemicals. On detecting a terrible odor, my unit spreads the powder over the area. Because of the visor, my gas mask does not fit all that tight. We all began to sweat considerably in our suits but succeeded in establishing a poisoned area and marked it off with small yellow flags. It was frightening to walk into the contamination area with the galoshes in order to detect the gasses, and the incoming enemy planes forced us to take cover. After having completed our mission, we were moved out. Our clothes were burned because everything was completely contaminated. You can imagine the opportunities open to any soldier who volunteers for each crappy assignment! I do it just to learn to save one's life. I do it in an attempt to preserve my life from a bullet or other such death at the hands of the enemy. In a few hours we will move on, carrying full packs. We will march 25 miles across the Loire River (naturally, we must first build a bridge) and then return to the base. I have diligently cleaned my feet and treated them with powder. For your loyal care, you deserve a kiss. I would, otherwise not be able to walk as well as I do. You can see that we are always on the move; the German soldier is sometimes more animal than human.

Since no one is bothering me just now, I have placed my beloved pictures on the wooden chair in front of me. Sweetheart, those were wonderful times – how long will it be before I can love you again? Thank God that I am not bothered with sexual deprivation. Must be the result of hard and rigorous service to my country. The photos of Distelhof are like sunshine to me. Again and again, they go with me, tucked into my shirt pocket. How often yesterday and today my door has been opened and closed again. Yes, yes, yes, Paulus has something special to offer – these splendid nougat bonbons are mine to give. A piece of home in the gray cabinet of war ... pieces of home, made by my lovely little wife.

You were with me today, on the march. I looked deeply into your eyes and received the radiating power of your love. I want to write to you again today and tell you just how I have progressed with this new power. Another hour has gone by. It is now 4:15 AM. In my dreams, Goldchen, I want to be with you in our bedroom, with a glowing fire. Love and oneness shall bind us together as it always has. Kiss the little ones for me.

From your soldier Papi. I love you so much and remain –
Your Paulus

Letter no. 39
France, September 10, 1943

My dear Little Goldchen!

You should know that, thanks to the therapy of Walk Well powder on my swift feet, I withstood the march in fine shape. We marched forth in the gray of the morning fog which lay cold and moist on the streets and the meadows. It hovered on the grass and drooped from the rooftops. The sun, however, shone through soon enough and bathed us and the land in a powerful glow. After 10 kilometers of marching, we stopped at the Loire River. We were supposed to be transported across, but unfortunately, the boats were overloaded, and so we had to wade out in the middle of the river and make our way to the far shore, looking like a bunch of drowned cats. Everything was a mess, and as you can imagine, there is not much marching to be done in wet boots and socks. So we got things in order as best as we could and continued on our way. Our commander took the lead, and we succeeded in getting everyone back into tip top shape. I managed to hold up pretty well. Afterward, we all showed our feet to the medic. But the Walk Well powder is splendid and had done its job, even on wet feet. So, Goldchen, again 1000 thanks for the foot powder.

And then, today, I received a lot of money from you. Let me know, as soon as you can, just how it went with the shoes so I can send the coupon. I will use the money for it. I will not use it on anything for myself. You know how frugal I am, and that is the way it is with all of the soldiers. I ate the last of the chocolates today. They were so darn great and made especially for a guy like me by a discriminating little wife like you.

This afternoon we had instruction along with a definitive statement concerning the question of the Italians. Please, my Darling, do not be worried. All matters are in the best of order. . Because I know that you are interested, I will write you a detailed explanation on Sunday. I write to you in the assurance and hope that through my letters you will find some joy and not be sad and tired.

Goldchen, I love you so much that, even from afar, I want to make you singularly happy. Enough for today, my Love. I am tired and want to dream of you. As an enormous gift, I still have a letter from you that I have saved to read. You will get a letter from me every day, and you should always know that my thoughts are with you and home.

10000 sweet, loving kisses from your Paulus

Letter no. 40
France, September 11, 1943

My Dear, Dear Goldchen,

Quickly, another few lines for you, my Love, before the transport arrives. I'm sitting in the soldier clinic in Orleans and have just completed a treatment. My back has forced me to go to the doctor, and I have received various muscle therapy treatments for rheumatism.

Your dear letter telling me about Detti's sickness shook me up. What you have to go through! Although I know that you can take care of his treatment, I know that you are certainly sad not to have me there, by your side.

I will write you more this afternoon. You know how much I love you.

1000 Kisses
Paulus

Letter no. 41
France, September 11, 1943

Dear Little Erika,

The mailman brought me a lovely package a few days ago with oh, such wonderful things in it. A warming box made by Mommy herself – a wonderful foot warmer for Papi's feet. And, yes, in the bottom of the package lay a lovely little letter from you, my little Erika. There, written in large letters was a beautiful and lovely greeting from you – you even sent a little kiss. That you can already write a real letter in ink has made your Papi very happy and proud of his big daughter. Your Mommy writes that you are well-behaved and that is wonderful, and I am proud of you, Eki. Your Papi is proud of you and loves you very much. Please tell your lovely, lovely Mommy hello for me, again.

Dear Mattheu!

Although you are too young to be able to write, you have most probably thought about me at times and wondered why your Papi had to go to war and no longer comes home every day. Yes, my son, that is also something that is hard for me to understand, and I can't really explain that to you, until you are older. Anyway, I'll bet that you'll like playing with the train set at Christmas time and building obstacles for the train – By being a soldier your Papi has learned that he was good at that sort of thing.

Do play with your little brother, Detti, and be well-behaved and obedient. Your mother will give you some candy for that, as will Detti. We men understand each other, right? Give Detti a kiss for me and be a good little Matti.

Loving greetings from your Soldier Papi

Letter no. 42
France, September 12, 1943

My Dear Little Goldchen
My Beloved, You!

Today is Sunday and soon it will be gone. It was filled with yearning for you – I long for your hands and your lovely mouth. I miss you so much that it is hard for me to hold my head up high today. You, yes, you have been a great gift of feminine structure and direction in my life, and you have filled it with sweetness and comfort. At times I have, however, been a bad husband. Forgive me, my Goldchen, for every hasty wound that I have ever caused you. My transgressions weigh like a heavy piece of lead upon my chest today. When I close my eyes, the most beautiful pictures form in my inner vision, and I can almost forget I am a soldier. You are then with me in a beautiful dress. Laughing but also sad, you stand before me, and I can almost physically feel the nearness of your soul. A love ignites within me, and I long for your embrace. When I open my eyes, everything is gray – only the desire is still there. Outside, somewhere, is the sun – how great it would be if we could live only for our dear children. I wanted to make you happy and now am so far away, am a soldier and see only duty and the gray of this Monday. Today, I am hardly able to look at the photos. They make my heart ache, and I want only to live.

What have I done to you, my dear, sweet little wife? . . . A wife whose very spirit lives in the word wife, ... my wife who has made me so sad and so intimately happy. I will walk out into the sunset. Perhaps it will help to restore my composure. The future is uncertain; life will go on, but we must be committed to win, and I shall help in the work of the liberation which only means murder to the people of the world. No matter, I have to hold my head up high so that you, my Goldchen, can travel the hard path of coping back at home.

You and the children are all that I have, and I can only have you if there is peace in the world.

Your letters, Beloved, are my intimate companions. They tell me how much you long for me – you! . . . wife, you! . . . lovely, soft creation. Today it nearly kills me to think about it. Don't be angry about my rambling on as I am today, but a dream that I had has slipped away, and I was forced to open my eyes when duty called. Until that moment, you were with me. You looked into my eyes with your lovely eyes. In your eyes I saw laughter and trust. Everything came together. You appeared so beautiful, so beautiful, as beautiful as you really are. Everything was very special, even me. Suddenly, it was all over, and I was alone again. All that I have left now is the memory of it, and it still speaks to me. Sundays are tough for both of us – burdensome for loving hearts. God should put an end to this war, but it must be a victory that brings it to an end for me – for the precious homeland and for all of you to be safe.

Goldchen, you, my Goldchen, be kissed and if tears come to my eyes, then it is because you are everything in the world to me, and I am filled with such an infinite love for you.

Your heavy hearted Paulus [34]

---

[34] Upon reading this letter, Erika made the following observations: "A profoundly deep, dark and disturbing letter. I can't help but wonder what it is that he knows. I can only wonder about it, and I sense that there is ever so much more just under the surface of the words. One senses his deep need to tie any and all future family happiness to the positive outcome of a war that he surely senses has no chance of turning out favorably. He indeed feels black with hopelessness when he writes: 'I can only have you if there is peace in the world.' This is powerful and almost overwhelming in its beautiful and poetic word use, . . . 'You, full of feminine structure and direction . . . I almost bodily feel the soul of your nearness . . . love ignites in me . . . . a wife, whose spirit lives in the word, wife . . . you lovely, soft creation.' A consumption of husbandly guilt in epic proportions. My own thoughts flood with ever so many questions, and I am suddenly aware of his direct touch on my mind and his substance inside my soul."

Letter no. 43
St. Fargeau, France
September 13, 1943

My Goldchen
You, my little Soldier's Wife,

Back pain has driven me out of my bed in the middle of the night, and for some time now I have been pacing around. I have carried the precious little letter which you, my Love, wrote last Sunday and I received this Sunday, with me so I can read it alone and without distractions. Yesterday, in my depressed state of need I went to see the second smartest cat in my unit, you know, my friend Schorsch. We both intended to write to our wives but ended up spending the late autumn evening, just talking. We talked about you and the children, our homes, and also a time of leave for us. Schorsch is an educated fellow with a big heart. I feel really lucky to have found someone from my home area with the shared appreciation for things of beauty and value. We discussed you and just about everything up to the edge of the city, and ended up with our hearts filled with hope. Unfortunately, it was consuming enough for us to never have gotten around to the writing.

You know, my Love, Schorsch is to become a father, and since I have been a Papi three times already, he has a lot of questions for me. Yes, he, Schorsch, wants to know everything, and I will tell him all about my three little urchins and how everything was and should be. Since the listener is such a good friend and great guy, you can imagine what fun it is for me to have the chance to talk about that. Yesterday he prayed, prayed a lot. Maybe you could look up his little wife in Gotha. He has told her a lot about you and me, and she already likes you. It would be nice if you could call her. Frau Ilse Leichte – Gotha Willig – Marschler Strasse 39, Telephone 1332. You know, Goldchen, although he is an older unit leader and my superior, he is very sensitive and shares personal matters with me because he cares for my family, my life, and my profession. I would like it then, if you, as someone in high standing, would contact her and become the seal to bond the two of us together here in the land of the enemy.

But enough of that. I know that I look forward to next Sunday. By then, you will see that my longing has been replaced with joy and hope. From your letter, which enumerates the trials of running a household without Papi, I see that you raise concerns over the optimistic flavor of my letters. I wrote to you a few days ago, my Love, that there is a reason for that. Your conduct in regard to the life insurance matters has my full attention, and I thank you for all that you have accomplished.

The situation in Italy has turned out for the better. Our division, the one to which I belong, is under that command. People write that Hitler has kept a close eye on it. More later. Please send me your wish list for the sewing thread that you need so I can organize it. I await your answer concerning school. This evening you will receive a few lines.

My dear Sweetheart, I kiss your inner and outer self.

I love you sooo much,

Your Paulus

Letter no. 44
France, September 14, 1943

My dear Goldchen
You, my Beloved,

Very silently I stole from my bed and sit in a quiet room in order to write a few lines to you, my Love. I can hear the breathing and snoring of my buddies. It sounds pretty wild around here. Now, in getting to your letter, my Love, I would like to send you many, many thanks. You are so good to me. Here, I would have nothing, were it not for you. You have managed to get the life insurance [35] reinstated, and I feel better now that I will be able to provide a little nest egg – just in case. Our military outlook has improved considerably. Mussolini has been freed by our troops and has taken over command of his troops, however, under German direction.

---

[35] Insurance from Siemens.

I am sure that the radio and newspapers will fill you in. Our troops have slapped the hands of the enemy, and they have begun to withdraw. I have taken your admonition about my statements to heart, and things are going better. I am glad for the comradeship of my friend Schorsch. I don't need to beat myself up as a noncom. I have lively conversations with Schorsch. He has been a godsend for me. He has succeeded in shepherding me far enough in my life as a soldier that I no longer feel lost in regard to my position here or my previous professional life, and now receive outstanding military treatment. When it comes to duty, it is another matter. He lets nothing pass. I must make the grade, and there are no exceptions. I must push my 31 year old skin to the same tempo as the 18 year old guys, and so far I have been able to keep up.

The French are very disappointed about the events in Italy because all of them believe in the victory of the Allies. I, along with Schorsch, visited my farmer friends a few days ago. I delivered two loaves of bread to them for which we received some wonderful fruit, peaches and some other fine things. Later I hope to be able to get some milk and butter. I plan to take your advice and move more slowly and politely in regard to the trading of goods with them. They will have the grape harvest here this coming Sunday. It needs to be accomplished, or the deer will start eating the grapes.

Tomorrow, we will have night exercises. Today, duty began at 4 o'clock and involves just about every demand that can be put on a person. But with the hope that the war will be over with by the middle of 1944, I will endure everything in order to do my part toward contributing to the victory. Hopefully all is well at home, my Love. I heard that Leipzig was heavily bombed. Two noncoms lost everything.

Just a little while ago I was out in the dark of the garden again. The leaves of the trees had all fallen and covered the grass. Overnight it has become fall, and still the relentless sun bears down upon us daily. My Love, please let me know what color sewing thread I can get for you. While everything is scarce there, I can get it here. Hopefully I will know about the thread and school in a few days. English planes have just roared over us.

Well, my Goldchen, again I have filled you in on life here. I have become tired and immersed in the love and beauty of wanting to be with you. I will sink into a blissful sleep. I know that you love me, your soldier Papi. Well, my Love, I kiss you intimately and wish you a very good night.

Your Paulus.

Letter no. 45
Fargeau, September 15, 1943

My Beloved, sweet little Wife,

Very quickly, I must finish getting a package ready to send off to you before night duty. I will hopefully be able to bring you a little joy with this and do hope that the size is right. Good luck. Thoughts of love and being with you are included in the package. I was really happy to have the chance to be able to send you a little something.

Otherwise, everything here is in order. We built bridges today, with all of us stark naked and without pants in the cold water of the Loire. It was a little windy, but everyone worked diligently, as did I. Hopefully I won't suffer any painful aftermath. I sent the children a package today and want to hear from you as to whether the first shipment of fruit made it through to you.

Half of September has flown by. How much longer until I will be finished with my training? We hope that the ban on furloughs will soon be lifted. As of now, it doesn't look good. As Germans, we can be proud of all that has happened in Italy. If it were not for the bombing attacks, we would now be able to successfully concentrate on the homeland. Still, I think that we have turned the corner here.

How are things with you and the children going? Hopefully they are all fat and sassy. As the henceforward immovable chief and executive of the household, you must have concerns. So many of the details used to be taken care of by Paulus. Well, I want to rest a bit and look at photographs of my loved ones. We are to have battle maneuvers during the night.

The most beautiful greetings are sent to you, my Beloved, – with the assurance that your dear Paulus will try to be stronger. I kiss you, over and over. While at the Loire this evening, I will have special thoughts of you.

Your Paulus.

Letter no. 46
France, September 15, 1943

To my dear Children
Erika and Matteu,

Well, I hope that the peaches that your Papi got for you taste good. I think they will. Your Papi himself is very hungry, but the war will soon be over, and he will soon be home again. Little Eki should write to tell me what she has learned in school. I am very curious.

Well, my Little Ones, give your Mommy a big kiss and tell her that Papi loves her very much.

From your soldier Papi.

Letter no. 47
Fargeau, September 17, 1943

My Beloved, You my Goldchen!

Well, we're finished. A strategic accomplishment has been completed. I will explain it to you in the following order:

1. Night maneuvers: Under the splendor of moonlight we took our positions, that is, we dug one meter into the ground, in teams of two men. We camouflaged the rims and covered our faces with mud or dirt and with our rifles ready, waited, ready for the enemy. We covered our positions with undergrowth and brush in order to face the enemy onslaught. The moon painted the whole landscape in a pale, white light and cast ghostly shadows. We could hear mice, rats and other nocturnal animals as they scurried through the

brush. It was really unnerving. I honestly didn't know that night maneuvers could be such a kick.

We lay there for almost an hour as the moon climbed ever higher. Suddenly then, high over the forest to our left, there appeared a ball of light, then a second one. Everything was lit up by bright light, and both of us headed for cover as the shooting began. Here, over there, then closer. Our guns began to hammer away, da, da,—— We were loaded, but a tree branch had jammed the safety, and the gun did not function. Dark figures, . . . there – in front of us was the enemy, low to the ground – but he could not see us because the moonlight was at our backs. We gave them time to approach – two here, three there, and then all hell broke loose. The guns let go, and the enemy attacked with a loud "Hurrah." Guns sounded, a second, a third, a soldier jumped up and there was a fight in front of us. My glasses somehow stayed intact. The battle was over, and we headed back, tired and dirty. But rest was out of the question because we had to first clean our guns, caps, gas masks and boots. By 2:00 AM it was all quiet in the room.

2. 70 kilometer march: On a gray morning we set out. Our songs rang out as we left St. Fargeau and crossed the Loire River to St. Denis del 'Hotel to Chateau neuf. I was still tired, and at times my legs wanted to give out but mechanically kept going in the cold of the morning air . The feeling of having the chance to be in the military – all of that kept me going. So, with many a beautiful song we marched on into the gray of late morning. I had one of your recent letters and my most beloved pictures in my vest pocket. And, of course, I carried my longing for you, my Goldchen, and the children, along with me. Shortly before reaching one of the towns, we stopped to make preparations for a counter attack across the Loire. In gray coats and boots we waded through the water onto an outcropping. Sand and rocks worked their way into our boots so that it hurt to walk as they pushed up against our feet. I was part of the reconnaissance party and went up to the dike. Once there, we opened up on the enemy with machine guns and carbines. We secured the land and purified it of the enemy. We then sat down and prepared a feast of peaches and pears. As with everyone else, from the officers on down, my feet were wet. We were all freezing, and it was quickly back to further

pursuit of the enemy. After a tough battle, we were on the move again for a six kilometer march back to Fargeau. My feet had remained intact. That stuff is really good.

So, My Goldchen, this has been a short report of my day. Because we have to clean and patch our heavily used equipment, we have the evening off. You were there with me, all of the way. My Love, I will write you again tomorrow – I'll be fresher then. I kiss you today and tell you that I love you very much. My love to the children but especially to you.

Your Paulus

Letter no. 48
Fargeau, September 17, 1943

My One and Only lovely little Wife
You, my Goldchen,

Although I have obsessed the entire day over getting a few free minutes to write to you, I haven't had the time. Yesterday, night duty 'til 2 o'clock. Up again at 5 o'clock to begin duty until 21 hundred hours. Up once more, at 3:30 for a full- pack, 30 kilometer march. So, that's the way it has been. In spite of that, everything is going well with me, and I am happy to be able to explain all of this to you. I sent a little something off to you yesterday. Unfortunately, our field mail arrives with things missing and taken out of it. I got a 100 gram package from my father with five pieces of candy missing. The package was wrapped in French newspaper.

May my little letter quickly fly its way to you and let you know that I think of you every hour, and that everything in the way of a purpose in life revolves around you. I kiss you and am off to bed. It has been a long and hard day.

Your Paulus, who loves you so much.

Letter no. 49
France, September 18, 1943

My dear, brave little Wife
You, My Goldchen,

It is night again. Millions of stars stand out there in the firmament, and they point the way home. Home is far away, but for me it remains in my heart with all the love. Your dear letters, my Love, bring me happiness here in France. Yesterday, I got your joyful lines about having received the first package. Yes, my Goldchen, I really did it out of my love for you. Your words brought me much pleasure particularly because you liked everything that I sent and are pleased about it. This is what I had intended – to make you as happy as I am when I get a package from you. This makes everything a celebration of joy and sunshine.

Not even roll call could shake me. A letter from you is always a joy. Since tomorrow is Sunday, I only glanced at it to see if things are going well, then put it away and carried it with me during my Loire training. It's a precious possession! Because there is a freeze on coupons, I have not yet been able to get the shoes for you and Eki. Sooner or later, I'll get another allotment and will do my best to take care of everything else. It is, however, getting serious around here, especially when it comes to edible items. I will do my best to take care of you, though. For my father, I have rationed the candy for weeks. He should receive the package tomorrow, along with some other things. After that, it's your turn again.

My dear friend, Schorsch, had a birthday yesterday. We went to a pub during the day and drank a Bonteille wine. We talked about our brave wives, and I talked about home. We chatted a lot, and the time passed very quickly. Goldchen, we pictured the way it will be when we get leave. I got rather wild when it came to you – the menu was important. Schorsch understands cooking and food, and we really got into cookware. The hours were uplifting as we talked about the happiness around our own stoves at home. We both want to get back into the French countryside tomorrow. Our

74

duty in this country has brought us a great and bonding friendship, and we have come to know the hearts of our wives.

Hopefully, the weather will be good so that we can enjoy the glory of the country. We want to visit the farmers and take them some bread for which we hope to be able to get some milk and perhaps some butter. As soldiers, we adapt slowly in order to set up trades. It has to be that way because the mess food is just not enough.

Finally, you should get a letter tomorrow and experience what I have seen and done. I have learned a lot more about the French people, and my skill with the language has improved enough for me to frequently have to serve as an interpreter. Often, I fall short though. Schorsch does a better job than I with the language and vocabulary, but I plan to succeed in mastering French.

The day before yesterday, I got mail from my parents. There was candy in a 100 gram package. My father wrote about the people in Hamburg in an agitated manner. I'm sure that he will fill you in. Otherwise, things are in order. It is 12 o'clock, midnight, as I finish these lines. Then, I will get into a comfortable bed. If only the war were over. It looks bad, however. We were told yesterday that the Italian question had been solved. Details, later. Have you heard from Doctor Todoroff?

In closing, my Love, I think of you, always...of you, my dear and of home. Just to make you happy is my most beautiful earthly task. I kiss you

Your Paulus

Letter no. 50
September 19, 1943

Dear Frau Claudius,

It may seem strange that I, as a complete stranger, would have the trust to write to you, but I believe that the friendship between Paul and me will permit me to do so. I think that we were destined to a lasting friendship from our first encounter, and I guess with us it was just meant to be that way. I can tell you that I feel very fortunate to have such a fine guy for a friend. In the meantime, I have written my wife with the wish that she may get to know the wife of my friend. We have told each other a lot about our wives, and she has so much in common with you.

I hope that you can understand this wish. The many hours of talk that Paul and I have had, and all that we have in common, have brought us to this ulterior motive and hope that we can get together as couples and that our wives can also get to know each other. Please do not be upset at my forwardness in writing. Permit me to also say that you and your lovely children and beautiful Distelhof are all that Paul ever talks about. With that, and my hearty greetings, I will close.

Your Georg Blichle[36]

Letter no. 51
France, September 19, 1943

My dear little Goldchen,
My brave little Wife,

I just read your dear letter from this past Monday. I really had to laugh at how the bullion cube brought you such embarrassment. A package for the disappointed Mattheu is on its way today. This should rectify the oversight. Your fantastic writing about home has reawakened my yearning for home in my heart. God willing, we will soon be so fortunate. Today is Sunday, and we are back at it. We have been running recon on the banks of the Loire and have talked about home a lot. We were happy and even celebrated with a cigar. I carried your precious letter in my pocket and your picture in my heart and struggled with everything to make it come out as well as it could. I longed for you with my whole being. Oh, what a joy you are in my life. What a gladness our children are in such a hopeless time as this.

Now, let me now tell you what I am doing. I am sitting in one of our farmer's outbuildings. Large containers of unfermented

---

[36] This letter sent to Paul Claudius's wife by "Schorsch," his special army buddy.

juice from this year's wine harvest stand before us, and both of us are writing about it. Later, we will try to get something to eat since, as active soldiers, we are always famished. We will get out the cheese and typical long loaf of French bread, but first, this long letter to you at home must be finished. Then, we will turn into a monstrous eating, raiding party. Unfortunately, it is beginning to be difficult around here in regard to food. Chocolate is no longer available, and so it is with everything sweet. That goes for sugar and sugar substitutes as well. All are very, very scarce. I don't anticipate going hungry though, but must get busy trading so that my stomach won't end up growling.

Some marmalade and baked goods are on the way and will be a great joy to get. Chocolates are also en route and with them that unspoken aroma of home in the wrappers. It lingers for me for days. I also need to get some things collected for Christmas. Hopefully, everything will work out. I have taken care of your wish concerning elastic cording and will be able to come through with some blue shoe polish, as well. I will also try to take care of your second request. The scrubbing brush will go out to you tomorrow. The kind of brooms we use in Germany are not available here. One must be careful here, not to let the soft-spoken French pull a fast one, and that also goes for the exchange of money. I will need a ration coupon for Erika's play pants. Things of that kind are a luxury here and not to be found. That, then, is the state of my plans for procurements. If anything changes, my Love, you will be the first to know.

Now, we will talk. The way that you speak of your lonely hours is very meaningful to me, my Goldchen. How often I feel the very same way when evening comes. Autumn has unfortunately set in with a vengeance. The yellow leaves fall continuously to the ground, like weeping eyes. The special scent of autumn hovers in the meadows, and the vineyards have been picked clean. The leaves of the vines have taken on that beautiful red color that you know so well. The sky is very still and so splendid. I see the Big Dipper, Cassiopeia and the Dragon and remember how often we examined them from the terrace of our beloved Distelhof after one of our evening walks. How big the world is, and how vast, space. At that, my thoughts return to Distelhof, and I relive my love with you, up there, on the last night before my departure, again and over again. Only an historical event like this war could tear us apart and away from the happiness that we knew up there. But I don't want to grumble. I have been spared the first four years of this war during which time my dear brother, Otto, was forced to forever take the alternate path. I ask the Creator not to destroy the great love that we have for each other, the children, and a lifetime of work.

My lines end, but I do not leave you. The longing in my heart is evidence of your love for me, and you, Goldchen, will look after me with your innermost being. So, we will walk in our city again, happy with our loved ones at home.

I give you a long kiss, my Love, and will write you again, tomorrow.

Your Paulus

Letter no. 52
Fargeau, September 19, 1943

My dear little Mattheu,

I hope that everything tastes good. Your soldier Papi saved some things for you all week. The clams are from the Loire River. They are mother of pearl and are tough to open. It is something for soldiers – Papi, shot it. You will know what to do with the other things. Do share them with your sister and Detti. Give your mother a nice kiss and a big "hello" to all of you along with a kiss from your longing soldier Papi.

Letter no. 53
France, September 20, 1943

My Beloved,
You, my dear little Soldier's Wife Goldchen,

What a gift from you today to make me happy. The package arrived in good shape – save for a little marmalade on the side. God, what a cake, and it is even better than the first one. In a state of greed, I have already nibbled on it. For some days to come, the good smell of home will permeate my locker and breakfast will be directly associated with the taste of marmalade. Really, Love, just as you write to me about the joy that my packages bring you when they arrive, so do yours for me here with the other soldiers. You have succeeded in making me very, very happy. I depend on you, my beautiful Goldchen, alias Distelhofer Kitchen Chef, because your cooking is exceptional . It is so very special. I have tried cakes from my buddies, as well as the farmer's sons, and the farmers themselves, but none can compare with yours.

Yes, yes, as it is with the splendor of the castle, so it must be with the cooking utensils. You are such a great wife – and I remain a humble bystander. My Goldchen, my Love, I always place my footlocker where I can quickly get at the baked goods. I think that a little piece will be left for me to have before I go to sleep. With that, I can rest in thoughts of how it was made, and slowly go to sleep. I really need that. My back is better, to a certain extent, and I am able to sleep through the night.

In the meantime, it has become very much like fall around here, and yesterday the old witch got me good, but in another place. I got some detox pills from our chloroform stash and am anxious to see if they will help. Other than that, I'm doing pretty well. A person gets used to hardships and obeys the orders of the "higher military."

The packages, three in number if they are not held up on a convoy, are on their way. You, dear Goldchen, have really taken care of me with the writing paper. There might be a bit of a selfishness in it, as you probably want to keep those white pages with my lines coming again and again. In any case, your good care of me has made me very, very happy.

The foot powder and cream are also most desirous items, especially, in the days ahead when we will be on the move again. I have put a thick layer of cream on a callous on the bottom of my foot. In contrast to my buddies, I am able to run well in my boots, probably because of the cream, and also because my socks are in pretty good shape.

We rigged up an electric stove today, and I did the wiring. We will want to be able to warm ourselves during the colder season when we come in wet and freezing from the maneuvers. We'll see if all goes well with the stove. Schorsch and I ate with our farmers for the first time yesterday. You know – the French bread, with the long sausage-like shape. Along with that we had rabbit and a fruit wine from this year that was excellent. Butter is scarce at this time, but it was not spared. It tasted so good, and we were even able to stock up on some food. The French were nice. Even a couple of children came to visit. The fields are empty now that the grape harvest is over. What will we eat? It is all so gloomy.

It is 10 PM, and your guy has to answer the military call – I have room duty. The esteemed noncom left me in charge. The room I showed him for inspection was spotless, as were the foot lockers of my comrades. It is a fact, and everyone knows that when it comes to me, things are clean and in order right from the start. I am that sort of an inspirational hero. If that is true, the guy that takes over after me will have a rude awakening.

May this little letter quickly travel to the home in which I physically long to be. It is often difficult to think about you and not be able have and hold your lovely body. But, we will have patience and trust in God and our great love for each other so that fortune will smile on us again. I now take you to bed where I will be happy in my dreams of you and the children whom I love so much. All of you come to me.

Thanks, again, for the things that you sent – they grace my locker, invigorate me and renew my hope. I kiss you and tell you that I love you, so very much.

Paulus

Letter no. 54
France, September 27, 1943

My One and Only Goldchen,
You, my dear Wife,

I just read the letter that came with your last package and had to laugh at the way that you take care of the kids. I continued to think about it while I tasted, and tasted again, until I had nibbled away about half of the things that you had sent me. It makes for a masterwork of dexterity to slowly bite away at such cooking with a spoon. I really believe that your baked goods get better during their 10 day delivery trip – as if they could possible taste any better at all. In other words you, my Heart's Desire, have baked me cake that I want more and more and can never get enough of – a genuine Goldchen product. Soon, on my leave, we will cook in the kitchen together with our children. That will be fantastic.

Many, many thanks for the 32 reichsmarks. They will fortunately be returned to you because I have enough money (80 reichsmarks) saved and want to shop for things to send home. I want to make you happy.

As I turned in my record book today, I saw an official paper on the bulletin board in the writing room concerning aid to our family. I don't know what that's all about, but everything is probably okay, or I would have received a notice. Today, the weather was bad – it rained the whole day as we were out on maneuvers.

We were running sharp-shooting maneuvers with machine guns and carbines. Unfortunately I didn't make the grade with the machine gun (the rain kept covering my glasses), but it didn't mean much, since I am not a machine gunner. The carbine shooting is more important. At 200 meters, in the morning dawn, I got a 25. To be sure, there are better marksmen, but with my bad eyesight I was proud to be able to make the grade. If I am picked as night watch officer, I am sure that it will be of importance and the shooting will have had something to do with it.

At the moment, we are on alert. There was some night fighting with house to house searches in Fargeau this evening. Out there, it is pitch black and raining. We have received a lot of ammunition, and apparently that is the result of the British, the Tommie spies working in this crazy area. They just won't go away.

Tomorrow, I will have been a soldier for exactly 8 weeks. You know the song, "Wednesday at the Station."... We often sing it: "and if you want to see me again, you must go to the station. In the big waiting hall, Love, we will meet for one last time." I will always remember the look on your face when the train rolled up, with soldiers stuffed like cattle in the cars, and the reality that I had to get on board. Everything happened so fast and maybe that was for the best. The 18 year olds make fun of such deep and genuine shows of emotion, and unfortunately, it is much the same with us. So much has happened since that day. It is as if you have been gone from me for many, many months, and it brings forth my physical longing for you. You appear as such a sweet rascal to me in the night. But like so many others, I must, in reality, remain a soldier to bravely defend the Fatherland. Again and again, I think of your words, that this war must end soon.

When I have finished writing these lines, I must get the equipment ready and then get some rest. It is so hard to have any peace of mind or get any real rest within barracks life. Any peace that exists remains at home with all of you. My longing, My Dear, and my heart fly to you. Our happiness pleases me so. Because of that, I write you almost every day. My heart demands it. The little ones are in my innermost thoughts, and all that you write me about them is so heart-warming. A little kiss for you, Goldchen, on the mouth and,.....oh, yes – I love you so much, my Love.

As always,
Your Soldier Papi,
Paulus

Letter no. 55
Fargeau, September 23, 1943

To my Loved Ones and my Goldchen at home,

A tough night and an even tougher day lie behind us. Everything is quiet right now, and I hear the peaceful breathing of my comrades from their beds. I, too, am tired and long for sleep and a night without any alarms.

We were awakened toward 2:30 AM. Paratroopers had occupied an important bridge on the Loire River, and were going to blow it up. In the driving rain, we made a frantic forced march, past neighboring houses, through gardens, wet fields, and sand to enter the city from behind. We had put sacks on our boots in order not to make any noise. There was a wild shootout in the middle of the city and high explosive shelling on the banks of the river. One could hear, but not always see it. Through it all, the French folks spent some rough hours, and I'm not sure just how it turned out because the only thing that could really be seen in the dark were the flashes from the barrels of the guns and the sound of the machine gun fire.

All but one of the paratroopers were shot, and one of my buddies who was in the conflict was shot in the leg and lies in our field hospital. Back at headquarters, we got an hour's worth of sleep, and then it was back to duty again with all kinds of mopping up to be done in the city. As the result of all of the shooting, I can hardly hear – but am upbeat and healthy. Here, that's the way life is.

(I have received notification from the court authorities in Leipzig that I have been totally absolved of any prison sentence and am really happy to be able to put an end to this unfortunate matter.) I believe this matter to have been the result of a bad business dealing from the time of my father's having owned his own engineering company and not having been able to make the full delivery on a large number of orders of electric motors.

I also got a letter from uncle Hermann[37] in Chemnitz. He writes that with the need for soldiers in Italy and the Russian war front, he will most likely enlist. The Russians have taken Smolensk.[38] How long can the Russians fight? It is frightening. Hopefully I will not have to be thrown into that hell. That would surely be the total end of any hope for life.

You know, Goldchen, we soldiers sing while we are marching, and most every song is of love, a fair maiden, and a longing for home. I sing right along and always think of my own Love and my children. But I also think of an uncertain future. Often, it also feels as if Otto's retaliating eyes are watching me with his glassy stare turned toward Russia. What has humanity made of itself after four years of war?

The homeland is hurting and must make sacrifices, day and night – but we can't allow ourselves to get downhearted. We must hold our heads up high and be brave. As a soldier, one is trained to be positive and think only of the best outcome – otherwise victory

[37] Hermann Claudius – a well-know German poet.

[38] Smolensk – City in western Russia, located on the Dnieper River, situated 360 kilometers (225 miles) west-southwest of Moscow. This walled city was destroyed several times throughout its long history, since it was on the invasion routes of both Napoleon and Hitler. It was the site of the first Russian counterattack against the Germans and changed hands several times.

in any attack would become impossible. Some new recruits showed up today, and we here are about half way through our training. The war goes on as our homeland dwindles and diminishes into a camp of women, sick old men, and wounded soldiers. I cling to your words, always, that the Creator will keep us together in our strong and clear faith.

This afternoon we are to get some further training as assault troops. That's damned tough. I have signed up for duty within a damned dangerous unit of soldiers. My Dear, please know that my head is always held high, and this evening I feel at peace because you are always the beloved partner at my side.

After some considerable effort, I managed to get a second shirt for the children and a pair of blue pants for Mattheu. The package is already on the way. The most beautiful conclusion to my day was your last letter and the pictures. The one with you on the swing – I cannot allow myself to keep looking at it. It is just too arousing (and the little man just somehow follows along). Do you have a decent photo of me? – Let me know.

The Tommies roar overhead, and I wonder where they will drop their bombs. I hold fast to you, my Love, and want to be with you, want to be the old Paulus – with you in bed. I kiss you with longing and desire because I love you so very, very, much. Paulus

Letter no. 56
Fargeau, September 23, 1943

You, Loved Ones at home,
My Goldchen and Children,

Very quickly before I go back out into the field: the first package of nuts should be ready to go and sent. Because the French people will no longer sell them to us, I gathered and hulled the nuts from a tree myself in the early morning Oh well, just one more thing. Other shipments will follow. Please do dry them some more. The children will be happy to see that their Papi thinks of them, and that even from afar, Santa Claus wants to help. Mommy will be able to read between the lines as to how much I love all of you. Well, I have to go.

I kiss you all.
Your soldier Papi

Letter no. 57
Fargeau, September 23, 1954

My Dear Little Congregation at Home,
My dear little Mother,

Very quickly, a few more lines: I know how things in the packages arrive after they are sent off, and so I have taken special care in the packing. I snuck in the dress and also the shirt for Matti and even a new pair of pants that are, perhaps, the right size for Detti. It's hard to tell since French kids don't seem to be as big as German children.

I am in the process of preparing two more packages and more will follow. It makes me so happy to be able to bring you some joy. I will write another, more thorough letter this evening.
Your soldier Papi

Letter no. 58
Fargeau, September 24, 1943

My dear Little Goldchen, YOU,
Dear Erika, Matthias and Little Detti,

So, your soldier Papi sits on a wood stool far away from home, and even if I have only a few moments before my night battle-duty begins, I am sending a dear letter to Mommy and my children. I must satisfy the relentless drive in my heart to write to my loved ones. I know how longingly you await the mailman at 9:30, and with the ring of the doorbell, your heart beats faster as Detti comes running down the stairs and Papi's letter is proudly handed over to Mommy, and everyone wants to know what it says.

Yes, my Dears, it is the same way for me. When my name is called for the noon mail roll call, I yell out a loud, "here!" and run up to the sergeant like a chased heretic, take my paper valentine and get back into formation. I received your long and precious letter of September 15th, and thank you immensely for your loving lines about me. Across the many miles of landscape between us, you described to me your longing, your thoughts about the war and the death of my fellow soldiers. Your words are so well-composed, confident and firm. They make me strong and happy to read them. We must firmly cling to one another so that we are not lost into the depths of these bad times.

The enemy in Russia marches on. We can only hope that the winter goes better. Otherwise, the outlook here is not good.

That V. D. Br.[39] had to fall so soon is shocking. He was such a good person, as is his wife. I have decided to write to Etzel,[40] but I must be able to take my time so it comes out as just the right letter. Would you please give her a call and give her my regards. As soon as duty and the alerts permit, I will write to her.

I just returned from a quick roll call – didn't amount to much of anything. Your description of Distelhof is interesting, and apparently you are making good progress. The meadow has really grown and will probably need to be cut this fall. Too bad I can't see the pretty flowers around the garden shed. I would also like to see what has become of the trail and the wild grapes alongside. Write to me. Should some sort of repairs to the cabin that I have not so far subscribed to come up, contact old Georg. He will see to it.

I often think about our spring walks. There was something so timeless and infinitely rich about that... the sight of the fruit-laden fields, the realization of happiness, and my approaching departure into a life of soldiering. All of that makes it so good that I think of Distelhof much more than I do about our apartment in Hochheim. When will I be able to work our beloved patch of earth again as a free man? When will I, Dear, be able to live up there with you and the children in peace and happiness? The world has no answer; we must wait and fight.

V.D. Breueck has no future, and he had great plans. Some new recruits from Frankfurt drifted into our unit yesterday – all young, skinny fellows, but I guess we weren't any better than they when

---

[39] V.D. Breueck – a family friend.
[40] Etzel – another family friend.

we first got here. Now, we are no longer the ignorant ones. Now, there are those who are dumber than we are.

Tomorrow is Saturday. Hopefully there will be the chance to write you a detailed letter about our situation out here in the country. In another half an hour we go out into the night. A restless life, but with your letters, pictures, and dreams I can do it. Last evening I got to spend night duty with Schorsch. We talked about you, dear wives, and our beloved children.

I kiss you on your small, red, little mouth and wait with great opportunity to be,

your, Paulus.

Letter no. 59
Fargeau, September 25, 1943
Saturday, 19:00 hours (7 PM)

My One and Only Dear Goldchen,
My Little, Sweet Soldier's Wife,

All work is done, and we of Group 1 will have "rest' until taps. So I have grabbed some paper to write to my Love.

Today I want to tell you about my buddies from boot camp and on into field service. At one time, we were all just one of many recruits who arrived at the barracks with our suitcases. Only fifty of us signed up as Pioneers. After a night of sleeping on the bare floor, we began to settle in during the next morning. I was sent to a room with a bunch of young guys, which is where I made some initial friendships. I kind of associated myself with the youngest guy from Erfurt, and as you have come to know, he was a transport leader. He was nice, like all of the superiors, and no one made a move to leave the room. The door was left open, but we had no roaming privileges, and were not permitted to read or, above all, talk. Being used to wonderful home cooking, we dumped our first few meal rations out for fear that the food was spoiled, and so some large hams and bacon were unpacked for us.

The noncom assigned to us was a good fellow. He was especially nice to me because he prized my writing ability, and so the first few days were spent in getting to know one another better and getting used to each other, and that reduced our apprehension about the barracks. The men in the room had gathered together, but things were about to change. We were divided into four groups depending on height and build, and so newly-formed friendships were quickly torn apart. With that, I was put into Group 1, the best section, and some new individuals walked into my life. That is how I got to know Paul Klute. We were locker mates; that is, each of us had half of a locker.

The change of noncoms was not easy to get used to, and the hours were tough. I managed to succeed in quickly making friends in Group 1 and also got along well in regard to the training and instructions, something that remains, even today.

The very primitive, five day train ride that followed brought us all closer together, and I soon knew everyone's name and what it was that he did. My name became known from almost the first day in the company. They called me the "educated one." Our altered lifestyle brought with it a different and "louder" tone that some guys found hard to live with. With me, however, the tone is always a more moderate one.

We were brought into France via various and extensive company vehicles, and since there was no rail connection to Fargeau, we were transported here in trucks during the night. We, the July recruits, were quartered in the Ecole-Fils, in the city. All schools and public buildings in France are laid out with red brick. Our beds are in four rooms and every second bed is a bunk bed. I sleep on the top. It is too dark below. There is a beautiful yard with trees with large trunks and a courtyard in front of the schoolroom. The teacher's house faces the street and completes the layout of the school property.

The toilets have been the greatest surprise since they are so completely different than the German toilets. They're just a hole in the ground floor; one has to have very good aim, something that we were able to do after some amount of practice. Doing wash is also primitive, and yet we have also gotten used to that.

During our first days here we rearranged the tables and chairs that stood in our room. Some cabinets stand in front of the beds or up against the wall. Each of us has his own assigned area to keep in good shape. The tables against the walls serve as suitable areas for instruction. Pictures of the school children make the room look very formal, and we have removed the pictures of French military and politicians. Only the "Old Pertain"[41] remains. We spend time in the room but are most often in the field.

The school is located in the city of St. Fargeau, but it is surrounded by splendid and well-laid-out orchards. The city itself has some 4,500 residents and is a spa resort city with a seasonal life. The "Loire" region is a very popular rest and wellness resort area for the Parisians from near and far. Nothing much happens here in the fall and winter months. The houses are not large, but all of them are surrounded by charming gardens. By German standards, the house furnishings leave a lot to be desired, even when compared to the less than wealthy. I haven't seen any apartment houses in the French wine cities like those in Laubegast. Every house has a wood-burning fireplace in every room.

Letter no. 60
Sunday, September 26, 1943

My Love, Goldchen – You,

My comrades just came in with food and pudding. It will strengthen me so that I will be able to tell you more about my life. This morning was room and roll-call. Everything must be ship shape, clean, ready for inspection, and God knows what else. I had everything in order. Last night I was prevailed upon to organize a procurement. We took off with a hand cart – four men across the bridge – to St. Denis de-L' Hotel. We found what we wanted in a school, acquired some stove pipe, and so the German countryman helps himself at the expense of the French population. The French soldiers, however, acted much worse during the occupation of the Rheinland.[42]

---

[41] Possibly a reference to Napoleon or some other French general.

[42] Occupation of the German Rheinland – Part of the Treaty of Versailles after World War I. The French stationed black soldiers from their colonial holdings along with the regular French troops in the Rheinland in an act to antagonize and provoke the German population. This, along with the annexation of Germany's previous land holdings in the East, originally known as Prussia, lit the fuse that eventually ignited World War II. The Germans had defeated the Russians in the

The French houses are quaintly built. The windows reach almost to the floor of the rooms and are covered with grates along with the usual shutters. Unfortunately the French understand nothing about the maintenance of houses, streets or other structures. A general disorder and disrepair prevails, especially in the many houses that were damaged by the Italian soldiers. On the other side of the Loire, connected to Fargeau by means of a rope bridge, lies the little city Saint Denis Del Hotel with a railroad station. The next largest city of any prominence is the wine city of Chateaunef with its castle. The Frenchman, these days, lives a wonderful life because of all of his free time. He gets up at 8 AM, primps carefully, does his business, goes fishing, well-dressed, or he puts on sporty clothing and rides his bike out into the country. He reads in familiar circles or languishes around in shady gardens – a beautiful life. The woman is dominant in public – always nicely dressed and pampered. The dresses are tasteful and appropriate to the climate. They wear light shoes and almost no socks. The legs are therefore brown in color and paint a splendid picture that can look good. I have noticed some older women, seen them again on a Sunday, and didn't recognize them because of the makeup. When a man and a wife go for a walk, the husband is on the right side and a little behind her because he is not as well-groomed as the woman. He often goes shopping with her. I frequently see men with shopping bags while they are out purchasing things. Family life seems to be harmonious, and the children are disciplined and always well-dressed. It may be that the French women find the well built German soldiers somewhat attractive even though we show ourselves to be rather rough and boorish. The easy going, laughing, and carefree French attitude permeates everything. The natural world has given these people the most beautiful fruit on earth. Yes, it is true, the Frenchman lives well –as well as "God in France."[43]

East during World War I, and regained what they considered "Gross Deutschland" larger Germany. The Treaty of Versailles returned the annexed territories to Poland, stranding some 400,000 Germans in the city of Danzig, and hundreds of thousands in parts of Czechoslovakia.

[43] A German idiomatic saying: Er lebt wie Gott in Frankreich – He lives the life of Riley.

I will apply for ration cards for your and Eki's shoes, as well as the leggings. Everything is unavailable this month. I must go to Paris in the morning because my glasses are still not right. With all the hard service, my new ones have been through the mill, and it is time to have them changed.

A dear letter from my Goldchen was waiting for me at the noon roll-call. I checked the heading, was happy, and slid back into the line. That is my Sunday, my happiness, and my utmost hope –you, my Goldchen, and my dear children. Each of your letters is an emissary upon which I build and believe. When I smoke the cigar that I have saved for today, it is then that I will read your little letter. It will make me happy and give me the strength and hope to fight on and care.

I kiss you intimately – hopefully you can read between the lines on the matter of my deep

love for you.

Your Paulus

Letter no. 61
Fargeau, September 26, 1943

Dear brave, little Mattheu,
And Dear, sweet, Detti,

Your soldier Papi has been saving his candy for you for many days (even though he himself has a bit of a sweet tooth – just ask your Mommy – she knows). I will wrap your package, and then it will go onto a train and through forests and across fields. And after 10 days, the postman will bring it to Wachsenburgweg. I know that both of you like lollipops and that soon they will be gone. But think of your Papi, who is a soldier and loves you, there at home, very much.

Your Papi wears large black boots, so large that Detti would disappear in them, and your Papi has a gun which he must shoot, but only at bad soldiers. They must be killed so that they cannot hurt Papi. On his head, your soldier Papi wears a steel helmet made of thick iron, and he wears a flack jacket. No bullets may pass through it; otherwise, Papi would be killed and then would not be able to send anymore goodies. But Papi will not be shot. Mommy would bravely scold the bad soldiers, and they would not have anything to laugh about. Papi has a heavy leather belt around his waist, always polished. We soldiers call it an ammo belt. A number of bad things hang on this belt, things that you little ones would not understand. The evil enemy must be rendered dead.

At our last Christmas, Detti, along with Uncle Jung,[44] we pretended to shoot a teddy bear, and it fell over backwards. Your soldier Papi carries a small spade on a sling so he can hide when the bad soldiers come close. Your Mommy does not know about all of these things, so I will bring them home at Christmas time and show you everything, and I will play war with you. We will take up a position behind the Christmas tree and then storm the kitchen, along with all of Mommy's goodies, and win a victory. Then, we will celebrate by devouring everything. The entrance hall will be the review stand, and we will march left and right. Mommy will play the part of the sergeant; I have already trained her.

Enough of that; it is better to move the war-play to Distelhof. There we can dig fox holes and make the garden shed into a bunker. In that case, I will first have to consult with Matti about battle plans. Hopefully it will end so Papi can come home to his dear Mommy whom he loves so much. Pray in your little beds and in your mind. Then Papi can be at peace here, and dear God will bring our soldiers home in good health.

In the next few days I will send you rascals another package. This time, a bigger one so you don't forget your Papi, and your Mommy won't forget that Paulus hasn't forgotten his loved ones. I will go to bed soon. In the morning, Papi must get up early for shooting practice. You will all be sleeping in your beds with packages you already have from the little angels. Little Eki will be getting a package, but must wait a bit.

Well, tell your Mommy that Papi loves her very much, and give her a kiss on the mouth for Papi.

---

[44] Uncle Jung – Music director of the Erfurt Symphony Orchestra. He and his wife were friends of the Claudius family. This afforded the parents the ability to attend various music events, opera, etc. The terms "Uncle" and "Aunt" were often used in addressing or referring to adults or older people of another generation by children or younger individuals.

Letter no. 62
Fargeau,
September 27, 1943

My Happiness My Goldchen, You,

Just a few more precious words to you. I'm tired and worn out, and am ready to hit the sack. I just came back from Paris, the worldly city of Paris. I saw a lot and have a lot more to tell you, my Love. Air raids forced me into the U-Bahn Metro Cellar. Then, an ugly night on a train, finished off by a trip on a truck.

Boy, do I miss my little wife, who is so clean, tidy and beautiful. What I saw on the boulevards in Paris and in the Cafe-houses was shocking, as well as understandable. More tomorrow, when time allows.

10,000 Kisses from your longing
Paulus

Letter no. 63
Fargeau,
September 29, 1943

My Dear Children,
Dear Eki, dear Matti and Detti,

I have another little something for all of you. I would like to have sent chocolate, but things are very scarce here in France. Even Zwieback is only available at markets. So Papi took your dear pictures with him to a bakery, and the owner was so taken with them that he made a Swabian bread. Have it with some sweet cocoa and think of your Papi who will be back on duty tonight.

10,000 hugs and naturally, also to your Mommy.
Your Soldier Papi

Letter no. 64
Fargeau, September 29/30 1943,

My Beloved Little Wife, My Goldchen, You!

So, after a hot day of mud and rain, it is finally evening and rest. All of my buddies are already asleep while I am still up, so that I can write to my Goldchen. The wood in the stove next to me crackles and gives off a pleasing warmth that radiates into my weary body. The floor is dark with the dampness of the falling rain, and because of it, the short, free time that we had was filled with cleaning, putting things in order, as well as cleaning clothing, leather and especially weapons. I needed to patch my clothing, polish boots, my belt coupling, cartridge pouches, side arms and a whole lot of other things. One does this over and over again, because not passing inspection is a very serious matter.

I will not go into anything about duty or what I had to learn today, because I want to tell you, my Love, about France and about my trip to Paris and hope not to bore you with it. As you probably know, Fargeau lies approximately a one hour drive by car from Orleans. Along with a noncom, I left at 7 o'clock in the morning; we traveled by truck to the railroad station in Orleans. We soldiers receive 4.50 reichsmarks for travel expenses, not much in my opinion – especially in France. It was pretty busy in front of the station, mostly with military since the French don't like to get up too early, particularly on rainy days.

The train was ready, and so we boarded the cars that were designated for the military. We found seats next to four female communication aides.[45] It was great to be able to talk to some well-educated German women, even if they were older. The train traveled past brightly colored houses and the flatland which lies outside of Paris. There, the Seine came into view, and the farmhouses with their gardens sat neatly perched along the river. Neat white boats bobbed on the Seine, painting a splendidly beautiful picture for the eye to see. After the broad limitless expanses, the giant city came into view. Suburbs appeared, then

---

[45] These females were part of the German Information forces and Recon or Reporting.

some barracks, then garden land again and quaint single-standing houses. Clean lines of demarcation were lacking, as one would surely expect in regard to farm land and developed areas.

From afar, we could see the Eiffel Tower. I always feel a reverence when I see this symbol of French engineering. In the meantime, a quick stop at the Austerlitz Station, full of colorful women with makeup and people with polished faces and ultra-modern hats. The porter helps an older, well-kempt lady who manages to... ignore the poverty around her. Next, some very elegant and tasteful individuals get on, and there is lots of talking and laughing. Very little of the seriousness of the times is to be detected here. Black women with glasses, umbrellas, and an elegant sense of mystery, board the train, and after them, a young girl. A touching situation, as she tries to sell flowers and other little trinkets – would, perhaps, even sell herself for a warm meal.

It is sad that this little piece of paper goes to you; I wish it were me. The exhaustion will not leave me alone. I want to write to you about everything. In the morning I will have a bit of time to tell you of my experiences. How are things with you, my Love? I am concerned about your stomach affliction. Please go to the doctor because these frequent inflammations can lead to more severe ailments. I succeeded in purchasing three meters of elastic cording, some safety pins, yarn and sewing needles today. I will send these on their way home, along with the beret.

I know, my Love, you are more pleased with the joy that I carry in my heart for you and the children than with any material things. I only want to make you happy, and that will make my heart yearn for my Goldchen. This evening, I have missed you so much – because I love you so, and you are so beautiful.

Your Paulus.

Letter no. 65
Fargeau, September 29/30, 1943,

My Goldchen, You, My Happiness,

I just read your richly informative letter of September 22. You are a splendidly dear little wife, and as a soldier I feel especially proud of you, not only because of the smart head on your shoulders but also your deft little hands – the real Goldchen (Little golden one) of life and limb. I am sure that you recognize my own shortfall with the written word.

Your assessment concerning the war and the whole situation of it is far too negative. As soldiers, we get a weekly company report as to the true condition of the Wehrmacht. And it is entirely different than yours.[46] As to my part, I am very optimistic that you face no dangers for the time being. I will explain everything to you when I get home. It is impossible to do so by mail. Our ability to produce weapons is in order, our Wehrmacht is strong, and the training of our troops is setting a yardstick for all the world, other than Japan, which has a different view about the conduct of war. You should, therefore, not get upset when the radio reports to the contrary; there are reasons for that. I believe and know from corresponding sources that the war will take some decisive turns in the coming year and that Germany will have things well in hand.

I'm glad that the hard-to-come-by socks have arrived, because I know that you can use them. I will try to get some more. After a lot of running around, I was able to get the beret for Mattheu today and have marked it as "completed" on my wish list. I will be very happy when all of the other things on my list have also been taken care of, even though it is becoming ever more difficult in regard to money. Still, when it comes to matters of the heart and being able to provide someone with joy, one can make anything possible, and I want to bring you, my Love, and the children as much joy as I can.

I await the three packages that are coming my way with a pounding heart, especially since I know of their contents which will slide right into my little locker snack space. Yes, you do know your little sweet-tooth Papi well. At the cost of many French words and a showing of every one of my photographs to

---

[46] Paul Claudius's wife was fluent in both German and French. She also knew some English and often listened to foreign-language, short band radio broadcasts, including the BBC. It was against civilian regulation to listen to such broadcasts. She therefore gained a different perspective on the war, a perspective quite different from that of soldier Claudius. Much of what she heard she kept to herself.

the matron in the shop, I managed to get a 1 kilogram package of Zwieback for the children today. The dear little ones should know that their soldier Papi thought about them for the entire 1,000 kilometer trip.

I have been a soldier for nine weeks now. In some six more weeks I will be finished with my training but most probably will go on to receive further instruction. For Pioneers, this is a must. Your information concerning the question of study is very interesting; unfortunately, our company is not suited for a reference of this sort. I will have to find another way. As far as I know, there are no possibilities for any furlough or study-program leaves available for K V soldiers. Regrettably, so much about soldiering is buried in propaganda and removed from reality that I sometimes have to figure things out for myself.

The small passageway to the entrance of Distelhof worries me. The barriers there are useless. Animals can run right over them. Please get in touch with the Heyds. He will fix the defects, and you will have peace and order.

Your information concerning Dr.Todoroff [47] is unique and interesting and is evidence of how much things in Italy have changed. Keep me posted. I am interested. That there is such a regular exchange of letters with my uncle Paul is colossal. Too bad that nothing came of it. Please say hello to my friend. He has written me a few lines.

In the meantime, please excuse the rather short content of this letter. We had a rough day of duty in the wind and rain today, and tomorrow is supposed to be even worse. However, the knowledge that you love me and that you are mine, gives me courage and strength. I will now go to bed and dream of being alone with you in complete happiness. I love you so much. I am always your Paulus.

---

[47] Dr. Todoroff was an Italian friend of Mrs. Claudius from her college days in Friedensau. He went on to become a doctor who practiced medicine in Venice, and later in Rome hospitals. Sometime during 1943 he was arrested by the Germans and spent some time in a German Stalag in Lemberg. A letter that he subsequently sent to Mrs. Claudius stated that he was innocent of any charges. He stated in it that he had always been a loyal friend of the Germans and expressed his fervent wish to be of medical service to Germany, hopefully in a clinic in Nüremberg. He subsequently did receive such an assignment.

Letter no. 66
Orleans, September 30, 1943,

My Heart's Love, You,
My Goldchen!

As I write, I am so deeply thankful for the short free hour that
stands at my disposal. I want to chat with you, my Love, and I
want to be with you. Quite an experience lies behind me. I have
seen a lot and endured a lot in connection to the horrible
developments of a war that uses modern weapons and devices.

Your question as to our ability to make weapons and whether
or not we could produce better ones was very fitting. Yesterday,
we were the guests of a tank company in Orleans. We were there
with the tank commander in order to observe tank combat
methods. A large number of soldiers were present, and we made
our way across fields and meadows, through mud and water,
toward a village. The tanks were covered and hard to see. My
uniform and gun were smeared with dirt. At the outskirts of the
village, we were confronted with strong machine-gun fire, as well
as regular gun fire. There was too much shooting to be able to go
any farther. That was the signal to bring up the tanks. They rolled
across the meadows and over the ruts, like noble ships. They
opened their fire on the village with their machine guns and
cannons, and the defenders were driven off. With a thunderous
"Hurrah!" we all advanced to mop up any remaining defenders in
close combat.

A comrade lost an eye to a blank, P-ammo. After it was over,
we took an afternoon break out in the open. First, we worked up a
sweat to the point of being soaked in our uniforms. Now, we rest
in the intolerable state of freezing in the incessant wind of the fresh
autumn air. Hopefully, I won't get a cold from all of this. After
the break came the counter attack. The tanks were to withstand
mines, cover grenades, and all kinds of neat things. We dug
foxholes in the ground in order not to be seen. We camouflaged
our helmets with straw. The tanks rolled over the foxholes, and we
made ourselves as little as possible in order not to be crunched.
Young comrades crawled out of the foxholes, and then all hell
broke loose, as explosives, along with gas grenades, were thrown

against the passing tanks. The poor chaps that were in them crawled out, fell down in convulsions and began to vomit violently.[48] We had done our jobs well. Yes, my Love, it is in this manner that we learn to kill men, brothers of another country. I learn to wage war with all sorts of modern weapons, means, and leadership. My wish, day and night, is for some act of fate to put an end to this part of humanity. A young lieutenant told me about the fighting in Russia. It was terrible as to what a person does there and what a person could become. But enough of that.

My Goldchen, my back is better, and for all practical purposes the pain is gone. I know that this news will put you at ease. All attempts to get a military pair of eye glasses have come to nothing. The specialists had to admit that I needed special lenses which can no longer be issued. Now I will have to try my luck with a Parisian optometrist. I am going to have to take great care of my new glasses and treat them (like raw eggs) with the utmost care. Without them, I am a helpless man.

Well, I have told you so much about soldier Claudius, and you wanted to talk with Paulus, with Papi. But I also know that you want to know about how I live and how things are going. I pray to God that he will protect you as my prized possession, there at home. I love you so much that I feel like going astray. When I go to bed this evening, I will get out your picture and your dear letter and be happy.

Paulus who loves you sooo much!

Letter no. 67
No Date – 5 PM

The Love of my Heart,

I am located in a field. We went out with the 17th Reconnaissance Troop Unit, and I came back as the leader. There were six of us. We scouted fields, forests, and meadows. After a lot of checking and talking to the French, we finally spotted the

---

[48] Grenades here were probably of the tear gas type. Detonating such a grenade near the air intake would draw the gas into the tank.

enemy on the banks of the Loire River. With good reports on the marching patterns, it was back to the base. I am resting on the dike; some of the men have moved out. Behind me the French farmers are hard at work making wine, and the sweet smell of the finished prerequisite floats to me across the fields.

But the French are our enemy and will not give us anything off of the trees, not even what falls to the ground. Before me, across the flat field and expanses of land, lies the city of XX.[49] The typical water tower is a symbol of the community. The watering troughs in front of the houses and around the farm yards are also characteristic.

Well, Schorsch has just come in with his men. I will see what is going on. At important times I always think of you, my Love, because you are always with me.

Your Soldier
Paulus

P.S. In a few days I will send you a group picture of us in our room. You will really be surprised at the outfits.!!!
Letter to follow this evening. Your Paulus [50]

Letter no. 68
Fargeau, Sunday, October 3, 1943,

Dearest little Mommy and dear Dettos!

There is something for both of you in this little package. Mommy's is in the middle, and everything in the back and to the right is for my sweet kid. Your soldier Papi saved the candy because he wants to make little Detti happy. The sewing needles are for Mommy. Hope that you like these little somethings. I will write a long, thorough letter for Mommy later on today.

Many, many, 10,000 kisses to all of you.
Your Soldier Papi.

---

[49] Claudius was clearly not allowed to reveal his exact location.
[50] These two entries were written across the side of the letter.

Letter no. 69

My Dear Little Mattheu,

Because your Mommy sent me a long list of things to get, some of which were for you, your Soldier Papi has purchased a real French hat for his dear Mattheu. All the kids here wear these beret hats, and you must give Detti the extra one. Then both of you will look sharp, and everyone will be proud of my two youngsters. When your Papi comes home for leave, you can pick him up wearing the hats. Many heartfelt greetings to you, my dear little ones!
Your Soldier Papi

Letter no. 70
Fargeau, October 3, 1943, Sunday.

Dear Little Mother,
My Goldchen,

After all sorts of bargaining and buying, I have been fortunate enough to be able to get some yarn and thread in basic colors and hope that you will be gratified with my efforts. I will try to get some more things before leaving France. The ration coupons that I have for shoes and socks have been declared invalid. Bad luck for me, again! But even without "this," or that, Papi will continue to fend for his little wife so that he may bring her some happiness. Anything else, wouldn't be important.
Lovingly,
Your Paulus

Letter no. 71
Fargeau, October 3,1943, Sunday,

My Beloved Little Wife,
My Goldchen, You!

Yes, today is Sunday, but the weather is dreary, and I can't seem to get into the swing of things. Your little letter, for which I waited so long, did not come today. It will certainly arrive tomorrow, and I'll hear my name called with the mail-call, and be happy again. So, I will reread your latest dear letter of last Wednesday and be filled with the warmth and happiness of it. As long as you, my Love, are alone and we both feel a mutual longing that is especially deep on Sundays, we will continue to converse, as such. How very much better it would be for us both to be at Distelhof with spade and rake in hand, ready to work the good earth.

In the service of duty, I march through the French fields and meadows, past gardens, and I look at the grapes, carrots, and other vegetables. The farmers leave all kinds of fruit on the trees and on the earth to spoil. I guess that they have no interest in selling all of their produce. French food has no particular appeal to me, and so it took me a long time to find a decent eating place the last time I was in Paris. I went into a rather plain looking restaurant. The waiter there led me into a special room. He told me that the food for the German soldiers had to be more substantial than what the French are served. On a larger serving plate, he brought a bean and vegetable dish with meat and French bread. There were no potatoes, and for lack of funds (marks) I had to forgo the bread. I had two helpings and was full.

The waiter went on to explain to me that the Parisians are served much smaller servings of fat, meat, and bread, but that a person could get just about anything he wanted if he could come up with the money for it. The French people are embittered because they know that the Germans and German soldiers in France are better-fed than they are. As to my retort on the French farmers not working harder to get more out of their fields, I got the answer that, in the past, out-of-country Jews acquired all of the agricultural produce thereby holding down the prices[51] for all agricultural goods. And so it is only natural that the farmers sought to raise only what they needed for themselves. It was through a flaw in the governmental leadership. Lastly, he drove home the point for his hope that the Germans would take over the distribution of food in France so that the damned, endless, shady dealing would fall apart. I could tell you more about France but will do that when I get home. We have other things to discuss now.

I must tell you about the special report that all seasoned and trained soldiers, including noncoms, have been ordered off of detail and that the company is to consist of July and September recruits only. Since we are the oldest soldiers, it will mean some cutting changes for us. Only the instructors will remain. Some of the soldiers have been sent to headquarters in Erfurt to be redeployed from there. Perhaps you will see one of them, and he will be able to tell you a lot more about our life here and about me, as well as my buddy from Hochheim. Maybe he will give you a few packages.

XXXXXXXX [52]

A few days ago I was assigned to some noncoms (they are like little gods to us) to draw up specifications concerning some bridge conditions. For that, they really treat recruit Claudius very kindly, even if he is not a construction engineer. I hit them with a set of calculations that were beyond their belief. No one understood a thing. Yes, I did the calculations, but get this, they turned my calculations over to the Lieutenant for examination with the notation that *they* made the calculations themselves. One of them told me later that the Lieutenant laughed out loud and said: "Yah, sure! This work comes from the pen of a very intelligent head, an educated engineer." I do not know anything more and can make no more of it but secretly get a kick out of this slick turn of events. It was not easy for me, but it was a fine piece of work. The brain

---

[51] Prices to the farmers were held down by not buying everything they raised. Prices to the restaurants and the public could then be set at the whim of the suppliers.

[52] Seven lines of handwriting are deliberately crossed out at this point and are not legible. The reason for this will become clear in writing which comes later.

still works, and I know that you will be happy to hear that and be proud.

It would be better for my own personal future and progress if I were an officer instead of a plain soldier having to learn every little thing. But I must continue to be competent, get my poor bones together, and be diligent. Training takes a lot out of you, sometimes more than I can physically muster. I should be able to get military work assignments that I can be 100% effective at and with that be able to help 100% with the victory. The snooping around can best be left to the 18 year olds. Well, we'll just have to see how everything turns out. Maybe by the middle, or end, of November, I will have something to do with the training – then everything will be different. If I'm still in the same situation, I will want to have a few words with Mr. Etzel to take notice of the fact that my pre-military vocation at Siemens involved more than most any ordinary person would have been able to do. I plan to write to the regional magistrate land officials and Master Schmidt so that you will be able to get help back there, in times of need.

You know, Goldchen, as time passes, my longing for you as a man grows ever stronger, and I often have naughty dreams in the night. In my imagination, I take you, my Love, into my arms and you are so soft and full of life that my heart begins to beat wildly. The photo of you at Distelhof provides me with such wonderful hours of thought about our time up there together. Distelhof made us both so happy – oh, what great hours they were. They made me so physically happy. But don't worry, my Love, I long only for you. My love longs for you alone. I will always hold you high, and seek to kiss and love only you.

My further longing is for a clean table, for good food and utensils just like home, the way you, my Goldchen, have always prepared things for me. Sometimes it is difficult to find comradeship with rough and unpolished people. I have, however, found one friend with whom I can spend hours in the field in conversation and thought about our wives. When I finish this letter, I will hold you in my thoughts and again be with my "Happy" memories of you. It creates a great strength for me to be able to focus on you and the children. Having your letters close to me brings me such a joy that it shows, and my buddies ask me why my eyes gleam with so much happiness.

So, my Love, that is the way I feel. Everything is fine when I think of you, Goldchen, and about our little existence together. I feel happy when I go to bed because I think of you. I would like to kiss you, my Love, and pamper you. The little ones can tell.

Well, Dear. I love you and I'll write again tomorrow.

Your Paulus

Dear Love, Goldchen![53]

What is crossed out on my last letter to you is something that I want to say to you in person – so everything is clearly understood. The military has plans for me, but I still have time to take care of it in relationship to you.

Paulus,

Letter no. 72

O.U. October 4, 1943,

My Greatest Joy on Earth, my Goldchen!

Today Papi sits in the watch room, and I am about to give the new black gloves a try.

I have just returned from two hours of watch duty and must say that my hands were kept warm. You have again made me very happy. Another letter from you, my Goldchen, lies before me. I have not opened it yet. I have put it off for just a few hours more. It is such a wonderful feeling to get mail from you, as though I am a kid at Christmas time again and can see the tree with its warm light streaming through the door. To be truthful, I have taken a quick look at the letter – just a peek – to inspect the heading and read the signature before sticking it into my pocket in a woeful bliss. I then went outside on my watch where the moon and the stars shone brightly and let my longing thoughts fly homeward to Distelhof. The stars were always close to us there.

Beloved, it will be three months before I can get any leave to come home. It pains me to have to tell you about that. The sergeant told me yesterday that I will have to ship out for officers training on November 11. The first part of this training will take

---

[53] Written on a small separate sheet of paper.

three months. That would mean until the end of January, and oh that is such a long time, but I will do just about anything to be able to advance my military position and standing. After the initial training, a probationary period at the front will follow, and I don't know how long that lasts. According to what I have heard, though, the probationary period is another three months. Should I make it back from the war front, I would then get advanced training in weapons which also takes another one-fourth of a year. At the end of all of that, I would become an officer cadet, be returned to a unit, and promoted to Lieutenant.

Yes, Goldchen, a very tough time lies ahead of us. I would have had it a lot easier as a plain recruit soldier, but it is built into in my nature to want to advance myself, and it may be better for me to be able to leave the military as an officer.

It is very difficult for me to be giving up Christmas leave, but January will eventually come and go along with many other tough things. Our duty here has been three times as tough as it has been inhumane, and my shoulders are bloody from carrying the boards and planks. We all long for an end to our training. Our clothes are thin and torn from the constant washing. As a civilian, you well know all about the nuisance of constantly having to have things clean and in order. It won't be easy, but according to what I have heard, things should go well for me in officer training. There is still time for us to write to each other about all that will come to be.

So, Love, I will now get a few minutes of sleep before the next watch and dream of you. I love you so much and long for you just as much. Beloved, please don't hang your head and feel depressed. Everything will turn out all right. Trust, as I do, in the will of God. I kiss you, my Love, and want so very much to have you again, forever.

Paulus.

Letter no. 73
France, October 5, 1943,

My Dear Little Goldchen, You!

I have just finished freshening up and have consumed a hearty soldier's breakfast. With that, I am fully awake, and that makes for much more interesting and stimulating writing. In terms of letters, I am so exhausted by the time evening comes that I can hardly put my thoughts into good order, and so I am now taking this quick break in order to talk with you.

First, Dear, many thanks for your letter dated Sunday, which I received the next Monday. From your writing, I can see that although you are in need of many things at home, you are also very innovative, even when the electricity goes out. Yes, my Goldchen, it is often evident to me that time and time again you have managed to come through for me. The fact that the children are all healthy under your care makes me very happy, and I thank you for your nurture, you dear little Mommy.

Your brief report about the Distelhof harvest made me proud and happy. I am always delighted to have you write to me about Distelhof. (It is uncertain as to whether or not I will be able to spend my first leave there). Concerning the censorship of letters, I have thought the matter over. In the future, please use the substitute address so that the proper delivery can be made with the corresponding address (and telephone calls and newspaper).

You silly little dummy, you thought that the attack by the paratroopers was real. No, Goldchen, it was only a very realistically played-out maneuver. We take ourselves very seriously, and I should have explained that. Yesterday, for instance, we practiced fighting partisans. The enemy had recruited locals to fight against us, and so the commandos took over. Your Paulus is not yet so brave, but that will come soon enough.

Yesterday, Schorsch gave me a letter from his wife that was meant for me. I will send it to you. She seems to be a dear little wife. As you can imagine, Schorsch is as proud of his wife as I am of you. I have enclosed this letter.

All of my *books are in order, (*everything is ship-shape with me), and we are permitted to sleep until 6:30. Then, we all get up and get going, but it is not as hectic as in the past. That will probably also change. Because time is tight, my Goldchen, I must bring this letter to a close for today. This evening, when duty is over, I will write you another dear letter. Until then, 1,000,000 dear hellos and kisses.

Your Paulus

Letter no. 74
France, October 5, 1943,

My Goldchen, You,
My Heart's Desire!

The concern of package stamps is a very important matter for a poor country gentleman, especially when he has such wonderful children at home and someone who can bake cookies and biscuits the way you do. So, for a second time today, I reach for my pen in order write and send you more of these costly stamps.

I just came back from roll-call and will have mail-call in just a few minutes. It would be great to find something there for me. After that, it's back to watch duty. That's how it is during the day, and during the night it is so cold that my fingers feel like they will fall off. It is noteworthy that southerly weather prevails here – hot at noon, cool and frosty in the evenings, with lots of fog over the Loire and the nearby meadows.

Tell me, Goldchen, how far in the building process have things progressed with the Jung's bungalow? Is everything finished, and have they celebrated moving in yet? Write to me and forward a big hello from me to the Jungs. I received a nice letter from uncle Hermann in Chemnitz, and I plan to answer it. He says "hello" to you.

I have to find something for Detti's birthday[54] this week. There is nothing good that I can think of in the cities around here, and so I will have to look for something to buy for him during my next trip to Orleans or Paris. Since we won't be getting anymore allotments, I don't know how I will manage to get Eki's pants. I

---

[54] October 22

will probably have to trade for cigarettes, and I also have some candy to swap. But that is as it should be when one loves his children as much as we do.

Be well, my Goldchen, and be kissed 10,000 times

by your Paulus who loves you.

Letter no. 75[55]

Fargeau, October 5, 1943,

My Beloved little Wife!

It is the middle of the night, and the stars blink at me through the bars of the windows as if to call me back out again. For the very first time I have had a real watch duty and am so tired that I feel like falling over. Even with a jacket on I'm frozen clear through in this room. But I wanted to send you a hello and tell you that I love you. I will get a few hours of sleep and then go back out into the dark of the day that will gray up.

Have you ever been so tired that you could fall asleep standing up? I can scarcely feel the pen in my hand and keep losing my train of thought. So that you will know this comes from the heart, Goldchen, I have taken only one piece of paper and hope that you will not be upset. Beloved, when it comes to you, you should write me about everything and then the stars will twinkle for me. Hour after hour will pass and the soft twinkling will be so great. Goldchen, I love you so much and am so lucky to have you.

I kiss you and lie down.

Your Paulus.

---

[55] Translator's note: This letter shows how tired and cold the writer is. The German words were run together, not finished or sometimes simply left to the imagination. He was tired enough to be leaving out a lot. His reference to using a single sheet of paper may have something to do with the fact that he wrote his name and the date of October 4th upside down on the bottom of the page . . . . something new in his writing.

Letter no. 76
France, October 7, 1943,

My Dear Little Goldchen, You,
My Little Wife at Home,

As you read this letter, the arranged and previously discussed visit of noncoms Schraeder and Sochank from Hochheim will already have related to you everything about our lives here together as soldiers. Most everything I could write in this letter will already have been said. The main thing, though, is that these two individuals will have assured you that everything with me is good and that I am healthy and well. If this unexpected visit, which does not come empty handed, has made you happy, then I am happy too, because that was my intention.

My Love, I had promised to write you yesterday evening, but for a short hour I fell asleep at the table. So I ask that you not be angry with me. Upon waking, I had watch, something with which we as the "oldest" recruits are saddled.

Goldchen, Dear, please send a pair of large size leather gloves to me as soon as possible. I am freezing miserably, and it is difficult to write when my fingers are blue. Fuel, such as coal and briquettes, is very scarce in France, and for that reason they burn wood around here. Today I will try to find something for Detti's birthday. As it is, it's getting harder from one day to the next to find anything nice to buy in France. The metal toys I was able to get during my train trips are no longer available, but soldier Papi will make every effort for his little golden boy.

I received a 100 gram package from Laubegast[56] yesterday. It contained worm candy and really came in handy. Because I always read any letters that I get later during a break, I didn't read any of the information that was on the package. Worm candy tastes just like sugar sprinkled pralines, and I ate them from the sack while I was on the train. Afterward, I looked at the instructions informing anyone not to eat more than two before eating a meal. Well, I am, as of yet, not dead and so figure to be able to make it until 1950.

---

[56] Laubegast – The suburb of Dresden where Paul Claudius's parents lived.

As you already know from my letters, our small Pioneer Company has been downsized, and at the present time there are all kinds of rumors as to where we are to be reassigned. A lot is being surmised as to the matter of place – which is something that I do not want to go into with you. For my part, if I am not able to come home, I would just as soon remain here, in Fargeau, and for the following reasons: #1 The food is good; #2. This small city is under our command; #3 In terms of location, our countryside district of Loire is beautiful.

The young soldiers are like nomads, always pushing for change. To them, somewhere else is always better, and a split is beginning to set in between the 18 year olds and the older soldiers. The older men are by far the better soldiers in being better organized and more dedicated, and for those reasons, the officers continue to use us as role models. Naturally, we bust our buns to keep it that way. Because of my relationship to the noncoms and the other soldiers of my rank, I feel caught in the middle. That creates a conflict. Any special treatment that I get makes life with my comrades that much tougher, and I must at all times be on guard not to give anyone a reason to get down on me. Furthermore, they also notice that my training is different, and that creates a sense of discord. Unfortunately, I am not able to identify with the logic of primitive-thinking people, even if it is up to me to set their work ethic for them.

Now, my Love, to you. . . . . In the meantime you have probably received a few little things from me. I hope that you like them. I was able to take care of a few personal details yesterday – or better yet – some precious things that are intended for Christmas. They were not cheap and will be mailed off in my next package to you. Your three, 100 gram packages have, as of today, not arrived. Will have to see what is going on.

I hear that you have done some painting at Distelhof. Father wrote me about it, and he was very upbeat about Distelhof looking so good. He also noted your efforts in regard to Uncle Paul and regretted that the matter went amiss.

Since I will be alone on the local watch, I will write you some love lines this evening. For now, I kiss you passionately and tell you how much I love you. Also the children. Your Paulus.

Continuation of Letter no. 76:

I am very pleased that my packages got to you in good shape, and am even more pleased and happy that they brought you the joy that was anticipated. I also have a few more things up my sleeve for you there at home. Your oh-so-beautiful description of the splendid supper brought tears to my eyes as I felt and realized how deeply I am bound to all of you. The little ones, Goldchen, because they are able to bring you such joy and happiness, seem to be the ones who relieve the burden of your living alone. Likewise, I too would have brought you considerable joy if I could have been with you at supper time, and that's nothing to be sneezed at!! As to the nuts, I want to try something different. Perhaps there is something better. Yes, yes, you will be surprised as to the contents of my next package.

The enclosed letter from engineer Doeges is something that I will answer. Perhaps I will drop by to see him on the return trip of my furlough; we'll see. As you already know, I have become part of the Recon-Commandos – a thing that is usually not the case with a soldier who has not completed his training. That the higher ups have sought me out in order to talk to the famous engineer has, however, happened quite often lately. While the other older soldiers deal with weapons, maneuvers, shortages, understaffing and dirty work, I sit at a table in the "Tech Office" and do drawings of the region. The bombed-out areas near the railroad station are part of our undertaking, and they must be put to useful purposes. The rooms are to have running water, electric lights, and big windows. Since I have been studying things with two other comrades, it has become clear to me that I could have a nice place here. Because I am an interpreter, a draftsman, and carry a lot of responsibility, the officers drag me all over the place because they want my opinion on everything. They are pleased as punch to have me think logically and to be able to take care of things. They want me to go out with them, but I have not been able to do that because of the money that is involved in doing so. I need every penny so that we, ourselves, are taken care of.

I am able to write these lines to you undisturbed during my duty hours simply because if someone says anything to me, it is because they need advice from intelligent Claudius. That gets old.

They don't just ask me about military matters but also delve into my most private things, like wanting to know my views on this and that, about good taste and even my personal life – the life of the other half of me. I am certain that they want to make me a reserve officer.

A fairly beautiful park lies near, out from this base, and reminds me of Distelhof. It will be tough for me to leave this place when our training is finished in a few more weeks.

In regard to a furlough, a train has been provided to run between Rennes, through Paris and on to Berlin and therefore through Erfurt. I wouldn't even have to change trains. But when will this great moment come?

You will be happy to know that I am very healthy and energetic. Hopefully, you are also in good health and have been eating well so that when soldier Papi comes home ——! Yes, you know, you sweet rascal! You will be getting regular mail from me now. Unfortunately that won't be the case with your mail, once our company starts moving around.

Darling, I love you so much that I am becoming fidgety when I think of you. I kiss you. Kiss the children for me.

Your Paulus

Letter no. 77
France, October 8, 1943,

My Beloved Little Wife, My Goldchen!

My cooking ware stands on top of the small electric stove with my water next to it. Next to the water I have placed my combination, multipurpose spoon and your, or better to say, the children's pudding. All will stay in place where it is. This evening I will get some milk from the kitchen, and the pudding will be cooking.

Yes, my Love, when I returned from Paris yesterday, I found all three packages waiting for me, and it greatly raised my spirits. I also found your dear letter, and in this overflow of happiness, even if duty scarcely gives me the chance to catch my breath, it feels as though it were Sunday. Darling, you can well imagine the state of my happiness. Hopefully, the large package will also arrive.

Papi has just finished the pudding and emptied the cooking water. I had a few Zwieback left and, therefore, have had a fine meal – especially since I am without the ingredient of any butter this morning. One just has to be pretty lucky to have such a fine little wife at home who knows the stomach of her Soldier Papi. Sweetheart, a great big thank you for the three packages and the letter. Your love and act of giving, mean more to me than the content. It also pleases me that the package of peaches arrived in good shape and that the children will be able to taste this magnificent fruit. At the present, every growing thing is now dead, and fruit here has become as scarce as it is at home. The feeling of ill-will against the Germans increases.

Because of the unfortunate situation with my eye glasses, I was once again sent to Paris. I was to pick up a new film at the same time. Unfortunately, the army is unable to supply me with any "special" glasses, and so the matter becomes a larger concern. My eyes require anti stigmatic glasses with specially-polished lenses. The army optometrist just laughed at me and commented that there was no way to get such glasses under the present circumstances. I have filed a corresponding report with the Company Unit, but have been given no advisement so far.

While in Paris, I had the chance to further my basic education. I visited the Dome Church in the Invalides' complex with the tomb of Napoleon, as well as the open area of the World's Fair Exhibition[57] where the vehicles are parked, and the Eiffel Tower. The most beautiful impression that I will take with me from the Invalides' Church is of the coffin of Marshall Foch, carried by eight soldiers. I will personally tell you more about it later when I have thought about it a little more.

I have not been able to come up with any shoes. Coupons for pieces of clothing or items of wool are temporarily not being issued. Delicates, especially women's things, are out of sight in terms of price, but all is not lost, and I will somehow manage to

---

[57] The World's Fair Exhibition was held in Paris in 1925. The International Exposition of the Arts and Modern Life was held in Paris in 1937. The tomb of Marshall Foch is located in the same building as that of Napoleon.

come up with something. Unfortunately, we will most likely leave our beautiful location in another eight days or so. My present directive is unknown. All is up in the air, but I must tell you that our military situation, except for the air attacks, is considerately better than you can know at home.

I want to have a large package ready to send off to all of you by next Sunday. It will contain something special for you, something precious even here in France. You must hang on to it. For Detti's birthday I have succeeded in getting a little roulette set, . . . something fun that all of you can play with. It is still possible to get metal toys here, but at 10 to 15 reichsmarks they are a real ripoff. As quickly as children lose their interest in most playthings, this should keep them occupied for all of five minutes.

I have all kinds of things to attend to, but it pleases me to be able to do something for our children. What will the future hold for us here, and where will each of us be sent? There is such upheaval in the world that a person could lose his mind. As long as you are safe and healthy in the homeland, and love your Papi, I will go on being the same old Papi. My Love, I will write to you again this evening. Live well. I love you so much.

Your Papi

Letter no. 78
France, October 8, 1943,

My Beloved Little Wife!
My Sweet Goldchen and Dear Children at Home,

Papi has just returned to the observation room from a night watch to warm himself by the stove. He is carrying his gun, cartridges, and many other lethal items. I want to talk with my Goldchen, but my eyes keep closing, and it is hard to keep going. So please excuse the brevity of this letter. I just wanted to tell you that I am thinking of you. You will surely be able to detect the beating of my heart between the lines.

Your package with the marmalade and honey has made the rounds, as have the cookies. Yes, my Love, they were, however, not as lovely as the hands that made them, and they didn't get splattered with egg. – Goldchen, I'm afraid I must give up on trying to write. My eyes just won't stay open. First thing in the morning, though, I will continue. That will be a better time for me to try to bring you some joy.

So, my Love, the early coffee will help me as I want to thank you for the dear lines and for the contents of the package. All of the married soldiers have marmalade on their bread this morning. The butter did not go as far as that. Because of the arrival of your package and the joy that it brought, I again and again get something, here and there, from the other soldiers to put into a package to send home to you. One will go out to you tomorrow. Everything must be out by then, because after that time I will not be able to mail out any further presents. I can't tell you any more than that.

My father sent a nice letter and some waffle cookies, but they were not very tasty. Beloved, I want to sit at a nicely-set table again, soon, and eat with you. And I want to love you because I have so much love built up for you inside of me. Yes, hopefully everything will go well if the scheduled transfer to who knows where, sometime in the not too distant future, allows. My Love, I am worn out, and I kiss you in the middle of your dear mouth. Your soldier will write more tomorrow... a long, dear letter.

I kiss you and tell you that I love you more than anything on earth.

Papi Soldier, Paulus

Letter no. 79
France, October 9, 1943,

You, My Happiness,
My Goldchen, You!

You probably detected a certain amount of exhaustion in my last letter. Yes, my Dear, these are the last lines that I will hastily write in the late hours of the night, from my beloved Fargeau. At 4 o'clock we will move out for Bretagne, near the channel on the Atlantic. Everything is uncertain after that – everything is in the dark. At noon, we will muster everything together. The recon troops and everything else must be made field-march ready. As a high profile leader, I was first on the list. We are ten men to be included in the entire company. Schorsch is also among us. All of my important things are packed including the marmalade and the honey from home. All is ready for the evacuation.

What is to happen in the future is something I will only be able to tell you in a few days, after I have seen the new area. Because I still had things that I wanted to send home, the dear packages I sought to get ready for shipment had to be thrown together in a flying hurry.

My intense wish is to see you again and gently touch the hands of the children once more. For that, I have a great longing. Yes, my Love, I will hold fast to that belief – come what may. As always, your Paulus. I love you, my Goldchen.

Letter no. 80
Frankfort, October 11, 1943,

Goldchen, You, My Happiness!

A few hours ago, we left our old location up to fate. In what seemed like a very short time, our permanent departure from a city that has become dear to me was filled with the activity of packing up of all sorts of gear. By early morning we were far away and with new responsibilities laid out in front of us. You may receive scarcely any mail from me in the next few days, but be certain that I will write when I can.

Your lengthy Sunday letter shines in my pocket, unread. I will take it out tomorrow when I get settled in. Again and again my thoughts dwell on the letter from you, and it moves me to think about you and your letter.

Today, my departure from Fargeau has come and been put into the past, even if I know that I would have liked to have stayed there. It is so invigorating and pastoral there. My comrades must now be thrown back into reconstructing their service career, something that is pretty rough to do. Yes, I suppose that it is necessary. I am proud, in my case, to be able to say that I have lately been given instructions that can only be assigned to an intelligent, recon soldier, and because of that, I sense some distance from them.

How are things with you my little Beloved? May heaven hold us in its common protection. All the rest will work itself out. Goldchen, You, my Love, I greet and kiss you intimately. I am so much in love with you.

Your Vagabond, Paulus

Letter no. 81
Soldier Paul Claudius,
Field Post Office #59345
Bretagne, France,
October 13, 1943,

My Joy, My Everything. You, My Love,
My Little Wife at Home!

Beloved – Goldchen, these are the first lines that I am able to write following our transfer from the Loire region to Bretagne. Our new station for the next few weeks is the old historic and, unfortunately, very dirty and worn out city of Rennes. Yes, if you want to find out where your vagabond currently is, take an Atlas, and you will see that we are not far from the coast. But before I continue on telling you about my soldier life, I want to get back to your letter of October 3. After a lot of stress and strain, something that a recon commando must get used to, we arrived at Rennes yesterday. We are situated in a former hospital and an adjoining park. It was there, under a large, magnificent tree, that I read your letter. Goldchen, Love, what love and sweetness your letter contained, and what great joy you have brought me with your description of the lives of our beloved three children. Oh, how fortunate I am to have you and what an immeasurable treasure it is for me to be able to call you my Dear Little Wife. Beloved, I thank you with warm tears in my eyes, thank you with as much care and solid love as can be torn from a man's longing thoughts. Sweetheart, I would like to pull you into my arms. My longing grows ever stronger and only my Goldchen will do.

I am ever aware of your greeting from home in my pocket, ...from you, Goldchen, from you and the children. They make me strong and even happy to be able to live on in the hope of an impending opportunity to go on living with you. And so, my Love, I will answer your questions, slowly, sentence for sentence. I have the time and will explain that later.

I can scarcely believe what you have told me about our little mail carrier, "Post." Did Detti really say that again? And to think that this wonderful time has passed without my being there. He must be a really great kid, our Detti. Yes, it is with me as it is with you, Sweetheart, when I know that I have one of your letters in my pocket, I am able to perform my duty, and so it's just the same for you at our beloved Distelhof. I am proud of you and very pleased and happy about what you have been able to do in our little kingdom, in terms of accomplishments and order. We have been fortunate to be able to work with our hands. The harvest is not complete because there is always more to do. The strawberry plants must be prepared for their winter sleep if there is to be another harvest for the next two years. Sweetheart, you talk of onions in your writing. It is the same here. It is just amazing what a good harvest we have had from ground that was not supposed to be very fertile. How were the Jungs crops?

A quick note just before leaving Fernau. Great writing Papi is packed. Therefore, the short letters. More later.[58]

Letter no. 82
D.V., October 15, 1943,

My Wife, Loved Above All Else!

Oh, how deeply I have felt the desire to write to you again and again, but there was some detail relegated my way that required my immediate attention. Outfitting quarters for 250 soldiers and officers is quite a job. Your two dear letters of Sunday, October third, were the only sign of life that I had from you and the

---

[58] These two lines were written on the outside of the Field Mail envelope.

children for quite a few days. As though you knew of my situation, they arrived at the end of the month, and oh, you wrote such dear things in both of the letters that my heart became restless once again. Again and again I am surprised at Detlef, and am totally unable to believe that the little fellow can speak so well. "Pappi – Post," is so loving and sweet. Yes, the little fellows no longer have a Papi. If only this wrestling among the peoples of the world would come to an end, soon. I often have to take care of all sorts of things in the city these days, and I have studied life here and the things that are going on. Rennes is a venerable city but also dirty and worn out, and enemy air raids have added their part. After orienting myself to the black market, I find that there are quite a few things available to be bought here. For a German, however, and because of the cutbacks on the flow of money, the prices are entirely out of the question. A large can of sardines in oil costs 22 reichsmarks. That is nonsense. I am looking for something useful for you – something that Mommy will really like.

So far, we are pretty happy with our quarters. My room is filled with the beauty of sunshine. Above all, I have running water and a porcelain sink. You can well imagine what that means to me in having to shave every day and do a little laundry. Yes, I have already heard lots of comments from my buddies about the special room for the "Old Warrior."

Sweetheart, the other thing is that I am going to try my best to divest myself of the role as the translator. The first lieutenant came to me yesterday evening with the request that I set several love letters into writing. Since that would have been a Ph.D. dissertation for me to do, and he knew that you are the genius at languages, he has now requested that you translate it and send it back to me. I know that you would be happy to have given me the ability to be able to speak of womanly matters in the French language. For you it would be much easier. So, please do your best. I am proud of you and intend, as a result of the letter, to get all of you something to eat

Have you spoken with Etzel? I just haven't had the chance to write to him. I wanted to go to the movies with a couple of comrades this evening. The film, "For My Sweetheart" was playing. The movie was free, but I have a lot of paperwork to do this afternoon and must go into the city again.

You, my Love, belong to my most beautiful thoughts, and I am so happy with your dear letters and photographs. I think about my first furlough over and over. Yes, Goldchen, hold fast to it, counting the days and hours impatiently. Hopefully there will be no events in the war that will impede my time of leave. I kiss you again, and again. The love and longing in my heart strongly draws me to you. I love you and will always be your vagabond.

Your soldier Papi, Paulus and Vagabond.

(Upon leaving Fargeau, a fellow soldier had sexual relations with a French girl. Yesterday, he was in the hospital suffering from VD.)[59]

Letter no. 83
France, October 16 1943,
Saturday/Sunday,

My Dear Little Goldchen, You!
Dear Children at Home, Little Detti, Eki and Mattheu!

Soldier Papi has just retuned to his room from the dirty city of Rennes and is unfortunately empty-handed. He wanted to find good things for his children at home but must wait to be successful at bringing you this joy. Yes, Dear Mutti, you will want to know what it is, but I cannot tell you. You will only find out what that is when you unpack it.

We have this afternoon off, and everyone is gone. Just Schorsch and I sit in a park, in the autumn sunshine, and write to our loved ones and our happiness at home. So, I want to talk a little with you, my Love, and to the children. As you surely know by now, our recon group has been transferred to Rennes and has received a food ration of 4.26 reichsmarks per day. Yes, yes, our good soldiers are running out of money and beginning to run out of butter, bread and cheese. It is a bad deal. I was a bit better off. I still had bread and cheese, but the butter is now gone, and it will be four to five days before any of us are given any more money.

---

[59] These lines were written upside down on the bottom of the page.

Lunch, however, is very good here. A good selection of meat and potatoes is available at the soldiers' canteen. In France, bread is also always available at the noon-time meal. I have eaten at the field kitchen at the railroad station as well, three to four platefuls with extra bread on the side, and realized for the first time today just how tough it is for you to make the marks last for a full month.

Yes, a soldier can't measure up to a housewife. Don't laugh at the poor bookkeeping accountings of a vagabond! More news is that I have had the further opportunity to observe life and the activities in Rennes, and I want to tell you about them. Rennes is an old city with beautiful buildings and parks. Unfortunately, all of these have been neglected and appear to be quite dirty. As a result of the British air raids, many of the citizens of Rennes live in make shift dwellings. The general population here is more common. At the same time, the women appear to be very elegant and well-kempt. To me, that is just a facade. The income is poor. A truck driver, for instance, makes 60 franks per month and must support a family with five children with that. The tax burden is enormous since the French are required to pay to feed the German occupation troops. But because our families at home are far less well off than the French who seem to be able to go wherever they want and wander about in idleness, we are not inclined to be very sympathetic. I like the rural population better, and they seem to be able to adjust to our transfer more favorably. There is a lot to be purchased on the black market: cloth, shoes, hats, socks, most anything that your heart desires. Naturally, everything is tax free, but the prices are so horrendous that just about anything is out of reach for us. I will hold court at the black market when I can get some money together from some of the other soldiers so that we can make some more purchases. Cigarettes are available for 7.50 per 20 cigarettes. Thank God that I have been relieved of this burden, since I no longer smoke. My fellow soldiers who suffer the pangs of needing to smoke pay dearly for that after dinner cigarette. To each his own. I made the purchase of a yellow scarf for a fellow soldier yesterday. It was a very light fabric with a distinctive pattern. Price in reichsmarks: 12.50.

There are a lot of military personnel in this city, especially Luftwaffe. The streets are decked in field gray. For me, unfortunately, that is not the case, since I, as a recruit, must wear the forest green and take great care to properly salute. Yes, that is the burden of a 32 year old soldier – to salute 18 to 20 year olds because they carry a higher rank and are dressed accordingly. When I get home, I am immediately going to get out my gray coat and put it on so that I can be with you without having to bow and scrape before every piece of meat in the house. Yes, all of this rubbish will be done with one of these days, and I will either have become a "top dog," or the lousy war will be over with.

Sweetheart, you write so beautifully about our Distelhof. Again and again, I take out your last letter. (And since I have had no mail from you for the past eight days, I read it over and over again.) Someone will most probably arrive tomorrow and bring mail for the company. I take out the pictures and am very happy for all that I have. I surely would have liked to have been there to see my tomatoes ripen, since I worked so hard on them. Have the children been able to eat any of the tomatoes? The red fruit must surely have caught their eye. Have you been able to make any tomato sauce puree from the harvest, and is it similar to that of last year? It is astounding that you are still able to pick tender little green beans at this time of the year. They have probably been the best crop that we have ever grown on the kitchen side of the shed. Well, may they taste especially good. Again, the little piece of earth along with all of the hard work has paid off and will hopefully be even better next year.

The wild grapes on the terrace have, most likely, also done well. I imagine that they have grown thick there, in the spot where we did our sunbathing, undisturbed. I am also happy that the lawn has grown so well since it was a tough job getting it started. I am especially happy about your new plantings, that is, the 50 new strawberry plants. That is surely enough to fill several beds. Did you get them as seedlings? Oh, will next year be a great year for strawberries for the children, provided that Erika doesn't pull up any of the runners again. Planting trees will be too hard for you. We must wait until it works out for me to do that. The eternal problem with the leaking roof seems to be OK for now, since you have not mentioned it lately. If everything is in good working order, please do tell me about it. My friend, Klute, is no longer with me. He is now part of Civil Defense. It has become late, and I must bring this letter to you to a close. Since I look forward to dreaming of you and me and Distelhof, I look forward to bedtime. Oh Goldchen, how happy I am with you and the children, and with everything back at home. But I must not allow myself to think too much about all of that, though, because it will make my heart beat too fast. How often in spirit have I imagined my first hours back at home, and that reality becomes ever more incomparably magnificent. I kiss you intimately. I will write more tomorrow.

Your Vagabond

Letter no. 84

Goldchen,

Had to pack in a hurry. Am in recon, don't know where. More later.

Your Paulus who loves you above all!

Letter no. 85
France, October 17, 1943,

My Dear Sunday – Goldchen, You,
You Dear Little Erika, Detti and Mattheu,

I just came back from headquarters with a walk through the Jardin' de Plante with Schorsch.

We are now sitting at a small table in my room, airing out our longings and further thoughts about our wives and our "existence" in letter writings such as these. It was beautiful in the park but also a little tough on us watching the French couples walking arm in arm. It made us sincerely melancholy, and so we left to come here to do some letter writing. It is very hard to restrain a loving heart, but I hold fast to the joy that we and the children will have at Christmas time.

Before my eyes lie the dear photos. I gaze at them, and I lose myself in the happiness at home. You, Goldchen, are the queen because I love nothing in the world more than you. Schorsch longingly waits for news from home. He was to become a father on October 12th, and we have not had any mail for over a week. It is tough to go without letters from you, my Goldchen. In the meantime, you should have received quite a bit of mail from me, and my two buddies have most certainly already visited you as guests. Corporal Achaeder was the instructor for our recruits.

But what are words to one in such a state of love and longing. My being away from the children also hurts, especially my missing out on these last stages of little Detti's life as a small boy. At Christmas time you will surely be able to fill me in on the little rascal. When you get a little more experienced with the camera, you can send me some more photos of you and the children. I know that you will find the time to do that, because in quiet times they are such a Godsend to you.

Sweetheart, I love you, and thoughts about you and the children cheer me up more than anything else, especially when I am on watch and the stars and the moon shine down on this lonely soldier. Schorsch and I plan to eat at the soldier's mess this evening. We want to save what little butter we have left for tomorrow. Oh, how wonderful the honey and the marmalade have tasted. This adds so much to our otherwise sparse rations.

To you, my Goldchen, live well until I can take you in my arms. I pray for that. I kiss you and call out to you. Again and again, I wish the very best for you because I love you so much, Goldchen.

Your Paulus

(Have you been in contact with Heydt at the bank to cover the cost of the beds in the cabin? On that matter, I will send a few lines to thank them for the extension. How is Erika coming along with riding her bike? That must be exciting for her. Please do write me about it.)

Letter no. 86
France, October 18, 1943,

My Goldchen, You, my Happiness,

Although the day is only a few hours old, I have sat down in order to talk with you. I want to let you know how much I always think of you and how much love I have for you. Today is Monday, the beginning of the week. For us, it means new assignments and new work for us to do. At the end of the days that we have ahead of us, our company will follow up on several things. We had some good news yesterday, for all of us in Recon. On Friday the sergeant stopped by and promised to visit us on Sunday. He also promised to check with the adjunct for any mail or packages that had arrived for us and would bring them with him.

I have been cut off from you long enough and am in need of hearing some loving words. He didn't show up, however. No news and no letters from home, and so I must go on cherishing our letter from Sunday. It is always so rewarding for me to read and reread the lines over and over again. We are not able to sit in the garden today. The weather here changes very quickly, especially in late fall. It is especially so at night, and I often lie awake because I am freezing cold. We dare not take off our long coats. The month of October will be over and the month of November will determine what will become of me in regard to my military service. Then, soon, it will be Christmas, and I will be home.

Hopefully, my hopes for this holiday will not be ruined. The children are no doubt looking forward to it, and you and I – You, my Love, are the most precious present of all, and I want you so much – so much that I do not think about anything that comes after that. I put all of that into the farthest regions of my mind. To hell with it; the struggle must come to an end, soon.

Yesterday, during the evening hours, we were hit with an air raid alarm. Every flak gun cut lose to fire out of every barrel. It was as if everything was on fire. The French went running and howling into ditches, and we soldiers sought cover under some ruins. The fireworks were pretty heavy, but to my surprise, nothing really happened. Also, to my surprise, I saw a French couple and the man was black. He was a frightening sight. God spare us such things in the fatherland.

May these lines find you, as well as the children, healthy and cheerful. It has been almost three weeks since I have heard from you. Little Eki should be diligently going off to school. Mommy will tell me about it if she walks along to school with her. If she rides the bicycle at all, do tell her to be careful and not let any other children ride it.

I must close for today and hope that these lines bring you love and happiness along with the knowledge that I am always thinking of you. Hopefully, all of this will be over soon. A thousand kisses to you, my Love, on your small, rosy mouth – and many more. I am happy to be your husband and your lover. Say hello to everyone for me.

Your Paulus

Letter no. 87
France, October 19, 1943,

My Dear Little Soldier Mommy,
My Happiness!

Well, I finally succeeded in getting the very first package of butter off, and on its way to you! I don't have an endless supply of it here, but I do intend to continue to put some aside for all of you. You probably don't have any, and it gives me great joy to be able to procure this for you. Surely, you know that, and I anticipate that there will be good things to eat when I come home on leave. It is probably evident to you that things like these are not easy for me to come by, but I will do my best to take care of you back home for as long as I am able to do that. I will send you one more kilo of butter in the next package. That will be a tasty treat for the little sparrows and make them think about their soldier Papi. So – that is that.

I have put out feelers about certain other things, but the prices are so damned high, incredibly high. Everything is so expensive that you really have to give it a lot of thought. Well, I will do what I can and spend wisely what little money I do have. I have a first-rate source for floor polish. You will be well satisfied with your vagabond. I managed to get ahold of a bottle of red wine yesterday ....drank it too – 20 Franks per bottle, just one reichsmark. The wine is excellent here and, most of all, cheap. You can be sure that I will bring as much as I can carry with me when I go on leave.

Yesterday, I accompanied our sergeant as an advisor in search of private quarters for our lieutenant and company commander. We looked at all kinds of beautiful houses. I acted as translator and everything went well. (You would have laughed yourself silly.) At first, the French were not very cooperative, but after a little forcefulness, things went better. Many of the houses have been damaged by air attacks. Some of the rooms were nicely furnished. I was even able to play a piano in one of them. To be able to gain some insight into the economic workings of a French household was very interesting for me. In many ways, they have it tougher than we do. Even some of the upper-crust live simply and modestly. The French people living in the cities are more aware of the war than those out in the countryside. On the other hand, Rennes is rather distinctive in what has been stored up in the way of groceries. Enough said... I will send you what I can as long as it doesn't get too frantic.

This afternoon we have to stuff 250 straw mattresses; that's quite a job! And so, my Sweetheart, don't be upset with me because I have to close. It's time for me to get back to it and slave away. Kiss the children for me and say a prayer that Papi will be able to bring all of his fabulous finds with him when he comes home on leave. And, soldier Papi will also bring something very special for his Love, oh Yes, Yes!

Your loving Vagabond

Letter no. 88
France, October 20, 1943,

My Goldchen, You, My Love,

Everyone has gone into the city, but I have remained here to cook and eat my homemade pea soup. Yesterday evening, I was given a whole basket of dried peas, or something of that sort. I put them in a pot to soak and began cooking them at 10 o'clock this morning. I had no potatoes and so substituted onions and salt. The stuff cooked and cooked, steamed and boiled, and they are still not soft. But hunger is a great motivator, and I have eaten two bowls full and discovered that I got carried away with the salt. I had hoped that without potatoes, the onions and salt would give the soup a heartier flavor.

I must interrupt this little letter. Things are starting to shake up.

Goldchen, I have to tell you something – and just think about it! At the time of our company transfer from Fargeau to Rennes, we received 4.50 reichsmarks per day for a 10 day period of time, for food and basic necessities. Due to certain orders, and because our company was to take care of its own, we were to get another marching allotment after those initial 10 days. We did not get that allotment, and as of today, all of our money is gone. I have four Marks left and am the richest. Now we poor fellows sit here with nothing to eat. About all that we can do is to go to the train station and slurp up some of the soup that is available there..... damn it. In all haste, my friend Schorsch took a train to Fargeau this evening to pick up the money, while we all anxiously wait for his return. To be sure, we will not starve, but things aren't all that great around here.

Oh Love, how wonderful it was, there, at home and how great life at Distelhof was for us. Yes, with longing memories of that, I watch the couples here arm in arm. The same goes when I see the children, even though there are not as many here. It awakens a longing in me for our three little dear ones. I know so little about what my dear Detti is doing and how Eki is progressing at school. And, yes, according to the older soldiers, this is only the beginning. It is atrocious to hear the battleships (seasoned soldiers) talk about their experiences at the front. Because of their brutal ordeals at the war front all hope of ever living a normal life after the war is over is lost to them.[60]   But enough of these dark thoughts. They lead to nothing good. We are not permitted to think that way – but by the grace of God must imagine a better future ahead for our dear children, who still have so many years of life ahead of them.

This afternoon I went to the military platform of the railroad station and played "Vacation." In spirit, I left immediately, taking care to imagine every detail. You were so nice to me and cried out in joy, and I was so completely wrapped up in the moment that I completely forgot to greet you. Yes, that is the way it went, and an officer even allowed me to go when he learned of my name and my profession. He said, "You should have a better assignment than to be part of the Prussian tank infantry."

Well, we'll see what they have in mind for me. Well, my Love, I have once again told you about myself and my little concerns. I long for a letter from you. Never have I had to wait this long for news from you. All of my hopes hang on the furlough; I think no further than that. Oh, you, my Goldchen, those hours of intense love and togetherness should give us both strength in further times of separation.

I love you so much. Look at the stars and the moon. I have told them so much about you.

Your Paulus

---

[60] During World War II life-altering, horrific experiences that produced devastating changes in solders were often ignored. "Shell-shocked" was a term often used in reference to "disturbed" soldiers.   In subsequent wars new labels were given to this affliction. These included: "Vietnam Syndrome," "Desert Storm Syndrome," and "PTSD – Post Traumatic Stress Syndrome." In wars following World War II more was done in terms of dealing with the psychological changes caused by war. World War II solders often returned "estranged" from society, and they and their families were "on their own" in terms of dealing with the depression and feelings of estrangement.

Letter no. 89
Rennes, October 22, 1943,

My Dear, Sweet Little Wife!
My Joy at Home!

Yesterday I had the great fortune of receiving a letter from you. You write such wonderful things that I have read the lines over and over again, drinking up every single word. I'm sure the officer and the little recruit have filled you in about our life in Fargeau so completely that there is nothing left for me to add.

As for now, we have been separated from our Recon Company. They are expected to be back in six days, and hopefully, the officer will bring me a package from you and be able to tell me all about the way things are at home. He is really fond of children and will tell me about little Detti's claims of compensation from his soldier uncle.

Your news of the death of dear old Georg deeply disturbed me. The dear old fellow is gone, and with him goes a beautiful part of the village of Hochheim and such great woodworking skills. He was taken amid his work. During my last visit to see him, I noticed how much he had aged. Now the shutter work will have to wait until I get back to Distelhof!

Father wrote to me from Laubegast all about your long letter and the latest news from you. I am writing these last lines in great haste so that I can take this letter into the city with me to mail it. I was just asked to translate this and that into French. Ha, when my furlough comes, you will, no doubt, laugh at the lack of my ability with the French language, but someone has to help out whenever he can. The food situation continues to be a calamity. The NVS-soups have been good enough, but I really yearn for potatoes and a solid meal like those you make at home.

I must close for now, my Goldchen, I have to go into the dirty and unfriendly city of Rennes.

Be greeted with my longing and 1000 kisses. And give the dear children a big kiss from their Papi.

Your Paulus and Vagabond

Letter no. 90
France, October 24, 1943,

My Dear and only Goldchen, You, my Joy,
and Soldier Mutti,

I write this letter with a very guilty conscience. Can you believe it! I haven't written since Friday, and today is Sunday. I did not intend for it to be that way, but then, my Love, I have not received a letter from you since last Wednesday. So, each of us will just have to out-wait the other in this long absence of mail. I know, however, that you, my Goldchen, have your hands full at home with end-of-the-month bills to pay and financial records to keep. Hopefully, you and the children are healthy. The way that it is, our exchange of letters can mean as many as 14 days in terms of a reply, and a lot can happen in that period of time.

We have had rainy weather here for many days now. As you can well imagine in having seen our uniforms, I freeze horribly in our thin drill jackets, especially when having to crawl across damp meadows and fields. Everything sticks, and is badly in need of a daily washing. In this rainy weather, our weapons rust easily, and we are instructed to keep them spotless. That is often just not possible. It takes all of my free time to keep things clean, and I am dog-tired by the time I reach for a pen.

Well, enough of that. Today is Sunday, and we are off duty. Sundays consist of what little time we do have for ourselves, but even that makes it all the more difficult at roll-call since by then our thoughts have flown homeward to warm rooms and clean clothes. Our children play and do not have to think about the tough times that shake and bleed our poor Europe.

You, my Dear, will sit at the radio with things to darn and sew with our little band, ...a blessing to you. Yes, yes, how much I would like to be right in the middle of all of you, reading a book and smoking a cigar. How often I have been in that position, looked into your eyes and felt the happiness in my heart. The children would then interrupt my reading as if to say, "Papi, we are here too and want you to play with us." Yes, those were beautiful times at Distelhof. Though they are gone for now, they remain strong in my heart and lift me up to carry me through the hard times.

A lot has changed in the last few days in regard to the make up of our company and in the way of duty cuts. Our company consists of some 200 men. One third of the men are older soldiers, one third recruits, and the other third, the new, September recruits. All of the older soldiers left France today to be reassigned with units at the front. We, July recruits, are taking their place, and it is up to us to continue the training work that, up to now, was their duty. There has been considerable speculation as to our fate, but I don't want to communicate anything to you at this time, since nothing is certain. Our little group is getting smaller, and the noncoms must work harder. A young April recruit whom I have come to know will deliver this letter to you, my Dear, in Erfurt, in person. He will tell you a lot about me, and he also knows Schorsch well. You will be surprised to hear that the messenger comes from Hochheim and knows of you by way of Schoenemann. If you have anything there for him to smoke, it would mean a lot to have you offer it to him.

In my last letter I wrote to you about France and my last trip to Paris. In the meantime, and because of my eye glasses, I have had to travel to Paris again. I also had to deliver a film for our theater at the front, all of which meant having to get up very early because Pioneer Claudius has room duty.

I have had the opportunity to walk the beautiful streets of Paris again, even the "Champs d' Elyse." I have seen a lot and want so much to tell you about everything. But writing is insufficient because I know how much you love France. Because I really want your input on all I have seen, I will wait so that we can talk about it together, later on.

Amid the polished people, I probably appeared like a large hulk in uniform, wearing Wellington boots, as a commoner, as big as a bear. And I believe that the French did see me that way. It is truly a beautiful, interesting and even breathtaking city, a world-class city that deserves to be one. There, life goes on as though it were a time of peace, as though France were not being occupied by us. I saw a lot of cars with well-dressed people wearing fine jewelry. In the parks, the young people talked and played cards. Also interesting was the international stamp exchange under the free sky. I took note of the faces of the intelligent individuals, as well as the workers, who sat on park benches exchanging stamps as they talked about their collections. Peddlers were there too, and as for me, Mr. Country Gentleman, I felt quite international to be among them.

The shops are splendidly decorated, a lot like Germany, with the exception that you could see some expensive but damaged goods, like porcelain ware, in every shop window. The food situation in this large city is not good. An allotment of butter, meat, fat, or bread is about half what it is in Germany. Sugar is really scarce, since France has a very small sugar beet industry and imports most of its raw sugar from its colonies. In a time of peace, before the war, the French farmer had the chance to sell his agricultural products to the public or any of the large grocery concerns. Now, many Jews handle the sale of agricultural products to other countries and keep the profits to the farmers at rock bottom levels. Because of that, the farmer today is reduced to rags, and the fields are either completely ignored, very poorly attended, or the crops are left to spoil. Every apple, every pear, all of the fruit is splendidly plump, but the worms are busy and the crops need to be harvested. The French allow a great part of their fruit to spoil. All of it is the outcome of very bad politics. In this, we Germans have been much more responsible. We wanted to plant as many fruit trees at Distelhof as possible. I told you so little about raising fruit. Maybe you can get some help and tips from Mr. Rastin about that, and perhaps our children will carry on with our little orchard.

A few days ago I completed my drawings and calculations for the noncoms (they are highly respected and godlike to us). The drawings were outstanding and were presented for examination by these gentlemen as their own work, but the lieutenant saw through their misuse of the engineer, and I came out of that one looking pretty good.

Well, my Love, I must close and remain diligent. I kiss you in the middle of your sweet mouth but would then go on to do something else (?) with you, but you, you sweet rascal are too far away. 10,000 best wishes and love

from your Paulus.

I have sent the children little packages. One for Mutti has also been included.[61]

Letter no. 91
France, October 24, 1943,

My Joy,
You, my Goldchen at home,
and my Dear Children,

Schorsch just returned from Fargeau and has handed Papi the letters that were waiting there for him – My Joy!, letters for which Papi has so dearly longed. They now lie before me and call out for me to read them and dream of my home and of my dear little Wife, of my Goldchen amid our lively children. Every letter is a testimony to how much you think about me and how deeply you care for me, my dear Sweetheart. I also am thinking and caring about you as my daily little letters home help to calm my poor dumb heart, and just the act of it makes me happy. The more I write, the more I want to write, and because you have asked me so many questions, I will answer them, letter by letter.

Letter of October 9, 1943:

You have received all of the packages that I have sent so far, but some surprising ones are still on their way to you. A live messenger will arrive and bring with him a large bag for Mommy. "Kitchen," is written on it in huge letters, and tomorrow it will provide you with the most beautiful greeting from me. My dear friend, Schorsch, will tell you all about me in the way that only he can. Ask him all kinds of questions and remember that he and I have been together since the very beginning, and the two of us have dreamed together the great joys of our peaceful lives back at home.

In my next big package, Erika will get fabric for some new dresses which will leave the boys standing in admiration. Your

---

[61] These sentences written across the side of the page.

report about the deterioration of the living room drapes had a happy ending, but what makes me most happy is that my smart little wife was able to put things back together again. I have always been proud of those drapes. Hopefully I will be able to look them over at home and in person, sometime soon. I have already commented on the news of the death of Georg, faithful old servant. I liked him a lot and know that the feeling was mutual.

Letter of October 10, 1943:

In regard to the specific use of the money, I am of a different opinion than Dr. Manus. Here, in France, I can get ham, belly meat, butter, bacon etc., in ungodly amounts and, naturally, also goose. I have some special connections that I made in talking with a soldier one evening, and now everybody in the company comes to me to act as a purchasing agent for them. If the money comes through, and if you give it to me, I can buy you anything you want. Schorsch will tell you about my abilities at organization and procurement. Dr. Manus should give his money to Schorsch in the form of credit vouchers from the bank and with it send a wish list. If any of this comes to you at home as a shock, none of it has anything to do with my reputation as a soldier. My official work as a foreign relations representative came about through my appointment to the Recon group. Otherwise, as one lieutenant said, had I been appointed earlier, I would have already completed the requirements to become a lieutenant. He said that I could become one in 3/4 of a year. I will peruse that further when the company gets back.

After a 3 to 4 months training period, I would have to attend weapons school, then, most likely, weaponry at the front with a following promotion to sergeant and finally, lieutenant. Because everything varies, my company is not able to spell everything out, and that includes the required length of service on the front. At any rate, the troops having to take care of the most dangerous matters concerning troop maneuvers are the Pioneers. All of the officers have told me that, and I have heard it in other quarters. The Pioneer is the man in the Army who carries the responsibility for the most difficult and dangerous tasks because he is correspondingly trained for that. Our highly trained and educated

Pioneer soldiers are also sent in as replacements for fallen Wehrmacht military men at the front. In my Recon service I have been informed by the Sergeant (an officers candidate for the academy), as well as other officials, that there are considerable differences among my buddies. A transfer was denied for me because my officers value me as an educated, well-studied man with multifaceted abilities and, privately, they didn't want to lose me. It is unspoken, but the academicians stick together and put pressure on the humble infantrymen. My own roll is rather peculiar in that I am also infantry. They often salute me and under their breath whisper, "Yes sir, Herr Lieutenant." Schorsch will fill you in on the things that I can't put down on paper, and you will better be able to understand all that.

I am somewhat let down by your description of the house warming for the Jungs. I would really like to know more about how everything looked and how the little house was set up. More, please. Everything else that you wrote about the bright shining moon and the beautiful fields was beautifully moving because Distelhof is my very special country place.

When you have the opportunity, pass on a big hello to uncle Kleineman for me. He needs to remember to winterize the pipes and turn the water off out there.

Letter of October 13, 1943:

I have a heavy sweater here with my equipment, but I have no gloves that I can send to you and don't believe that I can get any little mittens. I can buy fur-lined, leather gloves for 30 to 35 reichsmarks, but they are too nice for you to use as work gloves. Should you, however, want anything like that, let me know.

As I have already written, we are presently quartered in Rennes. Our Unit is in Italy, and it is unclear as to whether or not I will be transferred there. That Mrs. Manus would like to see me go to Russia is interesting, but certain Army officials would have to agree to that. Your observations concerning certain diplomatic figures are interesting; I will, however, most likely not get an instructional furlough until I have completed three years of service. Weimar is out of the question, even if that would be the closest to home and to you. Please don't give up, though. Perhaps I would be able to begin my instruction as a lieutenant there. You, my dear little Wife, are so ambitious in regard to me, and oh how the tears come when I think about your perpetual care and efforts on my behalf.

In oracle-like words, you have let me know, within the lines of your writings, that you have something special up your sleeve, and since I am anxious about your plans, I hope for some quick enlightenment. What can it be for me? You further write that you have money concerns. Yes, Beloved, even though I send some of my meager pay home to you, I can well imagine that, since I also cost you money each month in the packages that you send to me. Because of an improved financial situation here, I have been able to put some money aside. Dr. Manus's suggestion that some money be invested on your part is not at all bad.

This afternoon I must again play the part of the translator. Gradually, one learns to speak common sentences without having to think everything over at length, but a letter, the sort of thing that the sergeant wanted to put into French, would be another matter and best left in the hands of word-wise souls like you. At any rate, our composers of German to French are not able to do it. How are things with you, my Love? Are you healthy and adequately fed? In the future, you will have things like butter, bacon, and other special delicacies because your Paulus will see to it. (What that means in terms of difficult or even dangerous transactions I will explain later.) Our company is expected to return the day after tomorrow, and then it will be back to the old grind for me. Until then, we must keep busy.

Tonight, my Love, I traveled in the large wagon (constellation) 1,000 Kilometers across the stars just to declare my love for you. Because my joy is always with you and the children, my thoughts are constantly with you. I do not wish to humble you, and you need not bend to me. I gave that up in my previous life. I love you so much, and it will always remain that way. Greet the little children for me, and as for you, I cannot find the words to tell you what you mean to me and the love that I have for you.

As always,
your Paulus

Letter no. 92
Rennes, October 27, 1943,

My Beloved Sweet Little Wife,
My Joy in the Homeland,

With a heart full of longing, I reach for my pen so that I might send you, my Love, a few dear lines. Since I had to accompany a noncom officer into several far off villages for procurement reasons, it was impossible for me to write anything at all yesterday. Today, with the company having returned, there is a lot of work to do. I am, however, pleased to be able to get back into a familiar routine in order to be able to complete my training. Without doing that, any furlough is out of the question.

How are things going for you back there at home? Schorsch has most certainly already called on you and given you the butter and bacon that I sent with him. Schorsch, like no one else, can tell you about me, and he will paint you a picture of my life here. When he returns, I will ask question upon question, and he will need to tell me everything – what dress you wore, ... and if you can still produce that pretty little laugh. Yes indeed, I will interrogate him – the new father. Even though Schorsch had to leave here in a hurry, as I understand it, you are to receive an invitation to the baptism. You should take little Erika. Put a pretty dress on her, that would be appropriate.

The best thing for me to do would be to throw my eye glasses on the floor. That would get me a pass to Germany. Both pair of military glasses must be procured in Germany, and I figure that I would be able to make a quick jaunt to Erfurt. That would be heavenly, and oh, I would also bring a little something along to put into the pot on the stove.

Did Dettos have a good birthday celebration? Did my roulette wheel get there in time? On the 22nd of October the sweet little guy will have become two years old. If this war keeps going, he will have become a young boy by the time I get home and that just should not be. He must remain my sweet little Dettos.

I talked with several French farm women yesterday. They told me that their husbands had been working in Germany as prisoners of war for the past four years and had not been allowed a home visit for all of that time and were permitted to write just once a month. Can you imagine how embittered they are toward us? It is always very interesting to talk to the people of the land. There, I also happened to see a farm house interior with a giant fireplace eerily flickering with a large fire under a huge, ancient, three-legged kettle, as antique as you might find in any primitive kitchen. It was also hard not to miss the very large, old, bed that stood near the fireplace and belonged to the owner and his wife. Splendid, intricately carved cupboards, more than a century old, stood up against the aged walls. And, of course, there was the vintage grandfather clock with its richly decorated housing. High quality furniture and old customs, the culture of another time, were there to be seen. In most all ways, the farmers are diligent, orderly, and tidy. They keep a lot of chickens and cows, and so there is plenty of butter and milk.

Beloved, we will have much to talk about in regard to everything I have seen and experienced in France, but when will that be? A letter such as this can cover only so little of my experiences, especially when it comes to telling someone you love about them. I must close, I fell asleep. I will do better, later. Sweetheart, always remember that I love you and have the one and only desire that everything turn out well. I wish to see my home and you again.

Your Paulus kisses you,

Your Vagabond and soldier Papi.

Letter no. 93
France, October 27, 1943,

My Beloved Little Wife,
Sweet Goldchen, You!

Our company made it back yesterday evening, and unfortunately, things are really hectic around here, and so I am not able to write you a long letter today. It is only because of special circumstances that I can even now grab a few minutes to send these brief greetings to you.

Your desire to forward things to me via a guest came to pass quickly enough. So, yesterday, along with his thoughts about having visited with you, I received the light package that you had given to noncom Schaeden. He praised your culinary abilities and, in detail, went on to tell me all about everything back there, at home, about Detti and the other two, as well as about their Mommy. (This pen isn't working right.) Everything seems to be going well with the little ones. Oh, how much I miss the youngest one, the last of our cheerful line. And I want to thank you, my Love, for your morning greeting (I have to change pen holders) and also for your lines of October 5th, "43" which arrived late yesterday evening.

That you are pleased with my copious mail makes me very happy. I will strive, always, to write a lot. In reference to Detti's pants, I will put my pen to work on that request.

I have received a 100 gram package from my parents along with a few lines. Things are bad in Hamburg; couples must sleep apart.[62] Your wish not to say anything about the bicycle is already in play, and I haven't said a thing.

I have spent many freezing hours on watch duty this evening, am really tired and in serious need of some sleep. I must get a letter off to Schorsch's wife and send her my congratulations on the birth of the child.

---

[62] This probably refers to the bombings in regard to "family" survival in any of the designated public or personal bunker spaces. The British bombers came at night, the American bombers during the day.

Oh, my Dear One, today the business of soldiering hangs like a great and heavy weight around my neck. I will be ever so glad when all of this is over. I want to come home. I want to do honest work with my hands. Well, this too shall pass. Father has requested that the Claudius family register be returned to him. It is probably in one of our files. If it is not there, I can get another one from the army, so let the matter go until I can get back there on furlough. I hope to rid myself of this pessimistic attitude by writing another letter to you this evening. You deserve love, my Goldchen. Say hello to the little ones for me – and a big kiss for you.

As always,
Your Paulus

Letter no. 94
France, October 27, 1943,

You, my Goldchen, You!
My Joy on Earth,

I have just returned from the "dog-eat-dog" field bakery where I begged for some bread. Yes, Goldchen, because our food allotment that allows us to buy anything for marks is gone, I begged. All of us now go down to the soldier's mess at the railroad station at noon where we "dine" on a bowl of soup and a piece of bread. Hopefully, Schorsch will bring the food and the letter from you for which I so dearly long, from the company that I miss. It was helter-skelter again this evening. Somewhere they assassinated a German Wehrmacht soldier. I don't know any of the specifics.

Yes, the French are fed up with the war, and it shows. Even though we have marks, we are treated poorly in the grocery stores and shops, ...everywhere. You really have to be on the ball in order to get anything at all to eat and carefully watch the pricing. Hopefully soon, we will not have to be dependent on the French in regard to this matter. Were it not for the fact that he works for us as our "home front," the Frenchman would be left with little of an existence to be able to squeeze out. So he holds back groceries and goods from us. Under the same circumstances, a German table would be set with much better food. Yes, my Goldchen, war is war, and special measures are required to be accepted by everyone.

As I have already related to you, one of the sergeants (an officer of advanced training and a candidate for promotion in placement himself) has often taken me away from my assigned duties in order to talk with me. He did that yesterday and again today. He asks me about you, about the children, and mainly about Distelhof. He is curious about our building plans and plans in general. (He is a nice guy and engaged to be married.) He is also interested in furnishing and outfitting an apartment, and we often spend hours drawing up plans and calculating expenses. It is difficult for me to spend so much time away from my buddies, but an order is an order, and I can't do anything about it.

Yes, Beloved, our Distelhof...my thoughts are always drawn to that wonderful place, and I picture the two of us there, arm in arm as we spend our happy hours there, you and I alone, and also with the children. Oh, how much I would like to be up there right now, to take a long look around as the green colors fade and the leaves fall with the autumn season. Beloved, we will come together again, up there, just as we did when we said our last goodbyes. But our reunion will be much more beautiful, and what could be more wonderful than talking about these things, there, together, when the day is almost gone and the evening begins to darken. Yesterday evening, as the moon shone, I held you there, at Distelhof, and the young lady loved the old farmer, and he shared her feelings.

Goldchen, 'til our next chat... be well. I kiss you and want very much to be happy.

As always, Your Paulus.

Sweetheart, since Oct. 22, I have written to you every day now. If the mail doesn't come with regularity, then the fault lies with the problem of our mail having gotten mixed up with another company's, because of our transfer.[63]

---

[63] These lines were written upside-down on the top of the page.

Letter no. 95
October 27, 1943,

My Goldchen, You, my Heart's Love!

I keep thinking about the letter that I wrote to you this morning. Oh, I know that I wrote nothing that was cheerful or uplifting, and I therefore take pen in hand in order to explain, even if I am aware that you know that there are days when things, in certain ways, don't go all that well and leave a lot to be desired in terms of one's mood. That, however, isn't something to which one should expose one's little wife. You should get only nice letters from me.

I am sitting in the watch room, and the smoke all around me is so thick that you could shovel it. Those who are not smoking are talking and laughing. Soon things will cut loose around here with the running of the new recruits in the exercise square and everything will be covered with their dust. After everyone gets to know one another, we will become as one big family, as it was in the freedoms that we felt when we were in Fargeau, along the beautiful Loire valley and the great open country spaces of our maneuvers. Everything here is gray, and the farmers look toward the distant horizon for their liberation. I hope that we move on to other quarters and do not stay here for more than two to three months. As far as I am concerned, my stay is questionable. Some of the things that are necessary for officer training have been excluded from Recon, but when one is a soldier, it doesn't do one any good to be inquisitive.

Things can turn out differently than one thinks they will. Yes, you see, Goldchen, all is going better with me. The old Paulus has broken through, and it is then that I see that this miserable life as a soldier is a more bearable lot than that old pessimist sees. I know that it's the same for you, and I therefore I don't want to write anything other than uplifting letters that can bring you hope.

And still it is difficult for me to be in a good mood today. How did it come to be that our lives, our togetherness, our whole worth as human beings, is based on one thing or another. What did the German people really do to again and again be betrayed by their fellow men? During hours like this, I really miss you and also

Schorsch, when he is not here. When will I be able to work at Distelhof as a citizen again?... When will I be able to finish the wood cabin? I have such an insatiable desire for that still peaceful place that it makes me sick to my stomach to think about it – the open countryside and our deep meaningful walks through the fields. And when it grew dark and the moon shone, you and I, filled with the joy of our togetherness, would walk along the edge of the woods on our way back to Distelhof. It was all so timeless, and when you think about it, the way we have lived our lives over the past four years is hard to beat. Remember our wonderful hours on the terrace. Dear God, when will my heart be at rest again? In this hell hole of a manure pile it is hard to find life worthy of living.

With my collar up, my hands in my pockets and the carbine on my shoulder, I must soon again go out into the rain-drenched night weather. As such, I will trudge along for a few hours in the dark. But this too shall pass. My Darling, you, my Love, I need to be with you. I want to pull myself out of this world, but there is no way for me to get out of this mess. I must see it come to some sort of an end. Today is a tough day. My longing for home and you, my Love, is almost like a bodily pain. I kiss you, intimately, and do not ever want to forget you.

Your Paulus and Vagabond.

Letter no. 96
O.U. October 29, 1943,

Always near to me,
My dear Little Wife!

I will again try to get a few loving lines off to you in the hopes of being able to finish them. I have a few details to fill you in on that will be of interest to you because they affect me in a personal way. But first, so as not to forget to answer everything, I have reread your last letter.

By the time you receive this writing, Goldchen, you will already have gotten the gift for your stomach. Do write and let me know if I should send eggs. I can get 100 of them at a cost of 38 reichsmarks!!? Then you can tell the Thaunsens what Papi is able to supply and fill the gluttonous Dr. Green with envy. I received a wonderful letter from the Baltins.[64] It brought me a special joy to be able to get a letter from 52 Wachsenburgweg. They described life at home, along with all the rest of the gossip, and had a lot to say about the children. It is grand that Dettos is getting on so well and is such a fine and well-respected little young man. I would love to be able to watch him at play. I would, naturally like to answer (the Baltins) letter and thank you for already having done that. It made me happy to have gotten news from Wachsenburgweg #52.

Well, now to go on. You know from my letters that I have been helping noncoms with technical aspects. The Recon commando unit considers such work to be almost spiritual in nature, and so these things do not go unnoticed. Yesterday, the sergeant and other assembled noncoms praised me. The sergeant affirmed that he wanted me to be part of headquarters (fantastic). Besides that, he wanted me to know that, out of 80 men, I am the only one to be recommended for training as a sergeant. He and several other officers accompanied me into the city yesterday. There, they spent 150 reichsmarks on buying rounds of drinks. I am pleased to be able to say that I was very well-accepted. My services are sought out because I am able to talk to the French people. Naturally, this doesn't go over all that well with the other men, and so today I am again referred to as in "there he is again, the scholar." But I am happy to have been removed from all of the filth. Although I am certainly not afraid, it's a lot better than being a soldier at the front. Today I must finish a plan involving the countryside around here, a job that seems to have been left up to me to complete. And who better to do it? Well, any certainty as to when my assignment to the "Drawing Room" will go into effect has not yet been worked out – three to four weeks, perhaps. The rest will either fall into place quickly, or little by little.

So, Goldchen, Sweetheart, it is now your turn to talk. I am so pleased to have passed the grade among 80 worthy men. Hug and greet the children for me. They should go easy with the butter.

---

[64] Claudius's neighbors. They lived on the same street.

There will be more. Over 10,000 heartfelt greetings, and a very passionate kiss from
  your Paulus.

Letter no. 97
October 30, 1943,

My Beloved Joy, My Goldchen in the Homeland,

Well, I've done it. All is set up, and Papi sits at a polished table to write and talk with his loved ones at home. Sadly, Sweetheart, I haven't had any mail from you for the past several days. Perhaps the attack on Kassel, where the mail is sorted, is to be blamed for the delay. Of my buddies here, two have been especially hard hit by the war. Their whole apartment house has been destroyed and several have even lost their entire family. The telegrams arrived here just today. What great suffering and loss people are required to endure. The war lays claim to so much from all of us – everything that we have, from every single one of us. Engineer Doeges[65] wrote a letter to me. He wants to get me out of the army. I think he is jumping the gun. Anyway, I am still with the SSW.[66] Let me know what I have to do. In the meantime, I will send an answer. I will travel to Giessen in two months and will then check into this whole business.

As an honorable visitor, uncle Kleineman has also written to me with an inspired description of Distelhof and, above all, praised the diligent "Distelhofers." He was really impressed by your strawberries. That is the sort of crop that you work to keep going as long as is possible. Oh, how I would love to be there again, to help you. It is really great the way that everyone up there has taken us into their hearts in spite of our first impression of the Kleinemans. He was pretty prim and proper when we first got to know him, and then as we got to be friends, everything changed.

We have been in our new house quarters for three days now. Our room is outfitted with running water and wall cabinets. It used

---

[65] A colleague at Siemens.
[66] Schutz Staffel Wehrmacht

to be the doctor's room in a clinic with four beds. Now, those have become the beds of four old soldiers of Group 1. All are married and a fine bunch of fellows. We all get along well together in life and in our work. The younger soldiers are surprised at our industriousness. This evening, we all gathered together to share two bottles of red wine that we had purchased for two reichsmarks and celebrated the fact that it was Saturday evening. The others have gone into the city to spend lots of money and raise hell. As far as we, the "older" guys, are concerned, that is an option that is just out of the question. Tomorrow we want to check out the countryside. My friend, Klute, has been transferred to Erfurt. Since I was with the Recon unit, we did not have the chance to say goodbye. He just was not strong enough for the service here. Another one of my buddies, a 45 year old, died of heart failure five days ago, and three to four others have been transferred to other places. In another 14 days our training will end.

Well, so many things have changed so very, very quickly in the last few days. My Sweetheart and Love, I will write you again tomorrow because I love you so very, very much and have so much more to tell you. A long kiss to you, Sweet Lady of the Land – and hug the children for me.

From your Soldier Papi and Your Paulus

Letter no. 98
Rennes, October 31, 1943, Sunday,

You, my Sweetheart, You,
My Constant Longing and my Desire, Always!

I have just returned from my many duties as a solider of intelligence to find your letter of greetings from the homeland, and my three old gentlemen soldiers, waiting for me in my room. Completely lost in dreams, I hold it in my hand to feel its weight. It is heavy, most certainly laden with precious content, and with it I feel the joy of a true Sunday in my heart.

Unfortunately, I expect to be called to work the telephone and attend to other things that will rob me of the next few precious hours ahead. These people know that I am able to do things that aren't easy to comprehend, mainly because they aren't accustomed to thinking and analyzing. They also ask a lot of questions.

You are thought of as a very special wife around here....first, because you are beautiful and elegant, but above all, because you are very intelligent. I sometimes wish that some of the officers could talk with you, the wife of tank-infantryman Claudius.

Things around here are really beginning to change. Here and there, one after the other is transferred to various places. It has all the appearances of a situation where the best soldiers are needed elsewhere on the front, and we won't be together much longer. For me, thank God, that is out of the question. I have priority duty at the "drawing table" and after that, officers training along with a furlough. Yes! You can count on seeing me around the 15th of December, but before then, there are a lot of things to be accomplished so Papi can come home and arrive with full hands.

And now, to your little letter telling me all about Detti's birthday: Yes, my Love, now that was a letter, a real Hertha[67] spectacular! You wrote with so much love that it would make any mother weep. Papi read it with ardent eyes and laughed in being so completely drawn into the children's party. Yes, our sweet Dettos is two years old. That he is such a good eater is probably something that he got from his Soldier Papi. Your happiness will arrive when I come home on furlough. That Etzels' children were at the party was great. I will have to send them a few lines.

I must reread the birthday letter again and then, Goldchen, I will then write some more. With all of the changes around here, it is unfortunately difficult for me to keep body and soul together right now, and so I feel like I am really having a tough time. As someone who thoroughly understands what is going on and approaches things with a practical mind, you can well imagine how things are for me around here. I tell myself to just get through with all of it, and then it's home, home to you. Oh, I so often dream of the first kiss and the laughter and chatter of the children. Yes, it will soon come to pass. We will have completed our training in another 16 days. My Sweetheart, poor old Papi and Paulus want to come home. I have such a great longing for the peace of home, and you are the most important part of all. In just a few weeks we

---

[67] Hertha – Claudius's wife's first name.

will see each other again. Soon, soon, my Darling, I will be there.
Make some special plans as to what we might do together.

    Be kissed 10,000 times,
    From your Vagabond.

Letter no. 99
O.T. November 1, 1943,

My Joy, You, my Beloved Little Wife!

    Today, I will attempt to get a few more lines off to you – first
of all, because it does my heart good and secondly, so that you
won't have to wait until you see this Vagabond stroll into
Wachsenburgweg.

    Your letter about Detti's birthday was monstrously long and a
true work of art. What a wonderful scene that must have been in
our living room, and I know that you did some very special
cooking. In order for you not to have to go hungry, I will put a
kilo of butter aside. I know that it will please you. I will also try
to bring some eggs with me when Papi comes home on furlough. I
will spend all the money that I have saved so as to be able to buy
what I can. Dr. Manus will also get 2 kilos of butter, but he will
have to pay for it. That will help to pay for ours. You will surely
be amused and astonished at my wheeling and black market
dealing, but sometimes that's just the way it has to be done.

    I am so happy that our two-year-old liked the roulette game,
especially since it came from his Soldier Papi, so far away. When
I get home, I am going to give the little dickenses a real romping,
and that will be even better. Uncle Baltins writes that Dettos does
a good job of playing with others. Oh my, yes, how time flies. I
have been a soldier for over a quarter of a year and not been home
for all of that time.

    Sweetheart, I reread some of your old letters a couple of days
ago and found one in which you wrote that I should not do
anything to shame you by coming back home to you as the same
person that left you as a soldier. At first, Beloved, I didn't
understand this sentence and was surprised that you would write
such a thing. Now, I do understand. Goldchen, in regard to what

lies behind me and the past that lies behind us both together – for as long as I have been a soldier, I have never longed to be with another woman. I thank the Creator on my knees that he permits my heart to beat only for you, as it did with Hertha and Paul Claudius in the beginning, and as it did in the first year of our marriage. All this has nothing to do with the fact that I am so far away. This time of separation has made a different person out of me. I will remain a respectable man, and to you, my Love, for as long as I draw a breath I will always be a faithful husband. You will, hopefully, be able to understand what I have tried to express here. Certain thoughts and feelings are often difficult to put into words, but know that you can count on me. I want to make you as happy as I possibly can.

So, my Love, I will say good night to you. Sleep soundly and keep a place for me, next to you in bed. I kiss you and am happy.

Merely your Vagabond

Paulus

Letter no. 100
November 1, 1943,

My Happiness, You, my Goldchen!

You will probably be upset with me because, unfortunately, I am able to get only a short letter off to you today. Due to a very heavy duty schedule it is not possible to put together my usual two pages of writing. We have had a lot of work to do today, and it has all been tough going. It is late, and I am completely exhausted, but it is impossible for me not to write anything at all. That thing beating in my chest demands, categorically, that Papi send you something. It's good for my mental health, and is the only joy of my entire day.

I bought a few things for you today. Things that I am certain you can use, but I do not plan on sending them. I expect to deliver them in person. At any rate, I am slowly beginning to save and pick up a few items, here and there, so as not to come home to you and the little folks empty-handed. In the meantime, you will probably have met with Schorsch, and he will have filled you in on things in ways that I am not able to put into writing.

Your dear letter of October 26th arrived today. I was so hungry for a word from you that I read it immediately. Well, Goldchen, if one reads between the lines, the resolve of his highness is not to be shaken, and he is one tough cookie. You need not worry about me. I am not bothered by it. I have more pressing things to concern myself with here. Details will follow later. Your analysis, my Goldchen, is exactly the same as mine. The guy was probably dumbfounded to get the translation in your classical sentence structure.[68]

Up and Away! An order is an order! My situation is not as rosy here as it was with the Recon group. My last 16 days of duty are going to be rough for me and full of all kinds of work. The weather is bad, and we look pretty disheveled after duty. My socks are all torn up. They will require your darning. The gloves, the pullover, and other items have really come in handy, and I cannot thank you enough for your love and care.

Enough for today, my Sweetheart. Please know that I love you very much.

Your Paulus

Letter no. 101
November 5, 1943,

My Happiness!

Papi is getting organized, chiefly because the trip home to you is at hand. I thought that I would bring 1 Kilogram of French soap home along with several other things that I still need to get.

Everything here is good and well. So, now a quick trip to the post office and then with speed, home to Mommy.

Your Vagabond

---

[68] A reference to the love letter the sergeant wanted translated into French. According to Erika, Mrs.Claudius probably attempted to dissuade the sergeant from following through with the whole affair.

Letter no. 102
Soldier Claudius (6550A)

November 5, 1943,

After a full day trip to Rennes, I have landed back in my quarters to a rousing welcome from my buddies. They all tell me that the "Doctor" was missed all Sunday long. That's just the way things go around here. Since I had night watch, I had to put on my helmet and head off to the watch hall for duty.

I just read your letters of the 13th and 14th and let the dear words soak into my heart because they represent my latest messages from you. I always worry about you when I don't receive the comfort of your communications. But there can be no letter for me if you are to be released from the hospital at the end of November. I must therefore wait and hope.

Surely I wrote you that Mrs. Ludwig from Sohverburn, near Erfurt, sent me a package with Lebkuchen. I helped myself to them and ate ferociously. Today I received something else. Contents: two hard sausages and one package of cigarettes. Since they look so splendid, I will send one of the sausages to you. I always have the chance to get meat here. I hope that you like them. I also managed to get one half pound of candy for the children by trading it for the cigarettes that Schorsch had sent me. Again and again, by hook or by crook, I manage to get something for you and the children and I am so happy when I can put together a package the contents of which was not shamefully expensive.

Well, the first snow will soon be falling back where you are, and the trees will wear a furry white coat. It won't be that way here. Here, it will remain cold and rainy. Bretagne is very sun poor. When I got off of the train in Rennes today, the train on the opposite set of tracks was headed to Germany. You can well imagine how that made me feel. I stood frozen in my footsteps. But I am a soldier and must to be able to control myself. A buddy from Erfurt was there with me on the trip to the bridge, and we played "Travel Home!" One of the railroad stations appeared bush-league dark, but when one looked more closely, it was just a hostile illusion.

I have had quite a few chats with Schorsch. He is pretty disillusioned, poorly shaven and has let his hair grow. Because of some blunders, he has spoiled his chance for advancement in the unit and, at present, is doing penalty duty. I will thoroughly check things out before having any thoughts of cutting off my ties with him. There are some money concerns[69] at play, and he is being blamed for some financial problems. He doesn't know how to budget in appropriation to the mandates of his situation.

Father wrote me again today. Otto fell on the 29th of November 1942. It has been almost one year since my dear brother (and only sibling) was laid and buried into the soft earth. But the battles rage on, and now we have been issued our winter equipment. This consists of a thick winter coat, two pair of underwear and shirts, gloves and earmuffs. We look like the Russian troops. Oh, that damned Russia. It will mean a lot of suffering for our troops. Fortunately, I am still in France, and so you need not worry yet about my life.

Well, sleep tight this evening, my Love, and remember that I love you so very much.

I will write again, tomorrow.

Your Paulus

---

[69] Money problems here may refer to Schorsch's having been sent to Fargeau to pick up troop company money. Perhaps things did not add up when he returned.

Letter no. 103
November 5, 1943,

My Beloved Little Wife – Goldchen, You!

Papi just came in from the cold of night watch duty, and I am back in the watch room. Got myself a quick bite to eat, took off my gear, and sat down to write to you, my Love. Your long, precious letter of October 27th lies before me as a partially read composition, spiced with French expressions from, yes, my Goldchen, the interpreter par excellence. (My little Darling is allowed to speak).

So, the first package of butter has arrived, along with what Schorsch delivered to you in the way of butter and ham. I am sending another thick package to you today. It contains more butter and some sweets for Erika and the ruffians and a pair of pretty elegant silk stockings for Mommy. Should I not be able to make it home for Christmas, you will have these things to remember me by and how very much it pleased me to be able to buy them for you.

Yes, my Love, I must spend three months of intensive training in the corps for newly recruited officers and another three months in the railroad station for "in house" training before I will be able to come home to you and the three children. That will probably take 'til the end of January. We will celebrate Christmas at that time. Hopefully, the ruffians will be able to wait until then. I would really love to see them. Your description of the children's lives is so fantastic and vivid that it's always a joy for me to read those special passages. Yes, Goldchen, you should write a book. I miss your opinions and colorful terminology.

I have written to you about engineer Doeges's desire to get me released from my military duty to free me up to work in his lab. I sent him my reply that, for now, this is out of the question because of my training for the SSW – Wehrmacht, and I couldn't do it at this time, even if he had the wherewithal to get me out. But you don't need to count his idea out altogether. You would have to travel to Krofdorf. That is where Doeges lives. My buddies from Giessen tell me that Krofdorf is a very elegant place in the mountains – wine and fantastic accommodations.

I am established here in Rennes and am settled in. Banners here to Saint Michel are everywhere. My thoughts, however, always return to Fargeau. Fargeau lies 20 kilometers from Orleans in the direction of Chateauneuf, in the Loire region. It is my wish to travel to Saint Malo by highway, but I don't know if I will get the opportunity. I am working on the matter of some Christmas toys, but more about that in my next letter.

I want also to be with you, my Love. It is my constant wish as well. My greatest desire is to be with you – you, Distelhof, home, and the children. Now, for a short while I will dream of the future, of arriving at Distelhof. I feel so very close to you, Goldchen. For today, in longing, I remain,

Your Paulus,

. . . .and Vagabond, Love and Kisses.

Letter no. 104
November 5, 1943,

My Beloved Little Goldchen!

Yes, another two pairs of beautiful silk stockings for you. It is too bad that I can't be there to help you put them on. I had to do quite a bit of procurement in order to get them. If they make you happy, . . . then good, because making you happy was the motivation for my relentless effort. Should you need a couple more pair, let me know, and Papi will get to more wheeling and dealing.

Always, your Vagabond,
who loves you so much.

Letter no. 105

My Dear Little Erika,

Your dear mother has just written me that you have really done well in school and paid full attention. You will receive a sweet greeting from your soldier Papi for that – you know, that rascal who eats everything up. Papi is so happy to have come up with this treat for you, and even though it isn't much, it is wrapped with joy and love.

Your Mommy will make you understand how much I love you. Your Papi.

My One and Only!

My Sweetheart!

Well, I have everything packed. It is probably better that I send the nightshirt and the envelopes at the same time so that nothing gets lost. That would be unfortunate. I wanted to wash the shirt a little yesterday, but didn't have the time.

Dear, I must take my leave again, must clear my thoughts and begin anew. I love you so very much. I have received your letter containing the bad news and will address that again, later.

Your Paulus

With that, and the first 105 letters longingly sent home, soldier Papi, loving husband, Paulus, is finally able to realize his often dreamed of and eagerly awaited furlough home. His next letter is dated eight days later, November 13th.

Letter no. 106
November 13, 1943,

My Joy!

Because of a slight delay in train schedules, there is no connection to France, and therefore I must remain in Metz for some 24 hours. Everything seems hopeless. How could I have ended up in this bad situation? These hours feel like the saddest of my life. Only your love, given to me in the form of food from my satchel is of any consolation. You comforted me when I really needed it. I will try to get as far as I can this evening. I sit here, alone, needing to leave when all I want to do is go back home.

My Love,

Merely Your Vagabond

Letter no. 107
Rennes, November 14, 1943,

My Joy in the Homeland,
My Goldchen!

Well, I have arrived after being nearly 12 hours late and want to write to you immediately because I know that you are longing to get some mail. So I will get right to the details.

With moist eyes, I stood by the train window for a long while as I took leave of Erfurt and my beautiful hours with you and the dear children. It was only after we had brushed past the houses and high rise buildings that I went back to take my seat, gripped by an unbearable sadness and hopelessness. I felt hollow, as if everything inside of me was in the process of being destroyed. Oh, how oppressive and gloomy these hours were, but I don't want to complain because the hours that I spent with you were like heaven on earth, and I do not deserve such splendor. What a superb wife you are, my Love. The Lord God has surely bestowed you with very special powers.

There were only officers in my compartment on the train. For awhile, no one said anything, and I had a time of quiet to think and remember, but soon enough one of them asked me a military-related question, and a discussion about politics, the economy, art, and languages ensued. As soon as they realized that I was a person out of their own circles, they wanted to know all about me and were surprised when I told them that I was about to complete my basic training and, after that, enter officer training. This infantryman Claudius must be a rare bird indeed. And that's the way we passed the time until we reached Giessen. That's where they got off and, in all camaraderie, wished me a good trip and the best of luck.

After I fortified myself with more of your wonderful bread and butter, I managed to find a good, soft spot and fell asleep. Unfortunately, we arrived in Trier two hours late, and my train to France had already left. We were advised to take the next train to Metz and see about going on from there. Since every kilometer was taking me farther and farther from home and from you, my morale was low. Half frozen, I finally made it to Metz by 11 o'clock and, like an army worm, proceeded to work my way through the natives to the information desk. You won't be able to imagine what happened next. In a very matter of fact way, the officials told me, "No more trains are running today. You must remain here overnight and leave at 11:10, tomorrow morning." My orders were to be back in Rennes by 4 PM, and this latest information about train schedules could not have been worse.

The first thing I did was go to the Wehrmacht housing office, a really poor facility with scarcely room to sit or breathe. The awful congestion of the place filled me with a terrible sense of hopelessness and loss. What great love then streamed out of the provisions bag that you had filled for me and how ravenously I ate and thought of you, my Beloved. All of a sudden, I felt better and even encouraged. For that, my Goldchen, I have you to thank. It was you who placed the thread of life into my hands. Along with two comrades, I took off in an attempt to find another way to get to Rennes. A civilian train to Paris was scheduled to leave at 2 AM. This was a forbidden train for us to take, but since I knew that an express train left for Rennes out of Paris at 8:40, we decided to risk it. It would save us an entire day. This French train was seven hours late but we stayed put and waited out on the platform in order to keep track of our bags and make very sure that we wouldn't miss it. With a little luck, we ended up in a railroad car that was nearly empty. It was also unlit and unheated, but we were able to make it to Paris at around 4 o'clock. There, we reported to the officer who was in charge at the station and explained our situation to him. We had found a sympathetic and understanding ear and proceeded to lie down on our bags where we slept until 6 o'clock. We then took the underground subway to Montparnasse Gasse, where we waited a couple of hours longer to finally take the express to Rennes. I arrived in Rennes at 14:30 and received a warm, Hello. Our commander was pleased that we had been able to make a successful return trip.

I can't tell you, my Love, how often I opened that satchel and helped myself to eat the great things that you had packed for me, and each and every time I thought of my unending love for you. Everything that you did for me was perfect. The trip back was depressing, as well as exhausting and felt like the hours of my greatest fortune and also my most challenging reality. Goldchen, I do not deserve your love and your loyalty, and am constantly compelled to remember the shame and disgrace that I brought to you during an earlier time of hurt.

During the long trip, I read the book, *Andre' and Ursula*. It reminds me of you and me, and it seems fitting for me to read this book now. The plot impresses me as moving and artistic, and toward the end, I nearly forgot that it is a work of fiction – a story about Andre' and, conceivably, other people like him.

My buddies were happy to see me and welcomed me back. But early tomorrow morning it will be on to another world and other quarters for me, and there is still a lot of work for me to do. I received my first silver braid for my shoulder strap just now, and am to sew it onto my uniform today. Schorsch was very happy to see me, and we ate supper together in my room. We told stories and talked a lot. When he saw that I was sewing the silver braids to the straps, he sadly said, "Yes, you are being promoted and will soon become an officer, and I will become a lance corporal – in other words, a dead-end in terms of any promotion to an officer. That is for once and for all, out of the question." The poor fellow. His financial situation, however, is improving. He is sad that I will be leaving, poor Schorsch. You have to love him. When I am finished with this letter, I have to do some hand laundry: two collars, two pair of socks, one nightshirt and a handkerchief. I want to be clean when I begin instructions.

Oh, Love, how can I thank you for my wonderful hours with you. My heart is so full, and that is why I find the separation to be so hard to bear. I know that you wept, as I wept, when you went back to the apartment. No Paulus. It was just that way for me as the train pulled out of Erfurt and into the empty darkness. I want to be more competent and more diligent so that I can come back to you again. That is my burning desire, and everything in me yearns for you. Hopefully I will be able to write to you in the coming days. I will want to do so. I kiss you with love and great longing.

Your Paulus

Letter no. 108
November 15, 1943,

My Greatest Joy in this World.
Goldchen,

These will be my last lines written to you from Rennes. I am departing, leaving buddies who have become dear to me and a life that I have become used to, leaving also my assigned workroom and a familiar daily routine. And, yet, I am happy, especially for you because I am being promoted by managing to pull myself up by my bootstraps. I am proud of my braids and proud, also, of the special recognition. The lieutenant and first lieutenant shook hands with me upon my departure and wished me well. I will leave by car at 1400 hours. The training school for new officers lies in Montfort. It is said to be a very small city, similar to Fargeau. In terms of beauty and the Loire, however, it is a far cry. Be patient, I will send you a full description. At any rate, the cost of living is cheaper and, in regard to your and my bank account, that makes it tolerable.

Now, on to your last letter which I read this morning. As though by some special stoke of perception I can answer it without even having read its contents. I am truly shocked by what you have written. That could not have been me. Mrs. Jung certainly did a good deed for a little soldier's wife and her promising loved ones by bringing this bit of gossip your way. But I believe today you think otherwise because you have put the matter into a clearer perspective than what could have been concluded from the original statement of the letter. I, myself, have nothing to defend. I have a clear conscience, and for that I am grateful to God. I know, Goldchen, that I have hurt and betrayed you during the years of our marriage, but I also believe that I have regained some of your trust. I love you with every fiber of my body and soul and know how it may have looked to you when you heard those asinine rumors from Mrs. Jung. Oh, Dear God, in spite of my shortcomings give me the strength on earth to have the opportunity to keep you in love with me. This is my most sacred wish, and I worry about you every day. I have acted despicably toward you, my wife. I have realized my wrong and since I dare not lose you, am hopeful that it is not too late. It is not my being away from you or the stress of the times that we are in that has awakened my feelings toward you. It is very simply my heart that clearly and cleanly draws me to you. I am pleased with myself to be feeling this continual state of repentance and am even happier to still be so much in love with you. The image of you is imprinted on my heart. My Love, do not push me away. I know that I probably deserve to be, but plead for your forgiveness and mercy. I am so afraid for you, for the children and the entire world. In all that you do, may I be with you. By means of your selfless life, my heart and my soul are now very clean. I intend to honor and worship you like a goddess.

From here on, my Love, I want to go quietly forward. Your last letter shall mark the end of the chapter, and I shall go on in hope for a future, a future with you. Do not push me away. I have nothing in common with this woman, and I have not written to her.

Your One and Only Paulus, Vagabond.

My thoughts, again and again, return home. It is as if this wound is not to be healed, and it pains me to think of so much happiness and not be able to live it. Your love and care for me, what we have accomplished, and our home, these are the things that carry me through all of the hard times. I continue to see you running and waving as my train left the station, that little corner of your mouth making your pain visible. Then you were gone, and everything out there in the night was black.[70]

To all the little ones, Mattheu, Detti and Eki – many greetings from your Papi. He is far away again and can no longer play with you. Oh you dear little ones. You make life so sweet and help with the pain. [71]

---

[70] These seven lines written at the bottom of the first page.

[71] Written on the side of the first page.

Letter no. 109
Soldier Claudius FD #5651a
Montfort, November 18, 1943,

My Most Deeply Beloved Goldchen,
My Joy on Earth!

I sit in the "room," with stiff fingers, damp clothing, and hard boots, in a murderous cold that goes right through you. I have skipped my meal so that I may get just a few lines off to you.

I do not want to go into all of the details of what is new and different in this place but only to tell you that it is hell. Our duty here is a lot more demanding than it was when I was a recruit. We have a 10 to 20 kilometer march every day in the bitter cold and are not allowed to wear gloves because that would be "un-soldier like." Our instruction is so burdensome that it almost makes a German soldier feel unworthy and leaves no escape from doing penalty duty. I am the oldest and have to work very hard in order to keep up with the 18 to 20 year olds. The training methods are first-class and the instruction is well organized. We audit the training of foot soldiers and go into the field to give orders and actually lead a unit. It's all tough work, but that's how we learn to be "superiors." We must train them to shoot and wound a soldier and hunt him down. You must naturally have very accurate details on all of these things. The comradeship is "excellent" and much better than it was in my old company. All of the guys are first-rate and highly educated. A number of them are young guys from good homes. Conduct here is completely different – too bad that everything else is so difficult.

It has rained for several weeks here, and the ground is clay-like and very mushy. The quagmire begins directly in front of the door of our quarters. We look terrible, day in and day out. Our uniforms are constantly muddy, and we spend every free minute scrubbing and washing. We have night duty here almost every evening. It usually lasts until 5 o'clock in the morning with our needing to be back on duty again by 7 AM. Things are really hot and heavy with the reserve officers training. All of it is very stressful, but our instructors make things interesting. Hopefully, I will be able to keep up with the tempo.

If it were not for the scandal and my worry over you, I would retire to the secure confines of the drawing room, but this is the way that it has to be. I will accept the fact that this is to be the punishment for my transgressions against you and all of the pain and worry that I have caused you. One of my buddies, who will finish his Reserve Officers Training on the 14th of December, told us of all kinds of frightening things, and there are times when I think that I can't go on.

What concerns me most is that there is no free time at all. First duty lasts until 19 o'clock, followed up with a further obligation as officer of the watch, or something of a similar beastly situation that needs to be attended to or cleaned up. A lot of instruction has to be supplemented, and lectures about all sorts of things need to be given to the soldiers. It's all a little different when you, yourself, are in the process of becoming an officer and have to imitate all of that officer crap. Thank God that I will be done with this phase of the training by the 29th. I do not know what comes after that. At any rate, I find myself being afraid of each new day of the cold, the eternal rain, and the bottomless mud. It is horrible.

I think of you, my Love, always and with a deep innermost longing. As to the difficult hours of the surgery[72] from which you are recovering, I pray for God's help and offer you my hand and loving wishes for speedy healing and soon improved health.

Well, now you know the way things are for me. Next Sunday, I will write you in more detail. That you are getting no mail is really painful for me, but this is the best I can do. With deeply wistful greetings and kisses, I remain your Vagabond, Your poor and insignificant, fighting Raider.

The sweater has really come in handy.[73]

---

[72] Surgery – the repair of a fallen uterus which followed the birth of Detlef.
[73] Written upside-down on the top of the letter.

Letter no. 110
Officer Training,
November 19, 1943,

My Goldchen, My Joy!

I just took in one and a half liters of "Frugales," an energy drink, and since I have night duty until 5 o'clock in the morning have managed to set aside a little bit of time in order to get a few precious lines sent off to you.

I need to prepare a lecture on the theme of "The question of raw materials in the fifth year of the war." I have to stand before a group of recruits to give the lecture and then pose some questions for the recruits to consider. I must make the material meaningful and that's not always easy to do. We older commandos are called upon to speak with a strong voice of authority so that the recruits will clearly understand what we are talking about and immediately recognize its importance and the scholarship that stands behind our words. Many of the older soldiers have voices that are young and childlike enough for our lecturing to sound pretty comical. For me, the commands and instructions come out well enough.

The duty here is hard...hard, indeed. Our officers are trained with strict masculine discipline, and we are expected to accomplish a lot. Every Reserve Officer Cadet is required to have a part combed into his hair. I, also, need to get myself off to the company barber to have my sparse collection of hair cut so as to be parted.[74] You will surely laugh and be amused by my looks. The thing that I find most regrettable is that we are given such an anemic amount of free time for doing personal things, especially letter writing. Right now I should be doing other things, but my heart is restless and wants only to talk to you, my Goldchen. All of the young Reserve Officer Recruits are already in bed and asleep. Night maneuvers will begin in two hours, and I still have to write an essay on the machine gun. Then I must shave.

My strong need to write to you comes out of knowing that you are in the difficult hours of recovering from your surgery and are

---

[74] Citizen Claudius always wore his hair medium length and combed directly back from the brow.

awaiting mail. You should always know, my Goldchen, that your Paulus is true and always thinks about you. Other women are no longer an issue for me. That is the holy oath that I have sworn. Hopefully, I will succeed in being able to win back your trust. That would be the most wonderful joy on earth for me.

My Love, the last packages will certainly have arrived by now. It pleases me that my departure from Rennes went forth with good organization in getting everything sent off to you. As things are here, I would not be able to be so sure of that. Since we are free from 1500 to 2300 hours on Sunday, I will try to learn more about the region around here. I will also find out about being able to buy groceries.

I got a letter from Laubegast today but have not yet read it – will do it later. Oh, my Sweetheart, I really am afraid of what is to happen with me next in terms of duty... the crawling and running in the cold is really taxing. There are a lot of thistles covering the landscape, and when we crawl to take cover, the thorns get stuck in the palm of my hand and cause a nasty rash. I have one that began on my right hand. Knowing that the worst is yet to come, I would not go on with this if I did not have my eyes on a larger goal. My precious thoughts of you, my Goldchen, of the children, my loved ones at home, will always give me the strength and power to go on. I kiss you with all that is in me. I love you so very much.

Your Paulus, only.

Letter no. 111
Officer Training – November 20, 1943,
Saturday – Afternoon,

My Goldchen, You, my Happiness!

Although everyone around me is expected to keep busy, I must give in to the eternal pangs of my heart and begin this little letter to you. Since I may get an order to do something at any minute, I'm not sure just how far I will get. Yes, my Love, even on a free evening, rest and relaxation are out of the question. We are plagued and encumbered spirits. Two individuals have just been ordered to the writing room, and I have been permitted to organize foodstuffs. Our rationing is not a matter of life or death, but as far as I can tell from the older soldiers, it is very, very difficult to buy anything around here, and so I am very happy that you have a small stock of butter at hand and am nervous as to how things here will go.

It is morning, and we have just returned from night maneuvers. Out in the starry night, I was cold as ice. Everything went well, but my nose dripped profusely. I will pass on to you what my father wrote. He is displeased that I am to become an officer. He has a different point of view and is probably thinking about Otto's death. He also mentioned that you have expressed a similar opinion. The best of the recent recruits are gathered here in order to measure up, and the duty and training is dammed hard and very demanding. So don't think that father is wrong. Reinforcing the front, right in the middle of the action, is also an encumbrance. Everyone has to distinguish himself. They say that some 50% of the Reserve Officer Candidates are killed. You, my Love, were in agreement with things as they now stand. Since the dye is cast, I can only tell to you that there is little else that can now motivate or encourage me to keep me from going on. It is also a question of advancement. Perhaps I should have joined the Air Force.[75] I must now go on with this course of training, and if everything goes well, I will be at the front as a squad leader in either June or July of 1944. When that happens, I will talk to our first lieutenant again, and in no uncertain terms, I know that I can find advancement as an engineer, if not as an officer. On the other hand, my Love, because of the advantage that it will mean for me in the future, I would like to become an officer.

Filled with longing, I looked at the pictures again today. Oh, little Detti and little Eki with the dreamer, Mattheu. How precious that last time at home with all of you was and how loving and well-behaved the children were. All of my buddies go into admiration over Detti and blurt out sweet sentiments over him when I show them the photos. Yes, my Love, I am the most proud of you because you are the mother and the soul of the whole family. I am already very well-liked here in the Officer Candidate Training Company. They call me "doctor." Because the individuals here

---

[75] His bad eyesight would have prevented his enlisting in the Luftwaffe.

are all quite unique, they come to me for advice with all sorts of perplexing issues. Almost all of them hold the Abitur, matriculation degree or something similar in terms of an education.

My Darling, the one thing that you should always know is that I am constantly thinking of you. My prayers are long and humble; "God, give me peace, home, and health." The rest you and I will do together. We are so good together, and I am so ashamed to have hurt you, especially since you have been such a dear, dear wife to me. I want to tell you everything because I love you so much, and tell you over and over again that I want to do twice as much of everything I can to make up for my mistakes. Now, it's on to Sunday. With my inner-most greetings and kisses, I must take my leave. I yearn for my Goldchen more than ever.

As always, your Paulus

Letter no. 112
Officer Training, November 21, 1943,

To my Goldchen, to my Sunday Happiness!

Today is Sunday, and I am ever so happy to chat with you, my Joy, and be able to tell you all that is going on. I have spent the entire morning, as well as a few hours this afternoon, sprucing up, and I've got it all done. I washed the socks and dried them. Then I darned the gigantic holes in them just the way I have seen you do it. I cleaned my boots and made them look like a work of art. I washed the drill uniform and sewed on buttons. I thoroughly washed the suit-coat braiding with soap and warm water. The countryside around here is full of thistles, and so I also had to do some patching. After that came the rifle and leather sling, both of which I had to clean and polish. Next in line were the leggings, which were covered with clay, and to finish off, I did a general cleaning of the locker. You can well imagine how much work all of this took. We never have time to get any of this done during the week. I still have to do a written work on a weapon.

Because I love you so much, it is so nice to be able to sit here and write to you, my Joy, but I have more to tell you. Yesterday afternoon, I had the chance to talk to an older soldier (he has been here for quite some time) about the shopping around here, in the vicinity and with the local farmers. Listen. Butter and fat stuffs are neither to be gotten on one's own initiative nor through the farmers. The possibility of getting some by trading smokes, however, remains a possibility. He did not give me any direct leads, and so I must go out looking on my own.

Eggs are to be gotten from the farmers, but right now the hens are not laying much. So I'll have to wait. There seems to be a lot of meat around here, but only fresh meat like beefsteaks and cutlets. A lot of liver and beef suet seems to be available, and I therefore bought a pound and a half of liver and a bit of suet from the cook, along with some onions and salt. The liver is very creamy, and I had to cut it up. Anyway, it tasted good. Because the suet sets up and hardens quickly in this cold weather, everything had to be consumed rather quickly. I will try to get some suet for you. I know that you could use it. Naturally the butcher involved likes to smoke and can be bribed. Fruit is as scarce here as it is in Germany, and we miss it a lot. Because of that, several cases of skin problems have been breaking out here and there. Yes, Goldchen, one can eat well enough and cheaply around here, but everything is pretty poorly prepared. Vegetables and potatoes are hard to find. Bread and milk can be had for the right amount of Marks. The French bake a thing called "honey cookies." with real honey. So, there you have it – the story on the technology of nourishment. You will certainly get an opportunity for a taste-test sometime in the future because your Papi is always thinking of you. The rations must be improved, otherwise I will collapse and not be able to perform my duties.

Father and mother asked if I can come up with anything for them. I might be able to if the cold were not so bad. Even with two pullovers on, I am freezing, especially when the wind blows. I use the gloves that you gave me, during night duty. They have really come in handy. The thick sweater has also been very useful. Yesterday, every Reserve Officer Trainee was given a large glass of steaming hot wine, and it was really good. It immediately made its way into every cold limb of our bodies. Our lieutenant was also here yesterday. He talked to me. He wanted me to forward his greetings to both of my families. The cakes you baked for me lasted until yesterday. They were a precious reminder of you, my

Love. Say hello to the children from their soldier Papi and tell them that Papi has saved a few pieces of candy for them. I kiss you intimately and remain,

Your Vagabond and Paulus

Letter no. 113
Officer Training, November 23, 1943,

My One and Only Little Wife!

Yesterday and today were big days for us Officer Trainees. The new recruits for the next training session were presented to us for examination. They are double our number, and we are already the "older ones." Of the twenty taking the exams, nine failed. The others will begin their course of study and training on the 15th of December. Two from our old company will be included, and I have been told that the July recruits, that was my group, will be transferred to Erfurt.. You can well imagine how that made me feel, but I know the guys won't be in Erfurt long and will quickly be sent to the front where their lives as soldiers will begin in earnest. As for me, it will most probably be May or June. This time of the year is unbearable in Russia.

But now to the two of us, my Goldchen. Today, I am again writing to you during my lunch-break. I will have night duty again and have no free time. We had maneuvers out in the country this morning with special training for enemy engagement. In shooting at dummies, I had three hits with two shots leaving the barrel without results. In spite of everything, I have made an increased effort in regard to my physical demands. The training is to be spirited, very snappy and agile. We are often harassed in the process of our training. If I am involved with giving the orders, I try not to sound mean. The lieutenant talked to me on Sunday and told me that he wanted me to take over the cultural leadership of the young people. He wanted me to recommend good books, poetry and stories. Because of my academic education and training as an engineer, he expects me to be able to do that. I will now contemplate as to how I can best achieve this objective.

In the meantime, I managed to grab a few hours for letter writing before afternoon duty begins. Now I have just 20 minutes left. Duty is to be ten kilometers from here, and it will hopefully not begin to rain and make the night feel even colder than it already is. After having seen what a great soldier's mommy you are, my Love, I feel driven to write to you just as much as I can. Again and again, I think of our nightly togetherness in the park. Oh, where have all those beautiful hours gone? Do you remember how we sat in the park and ate and talked? So many days like that were before me just a little while ago, and then they were gone, and the time for me to leave all too soon became a bitter pill. I wrote to you how all of that went for me, but it can be no other way; I am a soldier and must follow my orders. How it will all turn out for me is something that I just don't know.

I will now hang upon and around my body all of the various things that I will need for the scouting party. It will take place in the dark. The stars will hopefully be out. They always remind me of our nights at Distelhof. When will I be able to spend more of them up there with you? When will we both be able to spend beautiful warm summer nights listening to the sounds of nature? Nights like tonight are the times that can be so gruesome.

I am, however, grateful to be able to complete this letter to you. It will let you know that I love you always and love you so very much that my longing for you is infinite. I also fear that I might, perhaps lose you. Love – You,

I kiss you intimately,

Your Vagabond

Letter no. 114
Officer Training, November 26, 1943,

My Heart's Love, My Little Goldchen!

I feel very sad. For the past two days I have not been up to snuff. I've been sick with a fever and have repeatedly fallen into bed like a nearly dead dog. That is why I have not written to you for the past two days. I've always had a weak stomach and seriously suffer with that now. My hands are also infected and full of pus. I will, however not dwell on that this evening and hold fast to my resolve to write you a long letter about my great longing for you. There are lots of interesting things to tell you.

Because I have been away from my home for so long and have received no mail from you, my Love, I am extremely concerned about you. Evidently, the mail connections to Montfort must be bad. How are you? Are you still in the process of recovering from your surgery, and are you resting? How did things go in the hospital? You must tell me all about it. In this wilderness, I hang on every line that comes from home. I still do not know how things will go in regard to Christmas. At any rate, it doesn't look good. All furloughs have been canceled, and time away is only given under extenuating circumstances.

We have night maneuvers again this evening and are ordered to get as much sleep as we can. Also, our rations are not all that great. We sit around a little cooker every morning to toast our army bread and have run out of butter and jam. I was, however, successful in the kitchen and managed to swap a few cigarettes in order to get some oatmeal and sugar which I brewed up for myself using water, naturally. It tasted great and did wonders for my ailments.

So you, my Joy, be well 'til this evening when I hope to get some news from you with which to allay my fears. I kiss you intimately and remain,

Your Paulus, Only

Letter no. 115
Officer Training, November 26, 1943,
Friday Evening,

My Desire and My Happiness!

It is quiet now, everyone is asleep, and I can hear the steady breathing of my young buddies. Only the old "doctor" sits up and writes. Yes, my heart's desire, I write. I have finally found a few small hours and with my hurting hands want to express the depth of the yearning that is in my heart. I have so much to tell you. I am finally improving in regard to my health. A semolina pudding has put me back on my feet.

How are you doing, my Goldchen? What have you had to endure under the knife? Hopefully you are lying in a clean, white bed and are on the mend. Unfortunately, I am not able to know the reality of the situation and can only think about it. I did not get any mail today. It's really tough when my buddies get news from home, and I get none. But I know that you love me, and I will wait. We have night maneuvers again from 3 AM tonight until 7 in the morning. I honestly don't know whether I will be able to make a success of it around here. Because of my physical problems, the sergeant has, unfortunately, repeatedly reprimanded me out in the field. If I am dismissed, I will have to find another duty, but I don't want to write about that. I want to write about other things. I have written you about the Lieutenant's request that I assume the cultural direction of the recruits, that is, the Reserve Officer Trainees of the 19th training group. I need to put together a literary course of study for the coming week and also make a speech about the "Raw Materials in Germany in the 5th year of the war." So, in addition to the strenuous duty, I have a lot of work ahead of me. But despite of all that, I am happy to have an assignment here, in Officer Candidate Training.

(Last Wednesday, we had an Officers' mess evening in the Hotel du Lion 'd' 'r', in Montfort. It was a test to see if the Reserve Officers Candidates could handle themselves with a knife and fork, with the pouring and sipping of wine, as well as several other matters. It was really quite a sight. Everyone, however, got along, and everything went well. We ate a consume' with potatoes and white bread, then a potato salad, which was very tasty. That was followed by roast oxen and French fries, and finally a wonderful roast of veal. I do, however, miss having vegetables and potatoes fixed the German-style. It was very good but not quite suited for a German stomach. There is a lot of emphasis on tradition and how to act in appropriate ways. Today, we are to be given instruction in social manners and how they apply for us in regard to women. The noncoms were dismissed because the first lieutenant wanted to talk about "keeping one's distance." That would not have been a good topic for that rank of soldiers. We are getting a lot of instruction on a variety of very interesting topics, and our already swirling heads are soon to also be filled with sessions on "tactics." I hope that I can learn all that!

In a few hours it will be back out into the night for me, under the stars and into the cold. This too shall pass. We will unfortunately have duty this coming Sunday. We are to have an on-duty training sequence and won't be able to get much sleep. So I'd better get to bed and dream of you and my happiness there at home with my Goldchen. I will pull my gray blanket up over my face and make believe that I am at home with you and that you are with me. Yes, in bed with me and I with you.

Your Paulus, only,

I kiss you with a desirous and intimate kiss

Letter no. 116
Officer Training, November 27, 1943,

My Dear Sweet Little Wife, My Goldchen!

A hectic night with frozen limbs and a runny nose... a forced, return-march in the morning that ran the sweat right through our uniforms and then a heated day of duty until 7 PM. So we were, as we often are, on our feet from 2 o'clock AM until 8:00 PM. This doesn't make for an enjoyable life but, then again, there are those hours of comradeship that are close to precious.

I must write letters to you, Goldchen, at times when I should be asleep. As for my younger buddies, they just have not been able to write because they simply don't have the energy that I have to do so. There is also the factor that our clothing must be kept as impeccably clean as a work of art using only standard issue soap and water. It must all be done, and it gets done, but after a while it makes one crabby and, unfortunately, obstinate. Do you know what it means to be obstinate? That is to be stubborn as a lonely ox, pulling the cart and enduring it all in a peaceful manner.

Early tomorrow, Sunday morning, we must rise at 6 o'clock, and in freezing weather, we have to get onto a troop truck for a land maneuver. I don't know any more, other than it is expected to be a tough exercise. For our previous night maneuver, the set up had gone as follows: For half an hour, we lay on our stomachs, on the ready, at the edge of the forest. I was the number two machine gun. There was a giant, flickering fire up ahead of us, and in its glow we could see our marksmen. Flares lit up the night, making our surroundings visible, and we could hear the cries of an attack group. Then, as we shot off tracers that stretched their ghostly fingers like ropes into the landscape, the fireworks started. We shot well and any stray bullets bounced helter-skelter as they hit the stones around us in the landscape. This went on for awhile, until the enemy fire finally burned out. We then stormed forward in the darkness. I fell into a brook, getting myself wet to the bone. With that began an eternal wait. My thoughts, however, were focused on you and the joy of our Sunday and Sunday evening together.

But duty was not to be escaped, with other duties and orders to follow. There is always more of that. The wounds on my hands have not yet healed and are constantly full of puss. In the cold, the dampness is really painful. Comrades from an older Officers Group with similar symptoms have ended up in the field hospital. The thistles that grow in the area of our maneuvers produce this infection. Hopefully, I will get better soon.

My Love, your Paulus has vented again about part of the crap that is involved with army life. Tomorrow, I will try to write you a more tender and affectionate letter because you deserve better lines from your Paulus, but then to whom could I send my concerns but to you, my Goldchen. I still have not had any news from you. I am so afraid that things have not gone well. That would be the end.

That's all for today. I am dog tired and want to go to bed

Intimately, Your Paulus who loves only you.

Letter no. 117

My Goldchen,

As much as I can make of the meager bit of free time that I have, I made a trip into the city of Montfort to buy butter, eggs and bacon, . . .unfortunately, without any success. All of the older soldiers have their own sources and will not breathe a syllable about them – not even for tobacco or cigarettes. One can be certain that enough tobacco is available so as to prevent any exploitation of it, but it may still be possible to make a few deals, and it would be most unfortunate if you were to receive no more "fat" from your soldier Papi. There is no point in sending any fresh meat, since it would spoil before it got to you in Erfurt. The farmers in the villages are very reserved and hide all of the good stuff, and we are not allowed to drink anything that is offered to us here because it is said to cause sickness. I have already written to you about the skin eruption that has broken out in our company. It has developed into an epidemic; our company commander is very concerned. It would be better for him to concern himself with finding a source of butter for our rations, since the food that we are getting is not enough in regard to the stress of our duty. I succeeded in getting some more oatmeal from the cook. With some water and salt, Reserve Officer Candidate Claudius cooked that into a fine brew. I had no sugar, since that is only to be gotten with Marks. None the less, it was something really special, and my envious buddies watched me as I wolfed down one sticky spoonful after another. I still have a little left for tomorrow.

Yes, my Goldchen, that is the way one fights for his life to survive as a soldier. Damned little happiness goes with it, and all too often, what little free time that we do have is mixed in with additional things that need to be done. In regard to a plan that I have currently laid out for myself, I can tell you the following: . . . listen: My Reserve Officer Training lasts until the 27th of February, 1944. As a Cadet, I must then spend two more months training the recruits of another unit. There is the possibility of a furlough during the interim break. Then, if I prove myself as a noncom cadet, I will be sent off to the font in order to prove myself once again. After another two months of proving myself at the front, this over 30 year old field soldier will take charge and remain there until he is promoted to a Lieutenant. The training at "weapons school" will, unfortunately, follow for the old Reserve Officer Candidate. But now to you, my little worry child. I am still getting no communication, while my buddies get lots of mail. My Love, if I only knew how things were with you, if you are healthy and that the operation went well. Goldchen, I am really worried about you. You are my hope, my joy, and my guiding light to the future for my living on with you and the children. I have been away from home for three weeks now and have not had even one line from you. I can only pray that the dear Lord God protect my loved ones and that He may help you through the difficult hours. I can only hope that you will be well soon. That will make me happy again. The uncertainty is painful, bodily painful. I kiss you intimately, my Goldchen. Please know that your Paulus loves you so very much and so deeply, in his heart.

Your Paulus, alone

Letter no. 118
Officer Training, November 28, 1943,
Night – 1 AM

You, My Everything, my Beloved Little Wife!

As I wrote you yesterday, my Love, I am so happy to have a few hours of sleep after the many taxing hours of a long day. As you will hear, nothing much has come to pass in the course of this day.

I was awakened from a deep sleep and had to take over the night watch from 1 to 3 AM. So now I sit with my munitions belt and steel helmet on. I must make the rounds and keep watch so that no plots are being hatched to attack us here. In the meantime, I write to you, my Heart's Desire, and with that put the time to good use by doing something useful for myself.

With that said, let me tell you about a recent experience. As I have already written, one can dine well in Montfort, as long as one has the time and opportunity to be able to do so. And so a couple of days ago I was invited by a buddy to do just that. At 7:30 PM, we took off for our destination, the "Cafe Cidre, Madame Duval." I was astonished to discover that a gigantic table had been prepared for us in the guest room. Families, some 20 persons, were seated all around this table, and across one corner of the white table-cloth-covered table was the special seating place of the Duval family. A large and splendid fireplace stood on the long side of the room. A genuine, crackling wood fire burned in it, and the waitress shuffled back and forth serving food to the guests from the grill that stood in the middle of the fireplace. All of the activity was centered around this mystical place of fire, and it was a beautiful scene.

The staff was dressed in special outfits, and the waiters were beet red from their endeavors. Little by little, the Duval cafe filled up with the French and my buddies from our company. Everyone wanted to eat – and eat they did. It was such a wonderful atmosphere to sit near the great fireplace and watch the sizzling pans. The Frenchmen wore adventurous suits, which made the place very colorful. The Duval children played in a corner of the room as though no one were there. Two girls studied from an English schoolbook in deep concentration. Before our food was served, the officers from our company came in and sat at another table with a white tablecloth on it. They invited me to come and sit with them so we might enjoy one another's company. It goes without saying that this really pleased me. All of us got into some very lively discussions about French customs, traditions, and food and the ways it is prepared. One guy from our group was from Vienna. He talked about Russia and of our industry of the spun rayon market there. In short, it was an interesting and upbeat discussion which also included various aspects of military duty.

After the meal, we went into the pitch dark and rainy Bretagne night together. Tired out, I fell onto the straw mattress of my bed.

I hope that I have been able to paint you a good picture of our culinary adventure, because I know that you would be interested in hearing about it. Yes, my Love, France today is still a country of good old traditions. Too bad that it is so dirty.

Letter no. 119
Officer Training, November 29, 1943,

My Goldchen, You Dear little Wife,

I just came back, frozen and tired from a trip on a truck, and I find two precious little letters from you. The spirit of life now flows with more vigor through my veins. I have been relieved of a nightmare. I know that you comprehend what it means to have to wait. You write that you will go into the clinic from the 15th to the 18th and look for a tough road to hoe. By today you will have been released and are home with the little ones, joking and laughing. My fervent thoughts and wishes have found their way to God. You are healthy again and have been released from the operating room. Please know, my Love, that I think of you from here and now write to you in deep love and tenderness. And now I must go to bed, since I am hardly able to stand on my feet. I will write again tomorrow. My Love, 1000 kisses from your vagabond.

Morning, 6 AM, November 30, 1943,

I have just finished my meager breakfast. I am always the first one done. Now, to begin a new day with thoughts of you by writing to you. Your dear letters lie before me, and now I know how you suffered when we last parted. Yes, Love, I traveled away into the dark night, far, far away, and you, . . .you were left alone to go to our home, knowing that I would not be there. To be sure, the lights were all on because the children did not want to go to bed without their beloved Mommy.

Just had a little interruption. Because of some shortcoming, everyone was subjected to a caustic lecture. Somehow the young guys have a different view of their duties here than the older guys.

I really want to tell you about "Mont Saint Michel." I have seen it and will tell you all about it in detail in my next letter, because I know that it will be of interest to you. Well, another interruption – I have to participate in driving school in order to get a military driver's license. So, be well until this evening. A thousand kisses – Still in a hurry.

Noon: 12 o'clock,

So, here it is shortly before lunch, and I want to finish this letter to you. Driver education on a giant truck begins for me this afternoon and training on armored vehicles will follow later. I will let you know how it all went. You sent me the letter from Doeges so I can exchange mail with him. I will write him that you will be coming to Giessen sometime during the month of December in order to negotiate with him. During the course of our eight years of marriage you have become well-versed on the scope of my business activities. It is a delicate matter, and you know how I struggled with the shop[76] and how much stress and energy I have invested in all of that. I know that you will straighten things out. You know your way in such matters and are so diplomatic and good at comprehending these things.

So far, I have not I been successful at finding a source for butter and bacon in this poor little town of Montfort. However, when I get a chance, I will see if I can scare something up with the driver training people in Rennes. I am glad that I left you with a little butter and bacon in reserve so you have something to fall back on. So, Goldchen, I will now be summoned with my charge of, "Attention!!" and be prepared to eat at the miserably laid out table. But the hungry can't be picky.

Intimate kisses from your Paulus

Letter no. 120
Officer Training, November, 29 1943,

My Beloved Goldchen, You!

So, now you have a large basket for shopping. It was not easy to get, but I know that you will like it and find many uses for it because it is just the right, "Distelhof" size. Yesterday was the first Sunday of Advent. Oh, what a beautiful time that always was for us and oh God, how many of these things have become lost to us at this time – and there is damned little evidence that this hubbub will end anytime soon. The way things now stand, it will be a long time before anything will ever become resolved. But we do not want to talk of such things. I will write you about my first Advent alone in greater detail this evening. Now, I must get back to it. We are about to receive more instruction on tanks and all of the "paraphernalia." I will tell you all about my further experiences later and hope that nothing will happen.

A big 100 hearty hugs

---

[76] This in reference to a still pending lawsuit over not having been able to deliver contracted work or parts from "Elecktrowerkstatten," the small business that Claudius once owned. This business centered around the production and winding of electric motors, among other things.

from your Vagabond and
soldier Papi

Letter no. 121
Officer Training, December 2, 1943,

My Joy, You, My Heart!

Today is the second day of December, and Christmas is very much in evidence, but not yet here. It has rained constantly for days now, and the locals say that it will continue to be like this for many more days yet to come. The roads and streets have all turned into mud, and we look terrible. Driver instruction is really tough in regard to big trucks and the mud. Our only free time is after 8 PM, and by noon we are usually somewhere out in the country.

Oh, where has all of the precious time gone? . . . gone and overshadowed by everything except the hope of a reunion soon.

But now to tell you more about my adventure to Saint Michel. Sunday, at six o'clock in the morning . . . we set out in full field dress and traveled out into the country by truck. It began to pour, and we were freezing cold. Firstly, we arrived at the city of Dinan and checked out the fortress, the castle Annas au Bretonien, in particular, a solid piece of masonry which remains even today as a pile of stone with giant cold halls in which one can still feel the evidence of the past. After that, we went back out into the field where we conducted maneuvers. The rain was relentless, and we did not make it back to the troop truck until 3 PM, exhausted, hungry, tired, and frozen. We sat on the board seats of the troop transport and headed out into a direction that was not familiar to us until one of the road signs read, "Saint Michelle." As our destination became clearer, I remembered your stories about the beautiful edifices near the sea. Unfortunately, our truck broke down before we got there. So for almost an hour we had to sit in the rain on the side of the highway.

By early afternoon, we finally moved on toward the English Channel. The view of the structures was so beautiful that we all leaned forward in the truck as we continued to travel on. In the distance, the giant cloister rose out of the fog like a Grail castle. A momentary awe of silence came over us as we came ever closer to reaching the foot of the walls. I simply stared at this overpowering piece of architecture. Unfortunately, the tide was out, but we could see the shimmering water of the channel just beyond the great structure. All of us were awestruck as we entered into the interior space through one of the outer gates. It appeared to me that all sorts of business enterprises seemed to be mixed in with the worship areas, a real Jewish carnival with one pub after another seeking to lure in customers with their profitable menus. Even girls offered themselves for sale by the hour. Everything was sinfully expensive and bad, very bad. Any dumb country bumpkin would have believed what was being advertised and paid for all of it. As officers, protected by a good education and higher moral standard of behavior, we are the exception. I ate for 4.50, but the experiment was not a particularly tasty one, especially when compared to my Goldchen's excellent cuisine.

Then I ascended the 1000 steps to take a look at the inside areas of the fortress. The rooms were beautifully built and in the architectural style of a time gone by. Ramparts surrounded the Colossus, and only one street led around all of the walls. Most beautiful of all, my Love, was the view of the surrounding sea, and I wished that you and I could make a pleasure trip to this Saint Michel[77] together. Well, so much for now, I will tell you more later on. But this edifice has made a great impression on me.

My Love, good night. My thoughts and all of my hopes and desires are with you. I will see you in my dreams, my Dear. I love you so very much and want to be

Your Paulus.

---

[77] Mont Saint Michel is located approximately 150 miles northwest of Paris in the Normandy region of France. The Gothic-style Benedictine Abby sits perched on a rocky granite islet in the midst of a three-acre sand bank between Brittany and Normandy, France. It was built between the 11th and the 13th century and dedicated to the archangel Michael. The small village of Saint Michel surrounds the awesome structure of the abbey which served as a prison during the reign of Napoleon. It was restored in 1866 and connected across the one-mile area of sand by a causeway that can range 46 feet between high and low tides.

Letter no. 122
Officer Training, December 3, 1943
To my Joy, my Goldchen!

As by means of a miracle, our maneuvers have been canceled
for tonight, and we can get to bed in a timely fashion. We can
hardly believe it, but you can't look a gift horse in the mouth. So I
reach for my pen in order to write to my Goldchen, my dear little
wife.

Well then, since I still haven't received any mail from you
because of your pending release from the hospital, I am plagued by
horrible thoughts about your operation. I can only hope that
everything went well and have prayed to God, often, that you are
healthy. At least I try to talk myself into that and still am full of
worry in my heart. Write to me soon. I need to know how my
Goldchen is doing. I am better. Having spent every evening
pulling the thorns out with a red hot needle, my hands have healed
and are in good shape. But then, I don't want to tell you about the
bad things associated with my duty. That is good for neither one
of us.

Saturday evening instruction has been canceled and postponed
to another time so we can attend the Bizet opera, "Carmen," in
French, in Rennes. As you know, the Lieutenant had assigned me
the task of educating the young guys, and both of us have seen the
opera in Erfurt. Did you know that? I also talked to students who
wanted to learn more about the architectural construction of arches.
On Sunday we will begin our trip to Malo, and the young drivers
will be able to show us what they have learned. During the process
of that trip, we will also conduct land maneuvers which are
expected to be of utmost importance. That's military life.
Operating an omnibus is a bit of a different ball game than driving
my Olympia.

Grandfather sent me some money from Laubegast. He expects
me to use it as credit to get things for him, and a directive to that
effect is on my writing desk. I will write to father immediately and
let him know that he has put me on the spot. My hands are tied
because money coupons have become unacceptable in France, and
they are useless when it comes to the black market. As of yet I
have not been able to come up with any butter, and our own

nourishment is so meager that we feel empty most all of the time. The company tells us that we should go into the city if we need more food to eat. Since we would not be able to make it through the duties of the day with the rations that we are getting, we have no other choice. As always, comradeship helps us to make it through the dark valleys of a soldier's life. We all talk about the beautiful things in our lives. It is very uplifting, and the various conjectures that are made by "Matthias," or the "Doctor," as they call me, seem to hold a lot of weight.

So, my Love, that's pretty much the way that things go on around here, one day after the other. The mornings are overcast and cloudy and the homeland, along with all of my happiness, is far, far away. But hope remains for us, and we will have to place that even higher when I get to the front. As the "old Man," I won't be required to take any more weapons schooling and will stay with the commander, even at the front. Good news.

Keep your head up, Goldchen, and God will not forsake us because our dear children need us. What is happening at Distelhof? Until tomorrow, my Love

1000 Kisses from Your Paulus

Letter no. 123
Officer Training, December 5, 1043,
Soldier Claudius,
Rennes – Field Mail no. 56510a,

My Heart's Love, Goldchen, You!

Today is Sunday. It is still early in the day, and it appears to be very cold outside. Right now I am writing to you from my old room with my old company – let me explain. I have written you about having been repeatedly vaccinated. One of them festered and got really painful, so the dispensary in Montfort sent me to a field hospital in Rennes. Since there were still some matters remaining to be settled, the sergeant suggested that I seek out my old company while I was here and use this opportunity to do so. With that, I have a leave of absence until Sunday evening. So, I sit here with my buddies at the table in my old, familiar surroundings.

All of them talk about a furlough in Germany and a transfer to Erfurt, but the news is that the company is to be transferred to upper Italy. Any more than that is uncertain. As far as getting time off for Christmas, only the stars know anything at all about that. Orders are that no one in the officers company will get any time off, but then our duty schedule until February 28th of next year is so heavy that the time will pass very quickly. Yes, that will be tough and make for a very sad Christmas for you and the dear children at home as well. I will, however, try to work something out for sometime around the New Year. I must at least try. The lieutenant has informed me that I am to make the arrangements for the company Christmas celebration. That is an extremely sad task for me, because all I can ever see is the way things were, back at home.

Have you done anything in regard to Doeges? I would like to hear from you about that as soon as possible. I spent yesterday evening with Schorsch. He is really depressed. Things are not going at all well for him in regard to his standing within the company, and he still has not been promoted to private, first class . . . yet one more sacrifice of the war, and there have been so many. The one year anniversary of Otto's death passed just a few days ago. Yes, the poor fellow . . . he is no longer with us, and his body rests in foreign soil.

How is everything with you, my Love? I know so little about the way things are with you in your heart because I have not yet received any mail from you. Haven't you been able to write? I am so worried about you. By the second Sunday in Advent, the children are most certainly hearing lots about Santa Claus and are assuredly having a glowing afternoon, as you sit at the table with cookies and cake and the little ones' eyes aglow with the light of the Advent candles. I won't go into the way things look here. I feel sad enough as it is. Well, Love, things must improve, and I will repeatedly pray to the dear Lord for that. I love you so much, my Goldchen.

My Dearest, I send you intimate greetings and kisses.
From your Paulus

Letter no. 124
Officer Training, December 7, 1943,

My Desire, my Happiness, You!

It is bitter cold in the room. The stove is out because we have
no fuel. That's the way things are with the military, and we must
concern ourselves with other matters. I still have not received any
mail from you, my Goldchen, and I longingly await it. Yesterday
was St. Nikolas Day for you at home, with a special celebration for
the children and probably also for the "big kids." What fun that
time would have been for us, but things are different now. I am far
away and know nothing at all about my Goldchen. My last letter
from you was dated the 14th, just two days after my last departure
from Erfurt. I keep thinking about your surgery and if everything
went well, if you are in pain and how you are feeling. Perhaps the
postman will bring me a letter from you this evening. Then,
everything will be all right again. . . . Oh, if I only had that letter in
my hands at this very moment.

Since this eternal, hit-and -miss eating has not at all agreed
with me, I begged the cook for some more oatmeal last evening so
that I could cook up some more porridge for myself. I couldn't
get any sugar. Things like that are hard to find around here, and
without marks, you can't even get salt. A lot of things have
changed in France. Military money and credit notes will no longer
be valid after December 15th, and on January 1st, 1944, transfers of
money from Germany to France will no longer be made. Prices
will have to go down since buyers, other than the soldiers, will not
have access to the black market. Many dealers will have to bite the
bullet, and that may be good, because at the present, prices are
god-awful high.

How are things at home? Have the children been good during
your absence? I'm sure that they danced with joy when you
returned home. Yes, yes, my Goldchen, you! No one can compare
with our Mommy! There is so much that depends upon you, and
you cannot let them down.

When I left my old company, first lieutenant Goellnitz forgot
to write to Hermann Jule and Son, in Oberschoenberg. He was
really surprised when I asked him about that last Sunday. He has

four children at home and was happy for the chance to talk about them. We decorated our room with tree sprigs yesterday evening to make it look festive. We had little success, so the room still looks rather odd. We will try again. How are things at Distelhof? I often worry about the roof, but think that there is little else that can be done. Again and again, I take those pictures of Distelhof into my hands. Here, one hangs on for the memories of those wonderful and beautiful hours of our past lives, especially in the very hard and trying times as these, here in Montfort. But this too shall pass, and the sun will come out to shine again.

Now, Love, I will try to get a bit of sleep. I'll be back at it soon enough.

With deep-felt and longing kisses, I am
Your Paulus

Letter no. 125
Officer Training, December 8, 1043,

You, my Desire, my Goldchen!

We all just got in for lunch. We reached our quarters, cold, tired, and half exhausted with everyone wanting to be "first." Need I say any more? Duty will resume in 40 minutes with scarcely enough time to eat and clean up our dirty uniforms. The atmosphere borders on mutiny, and everyone has had a belly full of it, especially the younger men. What is to become of us? I have just heard that England has formed an alliance with Turkey. Another nail in our coffin, that is, in Germany's coffin. It seems rather odd that all of the countries around us have formed alliances against us, especially the larger and more consequential nations. Whether or not the German soldiers can succeed can only be held as a blind hope, since the conditions indicate otherwise.

So, my Goldchen, I will now eat the soup that is provided and put an end to the growling of my stomach. As usual, it will again be another bland broth. At any rate, the moral of my buddies is very low. My oatmeal has spoiled, so even the little bit of additional porridge that I had will have to be thrown out.

Dear Lord, I have such longings for home, for a sense of order and the chance to be human again. Here we are no more than automatons or robotic life forms. I must see to it, however, that I show no signs of weakness and become discarded. Then, all that I have done would have turned out to be in vain, and everything would become an uphill battle for me. The comradeship of my fellow soldiers is the only thing that lifts me to feel any joy at all. Too bad that a person has to be reduced to this.

My bowl of soup is so hot that I can't eat it just yet. So I have a little more time to write to you, my Goldchen. We have had a good working stove for the last few days which manages to heat up our room as much as the holes in the walls will permit. That returns my thoughts to Distelhof, because a stove such as this would bring on smiles and fit in very nicely. In order to enjoy being at Distelhof it needs to be cozy during the cold and windy weather. I know that you will laugh at the thoughts of a countryman, but if he does not indulge himself in these fantasies, he gets a little crazy. So, he paints castles in the air, lives in them, and pretends that he is home once more. Yes, Goldchen, that is as it is with me. That's what comes out in me.

This morning, I held class for the company. The topic was "Auto Ignition." They all perked up their ears and sat with open mouths to see that the driving instructor has other talents in terms of teaching and learning. It was really something that I enjoyed, and I was pleased that they were satisfied. I have always liked this part of my duty – just not the treatment that a soldier gets in this 5th year of the war. Without family and loved ones back home, though, there would be no reason for any of us to be trained as soldiers.

The fact that I haven't received any mail from you makes me very nervous, and I feel uninspired in having to wait so long. I have written you faithfully and need to be able to thank God for the gift of your good health and well-being once again. I love you so very much. So, my Love, my time is up, and I am happy to have created this little letter.

Yours, as always, Your Vagabond

Letter no. 126
Officer Training, December 10, 1943,

Always, my Joy and Happiness,
My Goldchen,

We just returned from duty, tired and dirty all over again. The Advent wreath hangs over my head, just above my chair. I am worn out, sad and sick, and there is no mail for me from my Goldchen in the homeland. While my buddies were loudly living it up yesterday evening, I quietly crept to my room like a dying animal and lay there for a long time in utter exhaustion. I must have had a fever because I shook and shivered with freezing and then began to feel very hot. In the morning, I had a rheumatic pain in my spine again, but duty prevails, and I must go on. That's the way things are with me, my Goldchen, but I have no idea how everything is with you. If you expected your stay at the hospital to last until the end of the month, as you previously wrote, then you have been home for perhaps a week. Hopefully you have received my mail. I wanted to write you during this very trying period of time to let you know how much I love you and am thinking about you. Yesterday, I lay in my small bed and chastised myself for not having written, but that doesn't really accomplish anything.

We have not yet finished the driver training tests because the truck was needed for other reasons. Besides, there is little that the others can do. Without me, things could be tougher for them. As I have already written you in my last letter, I gave an instructional presentation on "Automobile Lighting and Ignition." My eyes are beginning to close... the body is begging for rest. We are poor souls, but that is of no consequence, and things must press on.[78]

Several days ago, I got a request to make some drawings. I spent two days in the writing room, where I did a lot of burdensome work. The drawings were to be very elaborate and needed to look official. In the end, they turned out very well, and

---

[78]A large ink spot marks the end of this page of writing. An arrow points to it with the words: "I nodded off here . . . ." His pen must have remained in a stationary position, allowing the ink to dispense.
Claudius must have leaned over and fallen asleep for a period of time.

the staff members just shook their heads at the quality of the work that I had done. Goldchen, even at those times when things go well for me here my longing to have everything in order lies deep in my bones. If you have already been to see Doeges, my question then is as to whether or not you were able to come to an agreement with him. In regard to my letter to Mr. Etzel, I have not received any answer from him. I am certain that he sustained damage as the result of the attack on Frankfurt, because his relatives, especially his parents, live in that city. I would really like to get my hands on a technical newspaper like JETZ (or IETZ) or something similar, since the technical spirit in me has not yet gone to sleep.

I have until tomorrow to come up with a song and evening lecture under the topic of "Homeland." I will have to get to work on that tonight, and since they are expecting something "special" from me, I will have to put a bit of hard work into it. Too bad that I don't have you to rely on. You could certainly be a big help to me . . . but then I could use your help in all kinds of ways.

Well, I can only cling to the hope that I will receive some sort of a good sign from you very soon . . . lest I remain sick and die. Please say hello to the children for me and tell them that I love them and that Papa always carries the pictures of his little group with him so he can talk about them with the others. Of you, my Goldchen, I can't bear to speak. One can get sick with the suffering of so much worry and longing. I remain, as always, Your Paulus, and I love you so very much. Your Vagabond

Letter no. 127
Soldier P. Claudius no.5651a
Officer Training,
December 12, 1943,

My Desire!

Today is Sunday evening, and a stillness has come over the barracks. The few stalwarts who have remained here in our quarters sit at tables, and, like me, write letters home. A lot of mail and packages came today. Unfortunately, there was nothing there for me, and I have to say that I am very sad. I have been away from home for almost four weeks and know nothing at all of anything that is going on. I will soon have to believe that something has happened to you. Dear God, don't let that be the case. I couldn't bear it. Write me, Goldchen. Write to me and tell me that you are alive and in good health so that I will no longer have to worry with so much desperation.

Now, I will tell you what has happened here in the last two days. Yesterday morning, we marched through a foggy forest to reach the staging area for our maneuvers. Freezing and with our hands turning blue, we were ordered to sing, which, considering our physical discomfort, was really a chore. I was the second machine gunner. All went well enough with the maneuvers and everyone was happy to have gotten that part of things over with. All of us were completely covered with mud as we made the 10 kilometer march back to headquarters. In the afternoon, we picked up the pace where we had left off, only this time in a meadow. The dew was so heavy that water ran into my shoes. I was the group leader and had to give the orders. Having become soaked and dirty from head to foot, the mud party later made its way back to the barracks where we once again cleaned our uniforms. My boots are pale from the repeated washings. After cleaning our weapons, we all fell into bed at 8:30. At 3 AM that morning, we started up again ... this time as a scouting party. Muddied up all over again and often stumbling over rocks and stones, we trooped along in a ditch beside a road in the early predawn mist. While making our way through some lonely farmyard, I was set upon by an angry dog, but managed to escape, uninjured . I found some ducks in an open pen, but "looting" is strictly forbidden. Around 7:30 we returned to the cold of our barracks room to have to clean our weapons before finally being able to wash and rinse eight days of itching grime off of our shins in the hot water. And so, we were clean in both clothing and skin. All too soon, though, we were ordered back out into the cold again, outfitted in our newly washed, but not completely dry clothing which instantly turned frosty.

On Sunday evening, we had "drill practice," something that we had not done here before. There is an area of ditches and large piles of dirt behind our barracks. We were directed to go there, and then put through a drill that was so strenuous that I became covered with sweat. Our boots disappeared into the mud, and it took only a few minutes for us to become covered with blotches of dirt again. We splashed around the terrain like lightning, as we followed every order that was given and managed to do well enough. Drilling is my weakness, but of late I have stopped needing to fall out. In fact, I'm slowly becoming "snappy" at it. Nevertheless, I hate it, and it still pisses me off to have to do it. We wandered around in the training area until 12 noon, and then finished up to have some lunch – for which we again had to scrub ourselves clean. Even the staff has to brush and dry themselves as a daily requirement. After the soup, we were ordered to clean the room and cut loose with rags and scrub brushes until not a speck of dirt was anywhere to be seen. We finally finished up at around 16:00 hours which meant that we had been on duty from 2 AM until 4 PM. That was 14 hours.

In the meantime, I had a lot of other little things to do and take care of which I won't bother to go into. I am tired and feel sad with the lack of any news from you. Everything around me feels sort of hopeless. We will have a church service tomorrow. It's optional, of course, but they do keep track of attendance. Only four men from our company attended in the beginning, but I somehow managed to get things started, and some of the others hesitantly followed. I want to be able to talk to you and so will be in God's house on Sunday to pray for his sanction that all goes well for you and our dear children. I like Sunday mornings because we are allowed to sleep until 7 AM. Still, I'm always the first one to be up. Very slowly and with deep yawns, the younger guys follow.

Yes, Goldchen, to be an officer, a real officer, is no small or easy matter. An officer is a special kind of infantryman. Well, my eyes are getting heavy, and I need to get to bed. In the darkness I will fold my hands and tell God of my worries over you. I love you so much and give you 10,000 intimate kisses.

Your Paulus and Vagabond.

Letter no. 128
Officer Training, December 15, 1943,
Wednesday,

Oh, You, my Love, You, my Desire,

Oh, you, my Goldchen. Your letter of December 3, the first one in four weeks, has made its way to me, and everything within me cries out in jubilation. "My Love lives and has returned home." Goldchen, I feel like a different person. Every heavy burden has been lifted from me. The magnificent song of love in my heart is strong once more, and all of the agony of waiting is forgotten. I am certain that you have not told me about the worst parts of it (the surgery) and that the many hours of my restless worry were not unwarranted. You have written quite a bit about the stitches. Are you still on IVs that need yet to be removed? Please write to me and let me know more about the real reasons for needing to have such an extensive operation and as to when you expect to be healthy again and whether or not you can "still have little children" when I am back home with you. Your explanations are not all that clear. (Excuse the handwriting. My pen has been sick for some time now, and it drips.) No matter what, my Love, I am thankful to the dear Lord that you are alive and live for me, your Paulus, who loves you so very much. Have the children been able to bring you some joy during the difficult hours, or have they no idea as to what you went through? But then, what would be the point of upsetting them? The times we live in will soon enough take care of that.

In the meantime, much has happened to me, and I want to tell you about it. It has also become cold here. All of the brooks and ponds are frozen over, and a light fog hangs over the countryside in the mornings. My knitted gloves are nice, but they cannot stand up to the wear and tear of weapons handling. I have stuffed every finger with gray wool, (I don't have any black wool). Send me a pair of old leather gloves. They work better. I have a cold, and my nose runs. I freeze terribly in my bed at night and would rather have a down comforter instead of the two blankets that I have. We are all fearful of the cold here. It pierces me to the bone and renders my fingers useless. We have had to put on gas masks lately and run to the point that our faces and bodies literally cook under them. It's only when we take them off that the cooling down can begin. Our last maneuver with a heavy artillery company was very interesting. The artillery unit lobbed shells over our heads and debris flew all around us. I picked up several pieces of splintered material. We moved forward under this bombardment until our hearts sank down into our boots. All of us were greatly relieved when the signal to regroup was given. Our commander had watched the whole operation from a nearby mountain. He praised us and was proud of us for our bravery. Yesterday we departed from our usual routine in order to greet the new incoming Reserve Officer Candidates. We now travel within the regiment as, "old soldiers." Tomorrow, I will be the Officer of the Day and be in charge of the new-comers and, if needed, "chew their asses."

Oh, Goldchen, take care of yourself and care for our home. I will try to get some leave after the holidays. Tomorrow, I will write you a Christmas letter.

Love, I kiss you tenderly and intimately and remain,
Your Paulus

Letter no. 129
Officer Training,
December 16/17, 1943,

To my Joy at home, my Desire,

By now I have received two letters from my Goldchen, and it breaks my heart to know how much you have suffered and that you continue to be in pain. Your lines of December 5th reach out to me like a solitary cry. Oh, Goldchen, if you only knew how that makes me feel. At times I've thought that I could not go on here in Officer Training. I wanted to give it all up and throw it away. But then the realization of the disgrace that it would bring to you back there at home, as well as to my old company, gives me the courage to press on. The older and better educated soldiers are sought out for this kind of training, and because of that, I now know that I would not be able to be released from here. A forty-year-old professor of Theology from the University of Jena, arrived here yesterday He is bald and is bunking with 18 year old soldiers. A tough assignment to be sure.

But, back to you. Your letter of the 5th was handed to me during officers' mess. My heart pounded when I saw your hand writing, and I quickly tucked the letter into my satchel. I had table cleaning duty but kept thinking about my little letter – like a great treasure from my Goldchen, and a happy quiver filled my heart all evening long. Yesterday the Lieutenant told me that company commander Goellnitz had asked that I take two days off to take care of some things. Since I am not permitted to be absent from Officer training, I will have to travel to Rennes on Saturday and Sunday and give up some of my precious personal time. It is so hard to get any kind of a break that I look forward to the weekend so very much.

They have shown just about ten movies here in Montfort during the time that I have been here, but I have never gone . . . firstly because I want to write to you, my Joy, and secondly because I need every minute of sleep that I can get to rest my tired body. That's the way it is for me this evening. I am officer of the day (UVD) which means that I have supervisory duty for the company and must be at my desk during all break and rest periods, as well as taking all phone calls. I must police the rooms, inspect the dishware, and see to it that the recruits make it to mess on time. In short, I have to be on watch late into the night with my regular duties beginning again at 5:30 in the morning. I unfortunately tore my coat on a nail and also had to take time out to reach for a needle and thread. And so it is for sleep and war. Friday morning to Saturday evening, morning to night, we are always on the move and doing something.   On Sunday our duty lasts until 2 in the afternoon. A lot is required of us, and I can endure all of these hardships because being sick in the military is even tougher than that.

Now I want to tell you about our driving test. I was the best driver. The instructor got all of the technical data from me during my lectures. Then came the actual road test. An engineer was to conduct it. Everything went along pretty well...... You will laugh, but my esteemed colleague singled me out because I couldn't get the old wreck out of second gear. The instructor was still talking when I finally managed to get it engaged and rumbled the giant truck through the narrow streets of Rennes. In the meantime, both colleagues got things in order, and all went well. Everything went especially well with the theoretical exam. In the end, 5 soldiers failed (two were sergeants), and I now have a Wehrmacht second class license for heavy trucks.

The hand on the clock moves on and on; day after day passes by and moves us on to a sad and quiet Christmas – for you, there at home, and for me, here. If it won't upset you, I will keep the sausages that I got from Mrs. Ludwig so that I will have something better to eat in the days ahead. I will see what the Lieutenant has to say after the holiday, but for now getting any sort of furlough is entirely impossible because the regiment would have to OK it. Goldchen, remember that I am always there for you and that your Paulus loves you very much

As Always, Your Paulus and Vagabond,

You, my Dear Goldchen.

Letter no. 130
Officer Training, December 19, 1943,
4th Sunday in Advent,

My Joy in this World, My Goldchen,

I reach for a pen in order to write to you, my Love, something that is beautiful, after so many hours of helping others. Goldchen, listen:

My old company called me a few days ago and invited me to celebrate Christmas with them and to arrange their Christmas program, but the Lieutenant refused, saying that he needed me because I am to set up the Christmas celebration here as well. He does not want to lose his most valuable resource. Yes, and so the matter went to a higher court. The final ruling meant that Officer Candidate, Claudius, will travel to Rennes on Sunday evening, but not before loading me down with a lot of other assignments to complete for the company here. After attending to those things, I was nostalgically received by my old company. I am to develop an elaborate program for their celebration, am to play the part of

Mister Christmas, to play the piano, and compose a welcome poem to be dedicated to all of the soldiers and officers who will be participating in the festivities. There I stood, in the middle of the gentlemen who were giving me the assignment they were unable to do themselves – so, who was to help? Only Claudius. With that, they handed me a pen and ink, and I sat down to compose and complete the work. I wrote a beautiful Christmas poem. Yesterday evening I was to have a meeting with my Lieutenant because he wanted to speak to me. The commander and the sergeant also showed up and complained that the best individuals of the company were being transferred and taken away from them.

With so much to do I really had to scramble to get this letter off to you. In the process of making all of these Christmas arrangements for others, a great sadness came over my heart, especially when I think about the way it would sound to you back there at home. There you are with the sweet children, you dear little Joy, back at home. You have my deepest promise that I will be there with you in my thoughts and that we will all be happy. I have tried everything to get the chance to come home. In that regard, my Lieutenant has also made every effort on my behalf, but the Division has refused on the grounds of a general ban on travel for all officer trainees. It was not easy for him to tell me, but he added that he could see a possibility for sometime around the beginning of the New Year.

Goldchen, how are things at home? How are you coping with everything? I ask the dear Lord to stand by you and the children since in all probability there is no one else that will. My roommate buddies from my old company all went on furlough yesterday, and I gave one of the brave fellows a package to take along with him. You can imagine how I felt. It took every ounce of the soldier in me not to cry and lose my composure. This evening I am back with my comrades. I have my letters from you and my photos. All of them know me, and they have been great to me.

My Love, be strong in your heart. The most difficult hours are those of the wives who have men at the front. I am safe for the next few months while my former buddies who are now on leave will be sent to the Russian front as soon as their furlough ends. Sit at the window in the living room, look out over the land, and think of me. I do that often in regard to you. Get the big train and rocking horse down. The children should have the chance to play with the things that I made for them. My thoughts revolve more and more around my home and the joy that I will find there again. My hopes for a belated Christmas celebration fill my mind, and I live in the knowledge that you, my dear Love, love me.

So, my Dear, another Sunday passes. My fourth Sunday in Advent. It has brought me work as well as pain. I love you, kiss you intimately, and remain,

Your Vagabond and your Paulus.

Letter no. 131
Paul Claudius, Reserve Officer Training,
December 21, 1943,

My Desire and my Goldchen!

Just a few minutes and then it is back to the city of Rennes for me so that I can take care of Christmas matters. The company gave me 300 reichsmarks and said . . . "Soldier Claudius, you know how everything is to be done, so go and find the things that you need. Nothing more need be said." I am required to do it, and it hurts me deep in my heart to not be able to do anything like this for you, back home. However, Love, save your happiness for the beginning of January. It is then that I have a duty trip and will be able to come home for three to four days. My lieutenant has done everything in his power, but nothing has worked out because of the no-time-off from duty rulings.

Yesterday, I was told to take a passenger car and drive to Rennes to pick up 30 bottles of red wine. On the way there, I was to stop at a mill and get some flour. Unfortunately, the car broke down, and we were stranded in a small village. A French repair shop determined that the rear axle was broken and that the vehicle would have to be towed. In the meantime, I, along with the forty-year-old doctor of Philosophy from Jena, managed to come up with 30 pounds of flour from a local baker. (Hopefully it is not rye flour.) We were successful in hitching a ride on a French truck that took us a few more kilometers in the direction of our destination. So, there we sat, two learned individuals discussing our wives and our homes. We also entered a nice Catholic church where some children were practicing children's Christmas songs. It was so peaceful inside that I seized the moment to fold my hands and pray for all of you. I asked that the dear Lord protect all of you, restore your health, my Love, and give you the gift of hope.

In the meantime I was able to stop a Wehrmacht truck for a ride. Back on the road again, we slowly rambled to Montfort, where I still had a lot of things to take care of. So I have had to interrupt this letter a number of times. But I don't always want to talk about these things. We need to talk about me. After much searching around, I was finally able to get a few items for the children today. So that Papi does not arrive empty handed, I will pack these away and bring them with me at the beginning of January. We now have a Christmas tree in our room. It has beautiful branches, but the top is broken off. I took five reichsmarks from the cash box in our room to get some ornaments and . . . decorations. I will go to Rennes tomorrow to take care of that. The fellow soldier who is to accompany me is a businessman. He handles the books, and I may just need some extra money.

I want to thank you for your last letter. It was waiting for me on my little bed yesterday when I returned. Your dear lines brought me real joy even though you are so sad. Soon, my Love, the telephone will ring and Papi will be standing at the door. I do not know exactly when it will be, but the first few days of January are not so far away. Until then, I will try to take care of a few more details in terms of food procurements. Our days of celebration together should be crowned with some festive meals, and I don't want to deplete your cupboard at home.

My Love, Papi will now seek out his bed. All of my buddies are already asleep. Kiss the children for me and tell them that Papi will soon be home.

1000 intimate, heartfelt greetings from your Papi.

Letter no. 132
Officer Training, December 23, 1943,

My Love, Above All in my Heart,
My Goldchen!

Today is the evening before the Christmas Eve celebration. My heart is very cold, and I   feel as empty as if today were to be Christmas. Outside it is raining in torrents, and mud covers the roads. A festively decorated Christmas tree stands right next to my bed in our room. Evergreens adorn the walls, and out of pity, even the holes in the wall are decorated with boughs. My buddies have procured food. Six chickens have been butchered and plucked. The professional work on the chickens was done by a dentist. Eight or ten rabbits have been slaughtered and dressed, and since I was in Rennes, I was unable to supervise this aspect of the preparations. I was, however, able to bring back some live rabbits which were put into some empty rabbit hutches. For myself, I have managed to save a few cigars, a container of marmalade, some cakes of the sort that I sent to you, a pound of butter, and the Ludwig sausage. I also sent the following things yesterday:
    1 package with close to two kilograms of wonderful cookies for the children. X
    1 package with three little sticks of butter and a one pound box of butter.
    1 package containing a beautiful honey cake.
    1 package with 12 eggs. X
    I have sent the items that are marked with the X along with a buddy who is going to Germany so that the cookies will not dry out, and the eggs will not spoil.
    It's great that we received money today, because I will now be able to buy a few more things. (1 kilogram of coffee beans for 13.5 reichsmarks.) These tightly packaged things will hopefully bring you some joy. For you, Goldchen, I "purchased" a charming little Stylo fountain pen. It will be in my next package to you. It has brought me much happiness to be able to do these things.
    I have taken care of all of the preparations for the celebration. Tomorrow I will need to get twenty heads of cauliflower and some sugar.   Somehow Claudius manages to get everything done

including the supervision of the preparations in the kitchen. Love, it is good for me to be able to make these preparations for my buddies to make them happy, but it also hurts because I ever see you watching me with your big, sad eyes and the children hanging onto you and asking, "Where is Papi? Where is Paulus?" He is far away and is not permitted to come home. Yes, Goldchen, it will be a tough time for us to get through Christmas Eve. The Holidays are to be filled with duty for me, and that will make it a little easier to endure the painful thoughts of home. I have to discipline my mind about all of that, lest the tears begin to flow. I will hopefully get some mail from you tomorrow. That letter will be my Christmas and my Christmas Angel. I will pray for it.

In the barracks, back a Rennes, I looked at the dear picture of you for a long time. I see the love and femininity in your eyes and know how lucky I am to have you. I must make a presentation to the company tomorrow and, as of yet, have not prepared anything. Perhaps I will just speak from the heart. I will look at the Christmas tree and let my heart do the talking. I wonder what it looks like at Distelhof . . . if everything is covered in winter garb with the building wrapped up in a white winter coat. We would most certainly take the children out into the country to look across the silent fields and remember the summer of 1943. Waves of golden fields, . . . you and I strolling on smooth paths, happy in our hearts and yet wrapped in the shadow of knowing that I must go and become a soldier. My Dear, I love you and the children are our joy. I will always strive to be Your Paulus. Each one of us should think of this happiness on Christmas Eve. Perhaps we will succeed in being able to break through everything that separates us.[79]

Your Paulus

---

[79] At the end letter no. 132, Paul Claudius asks his wife to think of their togetherness on Christmas Eve. He seeks to "break through" everything that separates them. In a transcendental way, he seeks to be with his family across the miles. Once, during the translator's study in Salzburg, Austria, he became sick. In the night, he found himself crossing the ocean, transcending his separation from his family and landing in the driveway of 120 Hillcrest, Hamilton, Illinois. If one longs for something long and hard enough, one seeks it out in a transcendental way.

Letter no. 133
2 Postcards:
Christmas 1943,

My Dear Little Erika!

Papi just returned from church where he spent a quiet hour of celebration with the dear Lord God as well as all of you. He always thinks about you and especially about your dear Mommy. It is quiet here, and Papi's thoughts are with you because he loves you so much. Be well, my dear Erika, and give your mother a kiss. Your Papi

Christmas 1943
My Dear, dear, Young Son, (Matthias),

You, also, my Dreamer, shall have a Christmas greeting from your soldier Papi. Next to me stands the gun that you played with. Yes – a memory. Please ask your Mommy to write to Papi and tell him about your Christmas at home.
You dear, dear Boy, Your Papi

Letter no. 134
Soldier Paul Claudius,
No. 5651a
Officer Training, December 26, 1943,
2nd Day of Christmas Celebration '43,

My Beloved Heart's Desire, My Goldchen!

Today is the second day of the Christmas celebration and some letters have arrived. All of the military hustle and bustle of the celebrations has ended, and everyone has gathered at the table to write longing letters home. For me, the days were a strain because the entire program for Christmas festivities rested on my shoulders. Still, everything went grandly . . . including my speech, which was inspired by the still, quiet spirit of Christmas in the field. It was well-received. All of the higher-ups have praised the wonderful little celebration and made the effort to tell me that it was very meaningful. So it was with the Lieutenant, who asked if we could do something similar for New Years Eve.

My Love, Goldchen, I have prepared all this to bring joy to others by bringing all of my work and worry to bear on the preparations, but you and the children were alone. I'm sure that it was most likely very quiet there, at home. With some fear, I even ask myself as to whether or not you even had a Christmas tree. Here in the room stands a Christmas tree – poor little thing, decorated with candles and tinsel. The branches reach all the way to my bed. I have quietly looked at it for a long time, thought of home, and held my heart in my hand in order not to lose my composure. It was a sad Christmas for me as well, because the letter from you, my Joy, for which I had longed and waited, did not come. And so I spent the hour of celebration alone, by myself. Just as it was so difficult for you to spend your Christmas Eve with just the children, I watched with moist eyes as my buddies read the letters that they had received on Christmas.

I often wonder if we will be permitted to be together –forever – or whether my undisciplined living will push us apart. I am often very afraid and filled with bad thoughts that can only be driven away by your picture and continuing letters. I hope that you can understand what I am trying to say by this. I know that you are also plagued by uneasy and disturbing thoughts and that you have to struggle to keep from being consumed by them. The weather today is rainy, dark and dreary, and I am filled with melancholy thoughts – so little hope and so little strength for tomorrow's duty for which I must look sharp. If I had only received a letter from you. Then Christmas would have truly been in my heart.

I received my reichsmarks the day before yesterday, and with them I will be able to pay for the large package that I sent to the children.

Now, I want to tell you about something special: A few days ago, while I was sitting in the barracks in Rennes, I noticed a young soldier who caught my attention. I felt that I knew the young man, and as I stood up to go into the city, he came over to me and introduced himself as tank soldier, Gloria, from Hochheim. Then it hit me. We went on to happily talk about home and about dear, old, departed Mr. Gloria. Now listen. . . .The young fellow began to tell me that he knew, early in the day, that I was to be in the vicinity. He had run into a buddy at the railroad station who was carrying a package under his arm that was addressed to Frau Hertha Claudius, Hochheim.   It was the buddy to whom I had given the eggs and cakes to bring to you. Truly a very special encounter.

I am so happy to have been able to send you a few packages and all of it made possible because of my continuing duties in Rennes. The little ones and you should know that I am always there for you, and it makes me happy to know that another little package is on its way to all of you. Has the package with the genuine French basket arrived yet? Well, I will await a little letter from you, but I won't count on it, because it is so hard to be disappointed. Yesterday, my Love, I was in a Catholic church and thought about you with all of my heart and completely sensed that I was there with you at home, our beautiful home.

So, now, my Goldchen, be well. My heart is always with you, my Love. I love you, always.

Your Paulus

Letter no. 135
Officer Training
December 30, 1943,

Always My Desire!
My Goldchen!

I have been in great pain for the past three days and have forced myself to go on. I've been sick with a fever and nausea, a flu of some sort that just drags on. My voice completely disappeared two days ago, and I have a tough time making myself understood.

Time and time again, I am tormented by the fact that I have not been able to send you my timely communications. I haven't received any mail from you, my Goldchen, and am very worried about what has happened to you in the aftermath of the operation. Hopefully, you have not had a relapse. Such things are often worse than the ailment itself. Tomorrow is New Years Eve, . . . a new year, 1944, to live through and fight through. It will probably be the toughest one yet, especially for you and me. My time here will soon be completed, and it won't be long before I get my orders to be sent to the front. That will mean a long time of separation for us.

Now, my Love, my heart beats wildly, . . . the mail is here, and there are two letters for me. I will open them right away.

There are two letters, one dated December 2nd and the other, December 13th. The letter of December 2nd brings me both joy and pain. I know about the unspeakable hardship that you have been through from an earlier letter. I have asked the dear Lord, again and again, to give you hope and restore your health.

It is quite another matter when it comes to your writings of December 13th. It goes without saying that I was very surprised about the contents of this letter. Unfortunately I did not write you as to why Schorsch was so suddenly transferred from the company. He was removed with malice as a swindler. Of the 100 cigars, he delivered 10 to me. Because of him, I was interrogated. Things were very hot around here. They wanted to put him in prison, and his only chance to avoid that was a quick transfer away from here. I won't say anything about the way he acted toward me. Leichte was found to be the guilty person in our company, and I also made some mistakes in regard to money. I gave marks to Mrs. Ludwig when she came here to visit, and because of all of the things that were going on here, forgot all about returning it. Leichte also owed me money which the Company has paid back. I will write a letter to Mrs. Liechte about all of that. As for the rest of your long letter, I am really surprised at the long list of accusations. I had given you soft hints about Leichte's activities. Hertha, if you want to treat me that way, then go on and down the path that you have so recklessly described. A bum like him comes to you and gets all of this stirred up in you. It's making a mountain out of a mole hill.

I have tried hard to do everything that I could for you during all of the time that I have been in the service. I have a few things up my sleeve even now, but this damned, eternal coming back to the same issues every time something happens has put me into a different mood. It has made my heart bleed. I've had a shitty Christmas, am now sick, and with this wonderful letter can really expect to enjoy New Years Eve. My parents along with the Etzels have already written me twice about your surgery... quite a few days ago.

I received the 36 marks. You and the children will be compensated a thousand times over.

I don't need any more packages from any of you; things are splendid here. I don't need any money. I am very thrifty and do not want to cause you any hardships in your life. I deeply regret having brought you into any credit problems with the noble Schorsch. I have not received any packages from Ingrid.

My mood and my hope for getting better have taken on a new meaning. Paulus

Letter no. 136
January 1, 1944

Dear Little Erika, Dear Dreamer, Matthew, And Our Sunshine, Detti!

On this first day of the new year, Papi has come up with a bag of nuts and a bag of candy for his children. His buddies have given him these things. The nuts and the candy are for your three little mouths. It is not a lot, but it is all that Papi was able to get. Little Erika shall be in charge of dividing it all up. Otherwise, I know that the two boys would get most of it. Maybe they can hold the sides of the bag to keep it from spilling. If I can find anymore sweets, then I will get them. Love and kisses. Your Papi is sick and has to take care that his fever does not get any worse.

The lipstick is for Mommy for when Papi comes home!

Many heartfelt hugs from you Soldier Papi.[80]

---

[80] This line encircled at the bottom left of the page.

Letter no. 137
Soldier Claudius
#56510a
January 1, 1944

My Dearest Little Wife
My Goldchen,

> Somewhere in France,
> we light the candles in the night
> so that your heart will find me,
> since I cannot be with you.
> Silently, quiet and unspoken,
> all my words
> are cast homeward among the stars,
> to the children and to you.
> Many thousand wishes wander,
> lightly through this sacred night,
> where one soul in worried love for another,
> reflects, and keeps watch.
> Claudius

Perhaps you have some conception of the pain and frame of mind of a soldier's Christmas away from home. A handful of men are somewhere, gathered around a lighted tree. They stare, steadfastly and quietly at the flickering candles. One is absorbed in a book, and I – I hold pictures of my loved ones in my hands and draw from the spring waters of my memories, a life that lies behind me. No one ventures to break the silence for an hour. We think of "home," and, for a heartbeat, the war dies away and before us stands the vision, the picture of a peaceful German homeland, our place to be home.

This, to my Dear Little Wife, from
Paul Claudius, whose heart weeps.
Paul[81]

---

[81] Notice in this letter that he signs it "Paul."

Letter no. 138
January 3, 1944,

Goldchen!

Our first order of duty for the New Year begins with forest camping, and today is an especially intensive day of preparation around here. We will spend eight days in the muddy forests of Bretagne to simulate Russia. Like primitive man, we are expected to pitch tents, spend our nights wrapped in blankets on the ground, and travel from place to place like the first people on earth. Since I have been sidelined with a fever, this will put a particular strain on me, and I am very apprehensive about spending eight days 'in "Foret de Talensak." But this too shall pass, and the sun will shine again.

I have had no mail from you during the entire time of the New Year since the New Years celebrations. Mail in general has been sparse. In my room, I am the one who has received the least amount of mail. I must assume that you are still very sick and weak, – or that I do not deserve any better. Judging from the tone of your last letter, I must assume the latter.

The Lieutenant from the company came to see me yesterday to thank me for the poem that I had written for my old company. Unfortunately, I had to go over a few of the matters concerning Schorsch. I have started to distance myself from him, but it is not easy to change one's colors. I have always thought of him as a true friend, and no one can ever replace him as that. I had wanted to be the first to write to you about this whole matter. If only some mail from you had reached me. In your physical condition, I could only hope that you would be anxious to await mail from me in which I would confide in you.

The New Years celebration in the circle of my buddies was a beautiful experience. The Lieutenant sat next to me at the head of the table. He had directed me to conduct the festivities, and I had ordered that the leap from the old year to the new one be conducted in a very down-to-earth and low key manner. I had written some poetry and read some stories. All of it was beautiful, but also inexpressively sad. Punctually, at the stroke of midnight, we could hear the clock strike twelve times over the radio from the homeland. I thought intensely about you, and my speech was festive enough to bring a gleam to the eyes of the young guys, who always call me "Papa Doctor," as they gazed at the lighted tree. Following the presentation we had a social hour. No one got drunk. It was one big family, and the higher-ups were very pleased with the good conduct and proud of the men for their discipline. I had a lot to do with that by having enough good things for them to do that they didn't get bored. All of the drinking was monitored. The Sergeant was very moved because I mentioned his little son in my poem and even poetically included the Lieutenant. He repeatedly said, "Paul, have a seat; let's talk." (He is from Warenhanle.)

I have no idea as to how the holidays went for you. Perhaps you were in bed and only the children celebrated the midnight hour of the passing year. Or perhaps you were invited to go to Dr. Manus's. Four, 1 kilogram packages of splendid white flour are on their way to you. I managed to get these things from the cook by trading him cigarettes. I still have 40 reichsmarks and will get some other nice things since we will soon be transferred from Montfort to Destination – Unknown.

Have you heard anything from Dr. Todoroff? The Italian army has been taken over by the German Wehrmacht. Have you received the French items? I sent the children some candy and a bag of nuts. Of the four or five Christmas packages that I sent, two were sent to Germany with buddies because they were rather heavy or contained items that could easily spoil. So, I will now take care of some of the things that need to be done in preparation for our forest camping and hope that all will go well out there. Everything gets placed on the shoulders of the oldest one. I don't really want that because it is just too much of a burden.

I remain, always, your Paulus

Letter no. 139
Foret de Montfort
Bunker 3, January 4, 1944

Goldchen!

Amid the dense smoke of a sooty lantern we sit around a little table and smoke and talk. We are in a forest camp that is to resemble the war conditions of Russia. Yesterday, we cut down trees which we chopped into smaller pieces of wood for use in the kitchen and bunker stoves. The Lieutenant diligently worked with the ax, and in the process of my using the timber saw with the large teeth, I cut my index finger nearly half through. It bled for hours and even the cotton wadding that was applied by the medic did not help. So, I just let it bleed until the flow was reduced enough to get it wrapped in a bandage. Because my hand towel was soaked with blood, I took it to a brook some distance away from here in order to wash it. Since we must get used to conditions as they are at the front, shaving with water is not permitted.

Our bunker is dug two meters into the forest floor. The roof is supported by thick tree trunks with a few steps leading down into the bunker space itself. The door, which can't be seen from the outside, is 1.10 meters high, and so it is a matter of having to crawl to get in. Only the constant smoke coming from the tin chimney gives any evidence that people are present – in this case, German soldiers. We have covered the walls with pine branches and so, we look green. The only pleasant thing in this dungeon is the little stove that stands in the corner to the right of the door. It is kept constantly burning and supplies us with comfortable warmth. The only thing standing is a little table on which a candle flickers in a sinister sort of way. We sleep on straw, eight men, side by side, like sardines. The sleeping chamber for the Reserve Officer Candidates is about four meters wide. At night, the air is so heavy with the spicy smell of pine, the stove and the men, that one thinks that he will suffocate. In addition to giving off warmth, the stove also causes the pine rafters of our roof to spit out sap which drops down onto my clothes and bed coverings. Needless to say, we sleep in our clothes and even leave our shoes on. That's the way we live, that is the way I live, and this is to be our home, this room.

The soldier on watch has just crawled in through the door. He is being relieved because we are expecting a surprise exercise attack by the older soldiers this evening. So we are to be on guard.

A wagon that delivers food is our only connection to the outside world. Today, that wagon also brought mail and everyone pushed in around the horse drawn wagon. There was, however, no mail for me. Well, in the last few days I have become used to it. Everyone has gone to bed; only old Claudius writes, as usual. It's too bad that this letter cannot be delivered to the field post station.

With that, I must close for now. Sleep well. We hear that Thüringen has been plagued by air raids – so make sure to take care of the children. Oh, this unfortunate war. When will it be over? 1000 heart-felt greetings from the bunker.

Your Paulus

Wednesday the –- (5th)

I just received an order for night watch. I am inexpressibly happy. I have a letter from you. You, my one and only joy. Your Paulus

Letter no. 140
ROB Claudius,
FD 5651a,
Montfort, January 7, 1944,

My Passionately Beloved Joy, My Goldchen, You!

Hurrah! I have just received mail from my Goldchen. Everything within me is jumping for joy, and with your letter of the 4th Sunday of Advent, just days before Christmas, there is light and hope in my heart again. Now I fear that you have the letter that I sent in answer to the "Schorsch letter" in your hands. I do not want you to be upset. Please, forget the harsh words in that letter. I love you so much, my Goldchen.

I just about fell over when I got the mail because I didn't hear my name called and then heard my buddies yell, "Matthias, – there is mail for you." Wow! My heart beat with joy, especially when I saw that it was from you. My hands shook with delight and excitement as I hurriedly read only the first and last lines. An unimaginable happiness surged through my body and filled me with inspiration. My Goldchen, my very being was reborn within me. Since the bunker was hardly the place to contain the excitement for this sort of a treasure, I tucked the letter away. While on guard the next day and lying on my stomach in the cold sunshine, I read the first lines. Oh, life is beautiful once more, and now that I know that communications between us have become reestablished, I have become a changed man.

Just one day after that, I got a second letter, the one dated December 8th. The mail has no doubt been shuffled around, and some letters were perhaps even burned in the bombing of a railroad station somewhere. It is evident from all of your dear lines that you are still suffering from the effects of the operation. You have not written me about the significance and intent of this surgery. As your husband, I would at least like to know if you look any different than you did before. Perhaps something has been removed. I beg you to write me and plead for you to get the best care that you possibly can. I do not believe that you would have allowed yourself to suffer and endure such unspeakable pain if I had been able to come home. How did you celebrate Christmas? I have asked myself that question over and over, and will certainly get some news of that in the coming days.

I was the coordinator of the Regiment in Rennes again today and had a lot of running around to do. They woke me up in the bunker in the middle of the night with orders to march a retreat through the dark pine trees. I was actually happy to get away from the underground bunker dirt for a few hours. After that, accompanied by a Company Leader, I traveled to Rennes by car in order to take care of a few more things. Little by little, it seems that I have earned myself a license of privilege when it comes to the procurement of things. I am now back in my quarters again, but everyone is gone, along with the stove. A real Siberian situation prevails. Hopefully I won't freeze during the night.

I am able to relate some good news to you and that is that I am able to live up to what is required of me. At any rate, I have made it through the toughest part, and best of all, I have successfully completed the training. Because of my ever-growing relationship with the Lieutenant, I have been given considerably lighter duties. I have become a sharp soldier for the D Company, and I get a kick out of that. I have had some interesting talks with the Lieutenant during our patrols. Bombers were here a couple of days ago!! I think that the British have something up their sleeve.

I have managed to warm myself up by moving around a bit. The cold can really be painful. Well, my Love, I need to tell you that I love you and think of you and the little ones – always. From here, it's all uphill again. Hopefully, I will be able to write to you from my hole in the earth very soon again. If not, you will have to wait for nearly a week to get mail.

In longing and love, Your Paulus

Letter no. 141
Soldier Claudius
5651a
Officer Training, January 8, 1944,

My Goldchen, My Joy!

Before the whole unit heads out for lunch here in the forest camp, I will attempt to write a letter to my Goldchen. As of now, I expect to be crawling around in the forest until Wednesday. Today I want to finally be able to fill you in on what is to happen next. After telling my Lieutenant that you have had a difficult surgery, that is, during our last field operation, he asked me about the content of your last two letters. He is also a married man and is the nicest officer that I have come to know. Because we were involved in a very important course of special weapons training, there was nothing that could be done until after the Christmas celebrations. Training as of now is set as follows: Our sequence of study will be completed by February 28, 1944, and we will then be transferred to a company somewhere in France to serve as instructors for the next two months. Our first leave comes due at the end of that period of time, after which we will be sent to the front. I, however, will travel to Germany on the 28th of February. Reason: A pressing family matter. Since I am not eligible for a furlough, I will be given a special assignment. This singular opportunity will naturally involve some sort of duty related assignments which I must take care of. But now you can clearly see what this means and be happy for it. If the transportation is good and we don't have to turn around, traveling Commander Claudius should be on the road on February 28th, and by then you will hopefully be healthy again. All of this is quite an undertaking and the Lieutenant has made a lot of preparations to make it happen.

I got a letter from Mr. Etzel. He wrote a lot of nice things and included his best wishes for the new year of 1944. How was the company Christmas gathering? Yes, my Goldchen, I had been thinking about that and remembering that I was the Santa Claus for the children of the Siemens employees two years ago. This time it is a bit different, but I know that our little ones had fun, and I await a report from you. Did you or Inge go with the children?

I have not seen the "combat Christmas package" yet, and I sure could use it. I'm living pretty thin. Did you get any of the many packages that I sent? I hope that the cookies and eggs that I sent off with a buddy got to you. Tomorrow, Sunday, I will be back in my bunker in the forest. Sure am looking forward to the cold. I'm freezing miserably, as it is, and have a bad cough. After sucking down four packages of lozenges, my voice has slowly managed to come back.

What are the little ones up to? On the train yesterday, I noticed a poor little child and wanted to take the little kid with me. Yes, Goldchen, when I am on watch in the French forests under the moonlight, my thoughts fly to you, and my longing returns. Those thoughts are so strong that it is difficult to return to reality. I long for those few days at the end of February and the beginning of March to come. Goldchen, I am thankful to be your Paulus and that I love you with such intensity. Say hello to the Benges for me, and to Inge, and to Erika as well.

I remain

Your Paulus

Letter no. 142
Officer Training, January 8, 1944,

My Dear Little Distelhofer!
My Goldchen!

I just got a letter from Franz Heydt. He writes to say that he will do some work at Distelhof. I will leave any specific decisions on this up to you. He could certainly be of use. He could help Inge with the early spring work on the garden beds. He won't go hungry during the work because of Inge. Being a roofer, he can also take care of the roof problems. Faithful servant. It will give you the chance to have some free time.

I am including some cigarettes and will write to the faithful servant myself, but I want you to give him a phone call.

I Love you, Above All
Your Distelhofer——Paulus

Letter no. 143
Foret de Montfort, January 12, 1944,

To the Love of my Heart, Goldchen,
My Goldchen!

Well, for the past two days we have sat around here in the rain and mire. The bunker roof leaks, and since no one can stand up, we hear the "drip, drop" coming down onto everything below. I got a letter from Laubegast yesterday. My father is back on his feet after a bad illness. He managed to start the letter but became so hopelessly tired that mother had to finish it. Yes, this eternal war has a way of quickly aging its mankind. It devours us, if we manage to survive at all.

We have maneuvers again tonight after which we will return drenched like rats and sleep in our stinking clothing. But it could be worse to be covered with nothing more than straw. Yes, the struggle in Russia is expected to be even more grueling.

I want to go on sending you a few dear lines for as long as I can and the situation permits. Yesterday, for instance, my love and longing for you was so urgent. I wanted so much to write to you because I know that you wait for mail from me. Are you still in pain? Please write me extensively about your condition. Say hello to the little ones from Papa. I proudly look at their pictures every day. I love you so much, my Goldchen. You, and you alone, are my whole life. I will try to write more tomorrow. I am always so lonely.

As always, your Paulus

Letter no. 144
Officer Training, January 12, 1944,

My Goldchen, My Beloved Goldchen!

Thank God that we are back "at home," if you want to call it that. We are currently busying ourselves, amid the mud, at the task of getting our clothing, and everything else, in shape. Our weapons are rusted and in dire need of cleaning. My socks are completely torn, and I must have all three pairs darned and washed by Friday. In the meantime, the Lieutenant has made me the senior soldier. The Lance Corporal was unfit for the job and had to be replaced. As the result of this, I unfortunately have a lot of work to do, even if it brings me special recognition.

Right now, my buddies are whooping it up because tonight is casino night, and since I have to give a speech, I clearly can't join them. Subject: "Vocational Choices and the Outlook on Employment Opportunities." I have gotten a lot of information together and hope that the "Speech" will go well. I do believe that my talent for public speaking has become recognized around here.

As of today, I have received no mail since your last letter of a week ago, and I am very sad. It's hard for me to believe that you write to me just once a week. So I tell myself that the act of writing is physically painful for you. I got a card from Uncle Kleineman, from Bishleben, today. He is a good fellow. I will answer him right away. He is a special visitor to Distelhof, and I miss him and that old clod of earth.

Again and again, I look at the pictures of our summer at Distelhof. I see the way I looked then . . . there. Then I look at the way I look now, . . . here. Still, little by little, I have proven that old Claudius is a "good soldier" and I am happy about that. Any shortcomings that I have in terms of being a snappy soldier, I make up for with my accomplishments at procurements and my special talents in the document room. They call me the "Philosopher."

In the coming weeks we are to have eight days of Pioneer instruction in Rennes!! I hope to be able to get some things for you while we are there. You see, I have some money saved and am always thinking of you. Is there anything that would suit your taste? I will try to find something special for you. It's too bad that there is only a frightful amount of useless junk available here. How are you and how are our little wonders doing? Please write me in full detail. I received the annual Siemens newsletter, and Etzel included a few nice lines for New Years. I have written back to him. Doeges also got corresponding mail from me. This man has apparently wrapped himself in silence.

As soon as I finish writing this letter, I will need to immediately go over the notes for my lecture. There are to be some important guests who are interested in hearing what I have to say. Do you remember my hesitant and faltering New Years Eve speech at Gartenstrasse? Times have changed, and I don't think that sort of thing will ever happen again. Events are slowly expected to change around here! We await the British[82], . . . exactly where is not clear, but most probably somewhere on the canal coast. In regard to my transfer to the Russian front, I may not have to go there. The front may just be right here in France. My Love, Kiss

---

[82] The Germans knew the British were coming, and although he cannot provide more "written" information here, Claudius's unit and other units were being trained to repel the invasion. It was common knowledge among German soldiers that Germany should have proceeded with an invasion of England after chasing the English forces out of France. The German General staff had drawn up invasion plans, and orders were issued during Dunkirk to prepare for a "crossing." Then, to the surprise of the German forces, the "crossing" orders were cancelled. In the years following the victory in France, Wehrmacht soldiers knew that their government had missed a chance to win a decisive victory, and possibly the war. Without bases in England, America would have had to concentrate on Italy and Russia as "invasion" routes," and the history of the war would have been changed.

the children for me and tell them that in 45 days I will be traveling to Hochheim.

In a loving spirit and with longing, I kiss you.

Always, Your Paulus

Letter no. 145
Soldier Claudius,
Field Post no 5651a,
Officer Training, January 13, 1944,

As Always, My Goldchen,

I just finished eating my soup and feel bodily rejuvenated. Still, I am constantly tormented with images of how things with you might be. Never getting any mail has put me into a considerable state of despair. My buddies ask me why I do so much writing and get so little mail. Goldchen, again and again my thoughts return to our home, and I try to picture you and the children. By now, Erika is probably on her way to school through the deep snow. The poor little thing. Please, write to me and let me know how she is doing. She is always so diligent and good. Erika is the oldest and has been with us the longest time in our eight-year marriage. A few days ago, I thought back to the time when you were Hertha de Veer, and you lived on Keppgrund Street. On Sundays, Paul would come by, dressed in his best suit with 10 reichsmarks in his pocket, ready for some high-priced fun. You would look out of the bedroom window. Your golden hair was so beautiful. It took a while before you were ready to come down, and then we were off. I especially remember our walks in the great outdoors and the evening meal that meant so much to both of us. Yes, my Love, many years have passed by since that time, and many things have changed. Your Paulus has brought you a lot of worry, but your steadfast purpose has always shown me the way. I do not feel that I will be too old to go on with our lives when I get back.

I am sending you a postcard that I got from Uncle Kleineman. I have already answered it and asked the "Steadfast Servant" to ask his roofer to take a look at the roof at Distelhof. Maybe you can go with him. By now, everything is white where you are. Here, the weather is eternally wet. Boots and socks are impossible to ever get completely dry and some have holes as big as a fist in them that I need to mend. We have shooting practice out in the water-soaked countryside this afternoon and will look like drowned rats again.

Duty calls once more, so I must interrupt this little letter. How about that, . . . I got lucky. The Lieutenant has given me an assignment to draw up a tactical map, and so I will pack my lunch and begin this great undertaking. This can take several hours because the maps around here are generally very poor and hard to procure. Our food situation has deteriorated again. I have been successful at buying just a little butter and a few eggs, now and then, and am only able get whole milk from a farmer's wife. With that I brew up a little pudding and fry a few eggs on a crude, little stove. Meals like this are a real treat for a countryman with a bad stomach who is expected to live on nothing more than cabbage soup. I will try to bring you some of these delicacies when I come home in February. Day by day, though, it has become more difficult to get any procurements of food.

How did things look for Christmas in terms of the special allotments that I sent? Did you get anything useful? For us, things were pretty pitiful. The Father State did little for its soldiers. On a chair next to me lie two little bunnies that are destined for the frying pan tomorrow. The butchering of six to seven live little animals per day happens quite a bit here, but it's the sort of eating that doesn't much appeal to me. There is a big difference between my personal taste, the way I like food prepared, and that of the eighteen-year-olds.

Well, Goldchen, my Joy, I will now slowly get myself ready for bed. I need to get some rest for the body before putting in some extra night duty. Your last letter and pictures will accompany me to bed until I fall asleep, overcome with exhaustion and longing thoughts of you. 1,000 intimate kisses from your old Paulus. Just like in the park, which was the most beloved place in the world for you and the children.

No mail again this time. Oh, my Love, what has happened! [83]

---

[83] Written on the side of the first page of the letter.

Letter no. 146
Soldier Paul Claudius
Field Post Office 5651a
Rennes, January 18, 1944,

My Joy, My Dear Little Wife!

I just finished acting as the advisor. The gentleman came to Papa Claudius to ask what type of wedding gift he should get for a dear friend back home. Well, the first thing I asked him was how much money he had and also about his "ability to send." I suggested a nice carved bread bowl, an ash tray or perhaps a suitable set of napkin rings. He left me and departed with a happy "thank you."

Yes, Goldchen, since I know that you are at this very moment looking for a little letter or a package, I am happy to prepare this little epistle to make its way to you. And so I will write you in reply to your letter of December 27th, 1944. It was with a heavy heart that I read how sad Christmas was for all of you. I am sure that you had tears in your eyes with the pain that you were in and the fact that Paulus, Papi, was not there with you. Hopefully, the three little ones were happy with their playthings. They are young, and it is the most beautiful time of their childhood years.

I have already told you about the way things were here among us as soldiers. Dettos made out well again, as he should, the little rascal. Everyone loves the little guy when I show them the photos. I spoke with a ranger's wife during a procurement trip into the country a few days ago. I showed her the pictures of Erika, Matteu, and Dettos and expressed my astonishment that the children here were so small, even though they were six to nine years old. The woman was very surprised. The robust figure of Dettos especially caught her eyes in wonder, and she told me that the countrymen from Breton were considerably smaller in stature than the other French races, but that the men are strong and hard working – something that cannot be said about the men from the Loire region.[84]

---

[84] Orleans and the surrounding area.

Were you at the Manus' apartment for New Years Eve? Does Manus live in the Baltus apartment? Did Mr. Baltus get to have a furlough for the celebration? Dr. Manus is now the only living Manus in the Wachsenburgweg district. My, things really have changed. One can certainly speak of the cock crowing over the dung heap.[85] Just be sure not to give him anything to crow about. Please write and let me know if he is living up to his assigned duties, or I will have to go after the Prussian master myself.

I have a vague and yet distinct recollection that Dr. Manus was our neighborhood air-raid warden. He was assigned to see to it that all window shades were in good repair, properly fitted and adjusted to darken out any lights that may be emitted during non-daylight hours. He also checked cellars and basement spaces, as they were utilized as air raid shelter accommodations, and diligently noted any (under no excusable circumstances – ever – whatsoever) – failure of anyone to report to his designated shelter area space in a prompt and timely manner. This was not always an easy task for my mother who had three small, sleepy children to roust out of bed. Air Raid Warden, Herr Doctor Manus, took his official duty to the Reich seriously and wore his official party armband with authority and a considerable amount of arrogant pride. He did not look kindly upon my mother's independent spirit and made that known to her on several occasions when she became teary and irritable with us.

It is so nice of you to plan a little after Christmas celebration for me with all of the children's toys when I return to you at the end of February. Mattheu is to get my carbine with three blank cartridges. Well, my Joy and Heart's Love, check out the things that I have come up with for all of you. Enjoy the cocoa and the full cream milk – a drink of the gods. If some is still left when Papi gets home, perhaps he can have a cup of it.

---

[85] Reference here to an old German proverb: When the rooster crows over the manure pile, the weather changes or maybe it doesn't. In other words, it is meaningless. The more things change, the more they stay the same.

Sleep in beautiful peace, my Love
I think so intimately about you
that my heart aches.
I kiss you in love
and am so happy with you.
As happy as a husband can possibly be
with his sweet wife.

Your old Paulus.

Letter no. 147
Soldier Claudius
FPO 56570a
Rennes, January 18, 1944,

My Most Beloved Little Wife,
My Goldchen, You,

I really don't know where to start in filling you in on everything. Goldchen, your letter, your long letter of January 6th, lies in front of me and has made me so indescribably happy and yet, also sad. Before I go on to tell you about me, I want to answer your letter point by point. But first, I want to let you know that Papi is always thinking about you. A little package with some special things wrapped up in it will be on its way to you tomorrow . . . a pretty black and white shawl for Matti or for Eki for cold trips to school . . . a pair of wine-red gloves that will go well with your overcoat. I hope that the gloves are not too large. No smaller ones were available. Lastly, there is a container of lightly sugared cocoa for the dear children. It was fairly costly, but it should let the little ones know that Papi always has something on hand to send to them.

Along with the white flour (there are 4 kilograms on the way) there is butter and eggs for baking, and a decorated chocolate cake. I wish all of you a big, "you are welcome." Thanks to Papi in France, you can all sit around the table in the living room on Sunday, and I will be there with you in spirit. As for me, I have been back here with my old Pioneer Company in Rennes for the past several days. It is quiet right now, and I am alone except for a lawyer buddy who, like me, is writing to his dear wife and two children at home. All of the others, the younger guys, have gone to a movie. I am just so happy for the chance to write to you, and with that, chat with you and tell you what is happening, and to "write" you some hope and happiness.

So, now I will begin with your letter, and it may take awhile to get to all of it. As I am sure you deduced from my letters, my duty trip for the beginning of January fell through. Dear, I know what it is like to have your hopes dashed and a joy abandoned. I have certainly chastised myself for not having written you about that much sooner, but Goldchen, just think about how my heart raced when the Lieutenant told me about my current, upcoming, trip. I have found no greater joy than to be able to write you about it, since everything that motivates me and keeps me going, everything that brings me happiness and upsets me, moves me to write to you. You are everything to me. My peace and happiness lies with you, especially in times that are as tough as the present. Oh, how difficult it has been for me to suffer under the nagging thoughts that you might be waiting for me in vain. But in 40 more days the telephone will ring. Then, open your arms and your heart to welcome me.

I have already related to you as to how things here have changed, and now my every joy and hope springs from my being able to come home for a few days at the end of February. As a soldier, I will personally use this opportunity to take care of things with the Finance Office in arranging to get military aid for the children. Goldchen, what a strong love you must have to have been able to open all of the necessary doors. I am really tired of the soldier's life. A probationary period, however, wherein I must prove myself [86]as an officer, comes first. That is a matter of formality, and I expect to get one more furlough with you before being sent to a much tougher life at the front.

I am happy that so many of my packages have made their way to you. Even some eggs have made it, and that is amazing when you consider that they were jostled around on the iron of the rails. The cakes were large and surprisingly good for war time. You can

---

[86] Claudius must do so "at the front."

see the real French retail price. The Hochheimer folks[87] will get a kick out of that. The butter and honey pastries, as well as the other little cakes, have surely been enjoyed and eaten up by now. The Episerie Bread is an original French product, a little costly for a countryman but not too exorbitant for all of you at home. Glad to hear that you liked the Stylo pen. I had to do a lot of looking to find such a nice thing for my dear Goldchen. The pens in France, for the most part, are inferior and poorly made.

So far, I have done all right with my money and have no debts. The company Christmas celebration and New Years Eve along with two company meals out, took up some extra marks, but I am a frugal man and always have a few spare marks in reserve when something catches my eye for all of you. In regard to the Leichte affair, I must tell you that I received two food coupons for January. I will send one to you and one to my parents. I have written to Mrs. Leichte and promised her the two food coupons that will come due in the days to follow. If Leichte telephones you and asks you for eight reichsmarks, it is because the bank has closed his account, a sign that he is unable to see to things at home. The eight reichsmarks are to be used so that his little wife in Gotha will not need to pay at the present time, . . .something that he, himself, will need to do when I, as his superior, run into him at a later time. He did not dare to remain in the Pioneer Company for even an hour longer and expect to remain among the living. Too bad . . . such a smart guy.

Goldchen, you next come to a description of the Christmas celebration, and I can hardly believe the difficult hours that you endured during those precious hours. How you, you poor little wife, must have suffered. Dear God, it is a wonder that you did not have a mental breakdown. We both have had so little time together with the children. It is great that Siemens had some toys for the children since Papi could not show up as Santa Claus this year. So, Uncle Etzel was able to come up with some surprises for the little ones. I will write him a few lines of thanks for doing that. I have already sent him timely Happy New Years wishes. Did you get a Christmas gift from Siemens? A profit-sharing bonus should arrive in January or February. You won't be short-changed since

---

[87] Claudius's neighbors.

these automatic payments come from Leipzig. (The office in Leipzig has bomb damage.)

You further wrote me that you and the children have been sick with sore throats and the flu, making the days even tougher than they already were. My Love, how bad all of that must have been for the outlook of your little heart. Hopefully everything is better now, and your pain and hard times are over. How very helpful it would have been if I'd been able to be there. I was in a Catholic house of worship all by myself today and quietly prayed for you and the little ones, and also for the German people.

I can scarcely grasp what you have written about the bugs. It is incomprehensible to me that Miss Brenniche did not thoroughly check things out. The lice certainly came from someone on furlough from Russia, or were brought in with some piece of luggage. The louse problem is a horrible plague, and old soldiers have described the infestation in vivid terms. I know all too well about the matter of crabs in Moldavia (Romania). That a large-scale plague such as that one could be repeated for all of you at Christmas time, is frightening. It appears to me that you are beleaguered with bad luck. Check in every seam and scrap of cloth. That's where the little critters hold up – but then, I know how thorough you are in such matters.

It is nice that the Manuses have helped you. I will see if I can find something to bring them at the end of February. It won't be as it was. Money is tight, and so it is with anything that is to be found. I'm glad that you gave a gift to Inge. It is too bad that the dear girl will soon leave us.[88] I have always liked her. I still have not received my battle packages. Too bad if they were lost or stolen, . . . I could really use their contents. I was very happy to hear that the side of bacon came in so handy. Really, Goldchen, that heavy thing hanging down in the cellar did manage to become good medicine for my sweet wife.

But now, my Love, I will close. I still want to put a few lines in with the package. Besides that, my buddies are after me to help them with the written part of being a Pioneer, and Papa Claudius has to say yes. Goldchen, even though your letter paints of so

---

[88] The German government provided help for German families with young children.

much hardship it has brought me a measure of joy for the days ahead, until, . . . oh my Love, until the next letter reaches me. Goldchen, I love you so much and am uncontrollably happy about our pending reunion.

Always, your Paulus.

Letter no. 148
Soldier & Reserve Officer Training,
Field Post 56510a
January 19, 1944.

My Dear Little Sweet Hertha, You, My Joy!

I just came back from the city with the Lieutenant. We did some shopping and other things. Picked up some fabric for a blouse, . . . white, silk, soft taffeta – cost, 20 reichsmarks for two meters. After that we got a delightful little girl's dress for a one-year-old child, one pair of white stockings, and some calf-high socks. Old Papa Claudius was in his element and having a lot of fun. I am supposed to go out again this afternoon and will have to check on my finances as to whether or not I can get something for my own urchins. Firstly, they include me for my value as a worrisome father,....and secondly for my familiarity with the language.

But back to me. As I have already written you, our Pioneer course of instruction has been moved to Rennes for the next eight days. Since we were allowed to divide up and chose our own living spaces, I have been fortunate enough to be back in my own bed. My former buddies, Mayfarth and Philip, are, however, no longer here and have been gone for some time now. Theirs was the good fortune to have traveled to Germany for Christmas and the New Year holidays. Since they were married, they were the very first to have had that chance. They will not spend another night in Rennes, but will be sent to the front immediately upon their return. Today, they are somewhere in Russia, fighting the enemy. There are so many new faces in the Company, . . . a constant stream of men coming and going up to the resident instructors. I am still known around here, but in a few more weeks, all of the lads will be scattered about.

I had a serious talk with the sergeant a few days ago. It again had to do with the morals of the young guys in Officer Training. Almost thirteen men went to a brothel on the first day of our stay here in Rennes. The same guys had gone there just eight days earlier, all of them 17 to 19 years of age. I chewed them out, telling them that it had to stop and that the higher command would hear about it, whereupon some of them would risk being put in the brig or penalized in other ways. Before mentioning these penalties, though, I had a talk with the command and managed to diffuse the situation a bit. I was, however, ordered to take over the penalty duty with the stipulation that it include some kind of learning and that this needed to be carried out by a man of my authority. It is not easy for me to talk about these things with engineers, but I do believe that I succeeded. I am to lead an hour of instruction this evening, that is, written work, about Pioneer duty.

That's the way it goes, day in and day out. Oh, if only we could get the better of this horrible war. But, my Love, believe me, no one can outlast it for long, much less in the homeland. How do things look for all of you there? How is life at home? You should eat the butter stored in the cellar. I would promise you more, were it not for the tightness of money. Yes, Papi will take care of it. Unfortunately, our own food situation is not much to feel full on. Regrettably, it is hard to understand why. How are things in regard to food with you? How is Schoenemann and the director? Yes, my Love, I will hopefully be given more time for my duty trip than the last time, especially since I will have a lot of running around to do. Oh, we will be so very happy – talking and loving. We have the verbal hope that in two weeks we will be together again – as one – with all of the tough times behind us.

Well, be intimately loved and kissed, 10,000 times – greeted and held by your Paulus and Vagabond. Give the kids a hug from soldier Papi. (More mail is on its way to you.)

Letter no. 149
Soldier and Officer Trainee, Paul Claudius,
Post O. 56510a
Rennes, January 19, 1944,

My Beloved, Brave Little Wife!

I have again been busy on your behalf and have succeeded. I must pat myself on the back. Thanks to you, Goldchen, I have been able to get almost two kilograms of lump sugar – real lump sugar. I have taken out just a bit for myself, but it will be a rare and fine gift for you. If I can, I will try to get some more before my duty trip at the end of February. Then Papi will really make the children happy. I have always been on the lookout for sugar. Firstly, because you wrote me that sugar was very scarce and secondly, because I like to indulge in it myself. Everything will hopefully arrive in good shape. A lot of things are being stolen. Boxes are being robbed and packages are turning up missing. As far as I can tell in keeping an eye on the packages that are currently on their way to you, everything has arrived, right up to the four kilograms of flour, the cocoa, and the sixty cigarettes. The battle package, as might be expected, has unfortunately not yet come. I don't think that it will arrive at all and that's a damned shame. I managed to get a scrub brush for Inge, for doing the dishes. I will send it when the opportunity presents itself.

With great concern, I took a look at my socks earlier today. They really look bad. I have washed them a lot and darned them over and over again, but they are becoming very thin and won't take any more washing or thread. I was able to get a near new pair of pants and a very clean uniform jacket from the supply sergeant for a package of cigarettes. The uniform jacket was formerly worn by a noncom. It has collar clips and a large eagle on the chest. Because I always take good care of my clothing, I am really happy to have it. Now I also hear that any extra combat uniform jackets and pants are to be collected for the new recruits because clothing is in short supply. That would be too, too bad. All of my buddies had to give up their boots. The only reason that I was able to keep mine is because I am a Pioneer. The First Lieutenant of the Pioneer Company visited my room at half past eight this morning and shook my hand. We talked. I believe that he is proud of me since he has spoken to me only during instruction sessions up until now.

But now on to you and the children: Is the delousing over with? The powder must have had a very special odor to it to have driven the little critters off. It is really hard to believe that something like that could happen in Germany. Have you sent Erika back to school? Something needs to be done. Please let me know about the situation when you get the chance. How are you, my Love? Are you, so to speak, back on your feet? Everything hit you at once and at a time when the father of the family should have been at home. Yes, the war is hard on everyone and demands everything of us that we cherish and cannot replace. I spent a lot of time in the city yesterday. Everything for the kitchen, the house and the garden could be found and was for sale, and everything was insanely expensive. But since I couldn't bring any of it with me, it really did not matter. I want to get a few plates for the children. I saw some nice ones in Bakelite.

In a few more days, the first month of this young year will be over. The end of instruction creeps closer and closer and brings me ever nearer to my joyful trip home to you. I will try to let you know as soon as I am certain as to whether I will be coming on the 28th or 29th with my leaving here sometime around 1:30 in the afternoon. I will keep you informed. Well, my Goldchen, be well and be intimately embraced and kissed by your Paulus. A hug to the children from Papi. (I will write more this evening)

Letter no. 150
Rennes, January 22, 1944,

My Love and My Goldchen!

Herewith, a few details. There should be more, but a sudden sortie in the direction of the Channel has forced an unmerciful interruption of everything. Yes, Goldchen, such is a soldier's life, unstable and uncertain. So, we will see what is going on. I am packed and ready. I do not know what is to happen next. The troop trucks are out there and honking. I have to run.

I think of you, and my love for you beats in my heart. Today, I really have a desire for you, as a wife and as a woman, but these thoughts are not good to have. They beat upon my brain, and for now, any response remains out of question. Oh, my Love, I love you, . . . this damned struggle of being in the service. I want my order, and I also want you. Please, excuse the crass manner of my writing, but I have had enough and am fed up. I have to close for now. I will hopefully not make you have to wait for further mail.

Intimate kisses from your Paulus

Letter no. 151
Reserve Officer Training – Claudius
Field Post Office 56571a
Somewhere in France,

My Love, my Goldchen,

I will make an attempt to write you even though it may be only a few hurried lines amid the helter-skelter of this place. I know that it will make you happy, and my goal will have been fulfilled. In the haste of yesterday's procurement, I did manage to send you one kilo of sugar and a small moleskin coat. The little fur coat was given to me as a gift. Perhaps you can make a few little items out of it for Eki. I will bring a few more kilos of butter, some coffee beans, and something to drink with me when I come home at the end of February. I will send you all of the other items ahead of time. Everything has really been helter-skelter around here. Right now, we are traveling in troop trucks in the direction of the Channel. What awaits us there is not known. I slept on the "bare ground" last night and was so horribly tired that it went well.

We are being called to lunch. I don't know what we'll be served, but just the thought of it is depressing enough. All of this, however, is just another preparatory stage to being at the Russian front. Well, this also shall pass. I will hopefully get a letter from you soon. The last one (January 6, 1944) has become worn out by my reading.

How are you, Goldchen, and how are things at home? What are our merry "three" up to? Hug them for Papi and say hello to

Uncle and Aunt Manus. Yes, the one thing that I can personally do as a soldier is to see to it that you are far enough away not to be attacked. I will be a lance corporal and with that, an old and seasoned warrior. I must tell you how very happy I am with you. Cool down the beverages so that I can satisfy my hunger for the homeland and for love. Well, Love, I kiss you and feel an uncontrollable happiness in you.

Your Paulus

Letter no. 152
Soldier Paul Claudius
Field Post Office no. 56510a
Officer Training, January 25, 1944,

My Joy, You, My Goldchen!

Using petroleum and other magic tricks, I have just spent a lot of time and effort trying to get the stove lighted. The room is full of smoke, but the stove is still not going. I'll have to give it a third time try. Yes, and what became of the letter that I promised to write to you yesterday? Everything continued to be rather turbulent, and so I did not have the chance to do any writing. Today it is 4:30 in the morning. That gives me the time to get it done, and I have a lot to tell you. We managed to get back to our quarters dirty as a mouse. We were dripping wet from head to toe with torn pants and gloves. It was really tough. In all reality we live in our barracks like a bunch of cattle.

How are things at home? How often I have imagined clean clothes and a beautifully set table. In all of my dreams you play a very special role. You are dressed so beautifully, have bathed and are wearing clean clothes. Since it all happens while I am asleep, nothing much is left out. But one of the two of us is in another place, so I will not occupy myself with such things on your time. In the morning I will repack the package that I sent to you. The post office informed me that it was too heavy, and sent it back. It's kind of an unusual matter to get bacon, sugar, and other things returned, especially when one thought that those things were off and on their way. The struggle that now starts all over again is:

Will I or won't I keep it. Because I am always so pleased to be able to send you a package, it will remain as yours. Things have cut loose again during the watch, and I have to interrupt once more.

Before the Channel maneuver began I was sent to Rennes on a special assignment. The Pioneer company sent orders concerning the execution of a PFC deserter. I was to arrange for a grave in the cemetery for this man, a place where deserters and criminals lie. This I did in Rennes in the God's Acre Cemetery. There I stood in front of the dug-out grave into which one of my comrades, a fellow soldier who was still alive, was to be placed. I am sure that he will have experienced many tormenting hours before the fatal bullets hit him. Next to the newly dug grave and amid the French graves stood the solitary resting places of other German soldiers who lost their lives due to dishonor. A wooden cross states merely the date of their birth and the date of their death. That's the way it is for a deserter.

In the meantime the stove has taken off and is supplying some welcome warmth from out of its place in the corner. In another fifteen minutes I will have to go throughout the room and call out the "wake up!" And because my buddies don't like getting up, they will complain with some measure of cursing. As you already know, I don't mind doing this. A talent such as this is one that the Prussians have always been good at. My eyelids are getting heavy, and I will have to get some rest. The night is gone, and duty will soon begin.

How are you, my Goldchen? How are your incisions? Are they healed? I hear so little from you. If you can't be with me in body, you should bring me joy via a letter. You are probably so weak that writing brings you pain. Yes, my Love, in a few weeks I will be there and then everything will be better. Keep the key for the bedroom handy because I will be very tired. Well, I need to shave and get ready for duty – and breakfast is very important. A long kiss. I will soon be there. A hug for the three children.

Papi.

Letter no. 153
Soldier Claudius
Post Office no.56510a Officer Training, January 25, 1044,

My Dear, Sweet Little Wife, My Love!

Even though I am really tired, and my eyes have fallen shut a couple of times during the instruction, I still want to write my innermost thoughts to you. Field mail has made me a present of one of your letters today. I read a few of the last lines of it, the part in which you described the hopes that I had given you about my coming at an earlier date and your deep disappointment at the fact that it had fallen through. Yes, my Goldchen, you have a right to be upset with your soldier Papi, but you do not know how hard it is to get any kind of a special permission from the Prussian army. To be sure, I have the best of relations with our Lieutenant of anyone in the entire instruction group. We spent many hours together just this Sunday. That I am allowed at all to come home at the end of February is a fantastic exception. Even though five of my buddies are also married and have children, I am the only one who has been given permission to do so. Please be happy for me. My arrival at the railroad station will be different than it was the last time. Yes, it will be dark when I make my way home to you through the park with the sure thought that you will be beautifully dressed and waiting for me. My Love, the heart of a countryman is passionately grateful for his little wife at home and rightfully so. You will be pleased with me. Take care that you don't get sick again. Eat a lot of butter; I will bring more with me. Well, I am dead tired.

With that, I fell asleep and an entire night now separates the above lines from the ones that I now write. My rheumatism has returned to my back. Right now it is just a little pain, but I'm afraid that it might get worse. I will hopefully be able to find a remedy for it in a French pharmacy. In four weeks you can give me a rub, right?

Yesterday evening was a good night. I read your dear, long letter. You poor little soldier's wife. The many daily things that you have to take care of! But I am pleased to see that you are able to go about your daily work. Things will only get better, and I await a detailed report from you including all of the local news as to how everything is going back there. It is wonderful that Erika has been such a joy to you at home and in school. She has always been the image of you. I am anxious to talk to the young maiden. In regard to their daily lives, the two boys are a "tempest in a teapot," to a certain extent, but they seem to be on the ball. Good genes, the de Veer-Claudius bunch, right? Your description of the "substitute Distelhofers" is right on. I sent the cigarettes to you so that you would have them on hand.

Since you have written me about the roof repairs in positive terms, I know that you have correctly understood my directions concerning that matter. I worry about the roof, so please be vigilant about it. You have shown yourself to be such an intelligent woman, and I am proud of you, really proud. In your conscientiousness, you have tried to do too much and have had to pay for it with severe pain. I have written to Heydt out of concern for you. When I come home in four weeks, I will check into the legal matters, and you will come with me.

There, in Erfurt, or in all of Germany, it must be very cold. Here, in Bertange, the power of winter has been broken, and we again have the eternal pouring down of rain. It is not a very happy situation here, and we are about to change quarters again. Do you have the Siemens package at home? If so, please do not send it. I would rather it remain there with you. As I have already told you, the packages that I sent from Rennes came back. They were too heavy. I took them back to the post office yesterday. So, Goldchen, again, "It is for certain that I am coming." Then you will get many real kisses from your Paulus.

Letter no. 154
Soldier Paul Claudius
Field Post Office 56507a
Rennes, Jan. 27, 1944,

My dear Little Wife, My Goldchen!

I will try to take a few minutes to write a few lines to you before the beginning of duty . The good life, here in Rennes, has unfortunately not been so good for some of the young soldiers. As the result of some disorderliness in the highest degree, we were forced to perform duty until after midnight last night. Even though we were not guilty, we were ordered to participate. The tough extra hours of duty were given out in the belief that it would teach the younger soldiers a valuable lesson, but that is a false assumption. It's understandable that there would be some ill-will directed toward me as the senior room supervisor. I only reprimanded the young soldiers in my room and informed them of the consequences, but the jug will only hold so much water.

I was again successful in my engagements on your behalf yesterday. A beautiful piece of marbled ham is on its way to you. It did not cost all that much because the layer of bacon is very thin, and the bone is still on it. The meat, however, is very tender and will taste very good to all of you. Hope that it gets there all right. The bottle of Maggi [89] that you needed so badly and a scrub brush for Inge are also included. I am broke, but there is nothing more wonderful than caring for all of you at home by sending you packages. So, Love, I must interrupt again. Duty for me begins right now. So, a little kiss from me on your rose-colored lips (a chance that I seldom get.)

It is 21:00 hours, and I will now continue. We had to do some written work, and that sort of thing can take up a lot of time. The writings that we did last night have already been checked over. Although I came away in good shape, I must laugh at their method of assessment. Yes, I am led to think that commission comes from comedy. I received a letter from father, in Laubegast, today. It was almost an angry letter. Let me explain. To start with, he writes about his illness and that he is now back on his feet again. Further along, there is information concerning the six page letter that you sent and they had been waiting for so long. Now my father and mother are better informed than your own husband about everything that you had to go through with your operation. Please write to me about the full extent of this surgery. Father could not believe everything that you had to endure. In regard to Distelhof, father suggested going half on a lease. Think it over, and we can discuss it when I get home in another five weeks.

---

[89] Beef broth concentrate.

After that, father went on to write me in a very uncomplimentary way concerning my enthusiasm for the military. He seems to have a completely different view of the matter. He read a horrible report in the newspaper that 70% of the Reserve Officer Candidates are killed at the front and goes on to tell me that my most important duty is to be with my family and to think about my Fatherland only after that. Goldchen, father is right to be sure, but how can I change any of this now that I am a Reserve Officer Candidate? My dedication to the military is more of a "fulfillment-of-duty" attitude. Considering the reality of the situation, I can't just pretend to be dumber than I am about the situation. I can only keep my back to the wall. My greatest and single most important hope is that I come back to you, my family, forever. We will talk about these things face to face in our own given time. Father further goes on to write that the von Droeses boy (the Berlin family) has died in Italy.

What are the mothers of the children to think about during this war? . . . the ones who have lost sons and those others who are raising children for whom there is no future and no real life ahead. I will tell you something very sad in my next letter but will write of this sad matter later. I am so tired that my eyelids keep falling shut. I will dream of my dear, sweet little wife whom I will soon hold tightly in my arms. My Love, a sweet intimate kiss, and a good night. I love you.

Always,
Your Paulus

Letter no. 155
Field Post Office 5657a
Somewhere, January 28, 1944,

Sweet Little Wife, Goldchen!

Well, I am among the nomads again, holed up with thirty buddies in a barracks, and I write to you by candle light. Water for washing and cleaning is gotten from a fountain some distance away. The path to it passes the ruins of a cloister. We are getting artillery training, and it is tough duty. We have to pull the heavy guns through thick and thin like galley slaves and everything is march, march, march. Little by little we are being trained for the war conditions in Russia. The village that we are in is without culture or even streets. The footpaths that lead to nowhere give one the feeling that his boots will surely get stuck in all of the mud. Yes, Goldchen, your vagabond soldier Papi and Baron of Distelhof, lives in this sort of paradise.

My buddy, Dr. of Jurist Prudence, Dr. Froehlich, and I went on a scrounging tour into the forests of Bretagne yesterday to visit with the farmers. We succeeded in buying 100 eggs, one pound of butter, a piece of ham, and some sausage. Unfortunately, part of that was for the Lieutenant who has been ordered to go to the eastern front. At any rate, there always seem to be some eggs, butter, ham, and sausage for sale. The eggs will regrettably not keep until my trip home, and so I gave them to the cook. He, in turn, will give me some later on. It was interesting to talk to the farmers. There is much to learn in regard to the local customs and traditions. Eggs, for instance, must be purchased in lots of five. My language skills have grown to the extent that I can now communicate with a Frenchman on an elementary level. I have a wonderful bottle of cognac put aside to be put to use during some happy hours spent with you.

I want to get a few bottles of red wine to bring home with me, and also plan to make good use of any time that I may have in order to procure some other nice things for the stomach. Other material things are just too expensive. Even though the credit voucher coupons for soldiers are all gone and the soldiers have less money to spend, prices for food are as high as ever, and there is a great demand for goods on the black market. Scrounging is really tough in Rennes, and when it comes to getting butter, eggs, oil and chocolate, one has to have good connections. Up until now, as you can imagine, I have always had those good resources. The cigarettes should have arrived by now. Please stow them away. Mr. Heydt is to get some, and I also get to have a few. I have been able to collect another 50 cigarettes which I can put at your disposal. As the result of our cigarette rations and as far as the tariff requirement is concerned, I have always had enough of mine left over to be able to use them in whatever way I want. I always have cigarettes on me and seldom smoke them, mostly because I have so little free time. By the time the instruction is over it's time for duty to start.

I have determined that your last letter took ten days to reach me. Mine take only four to five days to get to you. Well, my Love, I will soon be there with you in person. Tell Mattheu that since I still have claim to my half of the wedding bed, he will have to evacuate, even if I am seldom a guest there any more. When I finish writing these lines, I will get into what resembles a bed and pull the covers up over my head. Hopefully, I won't have too much rheumatic pain. I don't know how I am supposed to cope with that. I am always thankful for you, my Love, and ask the dear Lord to keep me safe for you and the dear children.

How will you look when you come to pick me up? What dress might you be wearing? Yes, these are the thoughts of a soldier. Are your thoughts anything like mine? A buddy just heard a rat squeaking in our room. Hope that we won't have to fight off any of these vermin tonight. My Love, a long kiss for you, until I am there with you, soon.

I remain, Your Paulus

Letter no.156
Field Post Office 5651a
Montfort, January 29, 1944,

Always, My Goldchen, My Joy!

After the completion of our instruction in heavy artillery guns, we were ordered back to Montfort from St. Gilles today. We made the trip in a troop truck and in an adventurous manner.

We piled in to sit or stand, to the point where I thought that the benches would break under the weight of all of the guys. All of our gear was stuffed under the benches. We managed to endure the trip with only a few minor scratches and were happy to get "home" to where our rooms and lockers are – and, also, no rats. We had been sleeping with the blankets pulled up over our heads because the rats were numerous enough to be running all over our bodies.

I immediately collected some wood and got the room stove going. It has turned cold again, and I have a head cold. Because of certain accomplishments, I was appointed as the senior soldier to the instructors group several days ago. I am responsible for the order and cleanliness of daily life, as well as the general activities in the soldiers' quarters. I have to assign the men to various work assignments, and because I don't want to play any favorites, that's not an easy thing to do. I've managed fairly well – but was more popular before than I am now. But you can read between the lines and understand that. They watch me interact with the officers, notice how the officers treat me, and see that as uncommon. But I use my authority as fairly as possible, and for a few hours anyway, there is order. I could write whole novels about it, believe me.

Today's mail has brought me the most wonderful present in the form of a letter from you, my Joy, your letter, dated January 20, 1944. My Love, I am so happy at the prospect of seeing you at the end of February. I have not yet read your lines but am saving them for when I go to bed. It is then that you are with me, as you were in days past, and I can escape the turmoil of duty and fall asleep in happy thoughts. Besides, knowing that I have a letter from you helps me to accept things as they are and gives me the strength to "go on."

Just had a little interruption. Consider this. Some of my buddies have just returned from a little "shopping" adventure. Their grand accomplishment includes six live bunnies and two chickens. Well, it looks like we will have a solid meal tomorrow. Since I view neither France, nor the French farmers as fair game, I really don't support this sort of thing. The boys are rather crass and violent and can kill, dress, and put a little rabbit out to freeze in about 3 minutes. Well, perhaps later on, when I am at the front and up against hard times in the way of staying alive, I too will begin to do some "buying." For the time being, I am still a pretty decent guy.

I also got mail from my parents today. It was a 100 gram package. Among the things included were some very tasty wafers, and yes, I couldn't resist eating all of them myself. There are still some things that I want to pick up for my furlough and hope to be able to spend an entire Sunday going to the farmers for eggs and other useful extras to bring home with me and add to our daily menu. Our period of instruction is just about over, and we will all be split up. Again, another little part of being a soldier has been lived and is over with. Like war, we smell bad. The English visit us daily, throwing out French language leaflets. All of it is propaganda and sabotage, and all sorts of explosives and weapons come down with the parachutes. Personally, I would rather fight against the English than against the Asians. Essentially, my greatest wish is for this terrible war of death and destruction to end, but that is a fleeting and auspicious wish.

Your report of the evacuation of the center of the city of Erfurt is bad news. How is it going? Has Hochheim been affected? Surely nothing will happen there. The English are damned good at their aim. Where are all of the poor people to go? If we were not Germans and able to successfully compete with the English, if we were an inferior class of people, no one would bother with us. Our best men and their sons die. Goldchen, I live for my furlough to come. I hold fast to that thought, and it gives me strength and hope. To you, my Love, my intimate hugs. I will write again tomorrow, so that you are always at oneness with your Paulus. I kiss you, intimately. Love, also, to the children. I love you so much.

Paulus

Letter no. 157
Officer Training, January 30, 1944,

My Passionately Loved Joy,
My Goldchen!

Oh, how my heart skipped a beat when the little package from you arrived. But Goldchen, I will certainly bring most of the wonderful things in it back home with me. At least the sugar, which I know you need from your having mentioned that to me. You are so kind to me. The splendid chocolate truffles are right here beside me, and I have nibbled and nibbled, until one of the bags is just about empty. For the gift of this package, my Love, my heartfelt thanks.

I am slowly beginning to get to work on my duty-trip at the end of February. My Lieutenant has granted me some money to pick up a few things, but I doubt that it will be as much as I was able to bring home the last time. This time I should be able to be home a day longer, however. Didn't the little ones look at the package with long faces when they saw you pack it full of chocolate for Papi? I am going to have to look around for something special so they will remember me, . . . or I will be just the "uncle," as Dettos so aptly and assuredly put it. That he has developed so well is entirely due to your special efforts. Yes, my Love, the dear Lord could not have placed them into better hands than yours, and I am thankful for that each and every moment. How much I would like to go to school with Erika. She has it the toughest of the three. The boys can still play, but the little thing has to go to school and do her homework. Mattheu will be the next in line, and I will try to find him a school bag, here in France. Leather, however, is another of the things that is not to be found here.

Before I forget, I am enclosing a photo of the Christmas celebration. I am standing in the first row, shoulder to shoulder with my Lieutenant. As you can see from their faces, almost all of my buddies are quite young. A noncom corporal stands in the front and to the right of one of the older guys. He is married and has several children and is one of the soldiers in my room. To the right, next to the Lieutenant, stands our sergeant, a plain and simple man who is also very sensitive and often at odds with us because of an inferiority complex. There were several distasteful incidents that happened while we were going through our training in Rennes that caused the Lieutenant and sergeant a considerable amount of grief. The young guys decided to visit a brothel [90] throwing all of my ambitious efforts to stop them to the wind. In addition to that, they left their room in such a pig sty condition that the commanding officer read them the riot act and wrote them up. It was my job to pull their bacon out of the fire. The first thing that I did, along with a few of my older buddies, was to get the younger guys together in order to take care of things and clean up the whole mess with the noncoms. Our Lieutenant was on maneuvers at the time and so heard about these highly disturbing things over the

---

[90] German: Puffhaus – brothel, in literal German: house of heavy breathing.

phone. On Sunday, the last day of our stay there, I met with the Lieutenant in Rennes so I could go over everything with him. He was really upset and in a peculiar mood. Like a father, he is concerned about the morals of his boys. We took a walk together, first to the field hospital to visit an injured buddy and then in the Jardin de Plantes where we sat beneath a little oriental tree together in the January sun, next to the Orangerie.[91] There, we carried on in deep conversation, two learned individuals putting their heads together with their hands folded behind their heads. It must have been a very curious sight, the Lieutenant and the Reserve Officer Trainee – Armor-Infantryman, Claudius. We made the decision to split up the cliques within the barrack group and to make some exchanges which would put the hard-core with the more educable. This news was announced that very evening, and it resulted in a giant uproar which, as the main enforcer, was naturally also aimed at me. (I'm sure, that I had been seen with the Lieutenant.) The lockers and beds were emptied that same evening. So, Goldchen, that is it.

I have such a strong longing for you this evening. The arrival of your package has made me even more homesick. I have not read your latest letter, . . . only took a peek. Have you, to a certain extent, become "my wife" again, so that you can give your soldier a real welcome home? So much stored and pent up love can be like a huge explosion. I love you so much.

Paulus

Letter no. 158
Soldier Paul Claudius,
Field Post Office no. 5651a
Officer Training, January 31, 1944,

Goldchen, You, My Dear Sweet Wife!
(A small twig from a branch is pinned within two slots of the front, top, right side page of this letter.)

---

[91] A glass atrium structure in which specimen citrus trees are wintered.

I brought this along for you as a spring greeting. It came from our maneuvers out in the countryside.

My Darling, your letter of January 19th lies before me like a beam of sunshine. It bestows me with happiness as well as a longing that is all wrapped up in the one wish – to be at home with you. I have waited all day long to be able to write to you and think about you. Again and again during duty today I have felt for your letter in my pocket. Now I can finally permit my thoughts and feelings for you and the sweet children to reach out to you. Things have recently been better in regard to letters from you, and your Vagabond no longer feels as lost as he did during the time of Christmas and the New Year. You should also be getting mail from me on a regular basis, since I use every free minute to write to you. Yes, my Love, I have a whole lot of plans for you and the children. Most of them center around our wonderful Distelhof and the sun and the happiness that we all had when we were there during my last furlough. They were splendid days and nights when we were husband and wife, Baron and Baroness of Distelhof. Remember our last night and the beautiful morning? That all now lies behind us by more than half a year. And, since every day in the military is a trial that I do not wish to repeat a second time, that is a good thing. None of the drilling and instruction up to now has managed to make me into the kind of soldier who focuses solitarily on army life and nothing more. On the contrary, the more I climb the ladder of military rank, the more I want to be a civilian again. I want to reconnect with your world, take up my profession again, and go forward with it. You will surely understand my words and their meaning. Believe me, these things are matters that are going to be serious problems for everyone, for wives, and for those returning with professions, and those who were simply soldiers. That will be even more difficult than having left wives and children behind to start with. I do not want to neglect you and lose the close contact that we have.

My Love, that you seek to protect Distelhof for the both of us makes me very happy.[92] With your abilities, you will, hopefully, be able to find some assistance in the matter. I don't want to think about the fact that Inge has to leave us. I know that it won't be easy for the dear girl, either. The children will miss her a lot, and she will miss them, right? I am happy to hear that you got the 200 reichsmarks from Laubegast, because I know that you can use the cash. I will thank father for it. This time he did it for you, and I know that you are very happy about it.

Please don't be concerned about all of the packages that I am sending. I will send more, and that way I won't have to drag so much along with me on my trip. Hope that I can continue to send you that sort of "concern." I will buy elastic banding at the "Marche-Noir," in Rennes. Some of the edible fatty things that I will bring with me on my furlough will surprise you. Our first evening shall be devoted to eating and drinking. We'll see if it remains as such by how beautiful you make yourself for me. Oh, my heart beats faster at just the thought of you.

I won't send any more flour. Please send some of it to my mother. She has very little, and I want to be able to look after both of my French ladies. In regard to the packages from you, I have not found it in my heart to use the sugar, but I have nibbled on the honey and the sweets. A very tasty meal for your tramp, but the sugar will most certainly come back home with me. It is smart for you not to send the Siemens package. [93] I will take care of that when I get home and send the proper thanks. I got excited to hear your short report about the Siemens Christmas celebration. I was a much better Santa Claus two years ago. I will personally bring you some envelopes. We have plenty here but they are plain, like the ones I send to you. So, my Love, we have had another long talk and my beautiful thoughts of you have put me into such a good mood that I am going to bed. My Love, I always want to be your Paulus. I love you so very, very much.

---

[92] At this time in the war, the German government declared that no one was permitted to have a second, unoccupied or occasionally occupied dwelling. Frau Claudius was fearful that Distelhof might be taken from her and used as housing for refugees from Poland and Romania. This did happen for a short while, but she managed to retain ownership of Distelhof.

[93] Company Christmas package.

Letter no. 159
Officer Training, February 1, 1944,

My Love, Goldchen,

I just reread your lines and gather from them that you have many, many worries about your daily bread. I have spoken with the accountant and found out that you are permitted to send me 36 to 40 reichsmarks. I know what to do in regard to the sugar. I will keep a pound of it for myself. As you can deduce from my lines of that same day, I have become pretty adept at being able to get eggs, bacon, and butter, and I will bring some home for all of you. Your money will hopefully arrive on time before the end of February, but I doubt it. I have pressed the issue with the Lieutenant, and he gave me the impression that any remainder would be sent to me in Germany. I will also bring pipe tobacco and cigarettes to Germany with me. I get any cigars that I may want for myself from my buddies or from my rations. (I smoke only cigars.) I will also be bringing an electric heater to my beautiful people at home. It will work on either 110 or 220 volts. From what you have written, I gather that vegetables are hard to come by. That just means that Distelhof will have to become more productive this year. I will get a reassignment furlough in the middle of April with some 14 days of being stationed in Erfurt. I could really make good use of the time. It would be good for you to try to get some seeds. If only we could work together, my Love, but my hands are so very tied. Since it is very urgent for me to get a reply, I am writing this letter very hurriedly.

As far as things for me here are concerned, I am pretty thankful for now, and have enough artificial honey and bread to be satisfied. I will survive. After all, I am the famous procurer of the Pioneer Company and the officer of the day. I want to bring a bottle of champagne with me so we can put ourselves into a good mood. My sources for champagne make it inexpensive enough for me to be able to procure some without reproach.

The most important thing for me is to have you as my wife and my companion. I am still young and you, as a woman, are even younger. You are so beautiful, and I often wonder why we feel so deeply responsible for one another. It is because we love each other so much. The French women are riffraff and of no consequence to me, and if I flirt with them, it's only business. I think about you always, of your beautiful white body and how we make love.

My Love, 1,000 intimate and loving kisses,
As always, your Vagabond and Paulus,
(I have to get my gun and go on watch!)

Letter no. 160
Soldier Claudius,
Field Post Office no. 5651a
Officer Training, February 1, 1944

My Happiness, always and My Desire,

Well, things have finally quieted down in the watch room, and I can think about you, my Joy, and write to you. My heart is full of happiness because the gift of a letter from you came to me today. It is dated January 25, and I haven't even worn your last one out before getting this one. Again and again I am consumed by the content of your last letter in which you wrote me so very lovingly, and for fear of bursting my good luck bubble, I don't want to get too overly excited about today's letter.

Goldchen, today I was very successful again. Let me explain (but first let me light up a cigar in celebration of a quiet hour around here). My buddy, Froehlich, the Doctor of Jurisprudence and I were given Company orders today to get one Zentner [94] of potatoes so that the guys would be fed with a better meal from the kitchen. (Potatoes are cultivated and very hard to find in France.) But the two of us are the best at this procurement sort of thing because we have a good knowledge of the language and can relate to the public in a respectful way. We took a truck, and, after several fruitless attempts, came up with one Zentner of potatoes (cost: six reichsmarks). We stowed the sack in the truck and went in search of further treasures . . . wanted to buy some eggs and butter. (Items that are available here but are hard for the military

---

[94] 110 pounds

to get because of the steep penalties for selling them to us.) Through persistent efforts, though, we succeeded in surpassing our old record by six eggs. One pound was booty for us. Being able to also come up with two kilograms of butter, some shaved meat, and a cut of smoked meat served as the crowning glory to our success. The company was very surprised, but then they trust the two great intellectuals, as we are often called. (We were even given a half day off with no duty.) Unfortunately, most everything is done to satisfy the demands of the officers. In this case, we managed to be able to keep a pound of the butter, 23 eggs, and the shaved meat. I have almost 40 eggs put away for the "trip home." We will see what happens in regard to the butter, and I will have to check as to how my finances are holding out.

Next Sunday I will be out on another procurement mission in the deep forests of Bertrange. A part of the French population has unfortunately been armed by terrorist deliveries from the British, and solitary German soldiers are being shot at, making these business trips very dangerous. A bomb was thrown into the midst of our soldiers in Rennes last Sunday while they were watching a movie. There were dead and wounded. For that reason we always take our loaded weapons with us.

Yes, Goldchen, Soldier Papi slashes his way through the world. I have observed and learned much in the way of the customs of the Bertrange farmers. At times I get into lively discussions with them and tax my abilities with the language to the limit, but things are going well in that regard. If I find myself having troubles in softening up a farmer's wife, I show them the beautiful photos of the children and your slight, elegant figure as well. I then go on to explain that you spent several years in France and that you studied the French language and also taught it in Germany. Then they understand everything much better. From the braids on my uniform they also notice that I am an Ecole-Officer from Montfort and those officers are well known here. We often get an earful as to the progress of the war, but what does one say? The French believe in the strength of the British and the Russians.

I just managed to get the stove going. A talker like me may just forget to breathe from time to time, and now that I have rambled on about myself, I want to focus on you, although everything that I do, I do for you. How are you, Goldchen? How are those mean wounds in your body? You will have to tell me all about it when I get home. All during my duty today, I was tempted to nibble at the sugar. I got one liter of milk substitute and wanted to make some pudding – but I want all of you at home to have some, and you will not let me go hungry, . . . (at least when it comes to cookies and sweets). Have you finished the liqueur that I brought you the last time? I will bring something even better this time. We'll both become tipsy, very much in keeping with the customs of our German countrymen.

So, my Love, take care of yourself and save your strength and love for me, and I will do the same. Your thoughtful Vagabond and Papi.

I kiss you lovingly.

Your Paulus

Letter no. 161
Officer Training, February 3, 1944,
Soldier Claudius,
Field Post Office no. 56510a

My Beloved, Little, Sweet Wife!

Despite the fact that everything is helter-skelter today, I must find time to write you a few lines, since I know how you wait for mail from your Vagabond, and I don't want to leave my Goldchen waiting. As of today we have been on night alert and are not to stray from our position, since every night has been interrupted. It is not difficult to lose your nerve here. There is something in the air. We are only allowed to go out with weapons loaded, since attacks on solitary soldiers by terrorists have increased drastically. Wehrmacht news from Russia is that Russian pressure is spreading. Hopefully they will be able to throw up a barrier to stop the Bolsheviks. It almost seems like our troop strengths are too weak; however, I trust the words of the Führer in his speech of January 30. You at Wachsengburgweg 57 will assess the situation in a somewhat less than rosy manner, but, my Love, we must not go so far as to lose hope, lest it become better to prepare a premature end to this life. My Love, please don't get hung up on my words. It should be clear to you that I have a different viewpoint as a soldier than when I was a civilian, and it is my duty to lift you up and give you hope. You and I live, above all, for the children, and for that we must stay the course until there is no longer a path to walk. Before I comment on your letter of January 25, which I have already answered concerning the money, I have to tell you something funny. Today we were having grenade throwing instruction in a meadow, and during a break in the action we found ourselves standing on the banks of the river "Meu." It is some 5 meters wide, and cuts into the valley with some 2 meters (of bank). We started making bets as to whether or not one could jump across it. (What, you say?) One of the young guys, a six-footer, bet 25 cigarettes that he could do it. With a good jump he went right over. My heart was pounding, and I said, good! . . . . for 25 cigarettes Papa Claudius will also jump over. A round of laughter erupted, and the entire detachment of men gathered at the bank to watch, offering the 25 cigarettes. Naturally they all thought that I was afraid to jump, since a miss would "wet my shoes right up to my neck." I took off all of my soldier things that had weight and took off on a run for the river. Unfortunately I jumped one meter short of the takeoff bank and landed a few centimeters short of the opposite bank, in the water. It was very shallow there. It was wet up to my butt. They were really surprised, and the sergeant told me he didn't think I had the courage. After my attempt, two other young soldiers jumped, but they didn't make it. They landed in the middle of the river, wet as drowned rats. Aren't you proud of me, even though it sounds like a rascal's (boy's) prank? But a soldier must also prove his courage. I just read your lines of January 25th. There is nothing there in terms of business that needs reply. I am so tied up as a soldier that I cannot help. It hurts me that I have left you to fend for yourself all alone. That is especially no easy burden for a wife who must give up her husband. On my part, I will try to supplement your food situation to the extent that you have a little extra to eat. I have plenty of eggs and have ordered butter. It has become damned difficult here. Yesterday I had to start out anew for the "Masters," to buy things (even took a car.) Our haul consisted of 100 eggs and some butter. What went on during that trip I will tell you in person. Franz Heydt wrote me. In a grand manner he explained that things at Distelhof are OK. The poor simpleton and braggart, what does he know about what is in order and what is not? Did you talk with the roofer? I have collected 4 packages of pipe tobacco here and will bring them along. (The sergeant just told me he spent the entire afternoon looking for eggs in a car. Result: <u>Nothing</u>. His people can't speak French.) So, my Love, the tough watch begins now, and I want to lie down for awhile, since tomorrow is going to be another tough day, and I have to get a lot done. You can imagine how it feels to get rousted out every night. I fear the call "<u>Get up!</u>" But these 3 weeks until February 28 shall also pass. My Love, I will now quickly travel home in spirit, but it won't be long till we meet again.

Tender thoughts of you always, the Vagabond
Paulus

Letter no. 162
Officer Training, February 4, 1944,

My Dear Goldchen, My Joy at Home,

I have to try to write you a few lines, especially since I may not be able to this evening because I have night maneuvers. So that you know I haven't started yet, I am writing you quickly, since I don't want you to think I am neglecting you. I am dog-tired as a result of my sentry outpost duty. Have to go back tonight with little sleep, and that wears me out. We have orders to stop any French man or woman that is on the street after 11:00 o'clock and request to see papers. One of us, that was my job, was to stand with a loaded carbine in firing position while my buddy checked papers. . . . a different type of war. I would rather have been in my little bed. On our night rounds in the city we go along the moon-lit little river "Meu." The pallid rays of the moon fall upon the dark, still waters, and the stars are to be seen in the river like a mirror. What a beautiful picture, ... here and there a light in a window. Who might live there. . . . Are the people happy? Those are the questions the lonely sentry mulls over in his mind. Really a romantic play with the first underground of the watch, and oh how happy I was to hear, at a distance of some 100 meters, the heavy footsteps of the relief sentry. It made me forget the cold and the pain in my feet. Made me think of the warmth of the bed.

How are things going with all of you? Do you still have snow? Did the kids take their skis up to Ahriaksburg? It was such a fun thing for the little goblins, bundled up by their Mommy, to play in the snow. How is your ouchie? Hopefully everything is healed, and you have no pain. Although I have repeatedly asked as to the reason for this operation, you have not provided one. I assume you want to tell me in person. Well, I will examine things for myself. You can rely on that. Although it is very early in the morning and I have time before getting started, I am horribly tired, and I can't keep my heavy eyelids from falling shut. I would rather be in my dear little bed at Wachsenburgweg, or better yet, on a folding lounge chair in the sun at Distelhof, sound asleep. When will I be able to enjoy myself without being disturbed, . . . naturally as a civilian.

My Love, the call to "report" just sounded.

Letter no. 163
Officer Training, February 5, 1944,
Soldier P. Claudius,
Field Post Office no. 56510a

My Joy, Goldchen, You,

It is now Sunday, and unfortunately I have watch today, but, Dear, I want to talk with you. First of all, I want you to know that I do not know the address of Mrs. Leichte, and I will deliver the two stamps (coupons) to you in person. I will put an end to this matter since this letter may contain a lot for us both. My Love, please remember that I try to think of you, write you and do things for you because you no longer have (your) parents. You are not to be alone. You are always to know and feel that I always want to be there for you. You write of air raid alarms. Yes, my Dear, I had a long talk with my Lieutenant today. It doesn't look good for us. I cannot and do not want to talk to you about that. We can only hope that the Creator will turn the tide and tip things in the Germans' favor. Unfortunately the reasons for our grief (bad predicament) do not lie with the average person, but rather in our political leadership. . . . But, Dear, enough of these dismal thoughts. Perhaps we will discuss these things when I come home in <u>three</u> weeks, as a lance corporal. At any rate, you have a tough situation there at home. You are among people, yet you are alone. The children are a joy, but only for the two of us. The state sees them as good enough to be soldiers. Hopefully this letter will not fall into the hands of a censur (some official to read). It could cost me my braids. Don't you get any help from people there at home in such situations? I will only have an opportunity to look things over when I come home. Dettos has become a real war child and knows what the air raid siren means. Really too bad that the little fellow must come to learn the horrible reality of the terrible situation in our country. Yes, Goldchen, it is a real fight, but the worst is yet to come. A British invasion in the west stands in the wings. We got that information in our officer training news from the famous General Guderian!!

I have run out of writing paper. Unfortunately I was unable to buy any in Montfort, thus the bad paper situation.

I'm really happy about the 50 reichsmarks from SSW. I am happy that I did not change anything, since *the worst difficulties* for the German soldier are yet to come, especially in regard to the proper arrangement and assigning of employment at the end of the war. If the racket (war) continues for a few more years, we will have become different men. (We will be changed.) That's why it is good when one has a foot in the door of a large firm. As to whether or not they will greet the returning soldiers with open arms and assign them to their old positions at the end of the war is questionable. I am rather reflective today, but I have to tell you something funny. I got orders from the sergeant to buy a <u>calf</u> and 2 zentners of potatoes. Potatoes are very, very rare in France, but I succeeded in chasing down some one-and-three-quarters zentners. The calf was a very tough matter. I did succeed in buying a calf from a very large farm. The price was *150 reichsmarks – for 75 kilograms*. The cook and I had to pick up the calf at night because it is forbidden for the farmers to sell cattle on the black market. Three of us went on the fly. Everything went well. I even succeeded in buying a few eggs and 3 lbs. of bacon. We will smoke the bacon. But to go on: Did you ever see a calf on a leash? No? – well – I bet not, since a calf is about as stubborn as a donkey, in reality even more stubborn. We hit the animal, pulled on its tail, pulled on the rope until no air was left in it and the poor animal was exhausted and laid down. It took us some 4 hours to go 2 kilometers. We had to carry the thing. It was a lovely sight. But three German soldiers can do anything. At two o'clock in the morning we passed the watch at the camp and there was a lot of laughter at the scene before them. Today we have already eaten part of it. We now get a daily helping of meat. Claudius takes care of everything. So, my Love, that's the way it is. Would you ever believe that I would do such a thing? My Love, I will close now, and seek out my bed in order to be strong for the watch and the hard duty tomorrow, as much as possible. Goldchen, only a few days and I will be home with you and the children.

I kiss you intimately and think of You with Love and Longing.

Your Vagabond.

Letter no. 164
Officer Training, February 6, 1944,
Reserve Officer Training,
Field Post Office no. 56510a

My Dear, Sweet Goldchen, You My Homeland and Joy!

It is Sunday, and the sun shines. The hoarfrost lies on the trees and on the telephone lines that pass by my window. It is Sunday, and luck is with me. I have two letters, so thick! That makes the greatest gift for my Sunday that you could have given me, even more wonderful than a package. Yes, yes, I always want to know how things are going with you all. Well, let's talk about your dear letter of January 23 and about you and the children and also about me. Your description of the lives of the three children is so vivid that I feel like I am almost there with the little ones. You write that Dettos has a fever. I hope the little vagabond is healthy again. (I haven't read your precious letter of January 29. I will read it Monday, after my hard duty!!) So Dettos is beginning to develop intellectually. He probably got that from you and me? Good for him. That is a good prep school. You can see that in Erika. What you wrote about our little maiden made my day. Of the 74 children in her class, Erika did the best math work. That is unbelievable.

She certainly got that from me, from her father. You said that you were no good when it came to math, minimal at best. I will enjoy being able to talk to Erika, since she appears to be so smart. Hopefully she will have a lot of strength (be healthy) so she can retain these intellectual accomplishments. However, I can certainly assume that Erika is very tough (healthy). You gave her your best at birth. Yes, my Love, our children, ... just yesterday I spoke with Dr. Froehlich on one of our procurement tours about children's education in our schools. You would have trouble not smiling because I gave you all the credit.

Later I proudly read him the letter while lying in bed. I am really so proud of "our" daughter. Please tell her that her Papi said he was so proud of her and that Mommy should give her a thick cup of chocolate with French lumps of sugar as payment. It is really something that the children think about the contents of my nourishment. The food is always the same. The cook doesn't have any seasoning, so everything we eat tastes like cabbage. A couple of days ago, I succeeded in getting a tin plate, on which I now eat. When it comes to meat and potatoes, I really have something nice to eat on, and it tastes more cultivated. A good education is not to be denied. Outside of Dr. Froehlich, I am the only one. In times of need, men are good friends, but this is unfortunately not so in times of peace. This evening I want to tell you more about my calf purchase and my visit this morning with the Lieutenant. But before I end these lines to you all, I want to tell you that the Lieutenant finally told me that at the end of February, immediately after inspection I would travel to Germany for 10 days (of duty) and that there would remain 6 days for the two of us, so make note of that!! You write so wonderfully of home, and I am only able to write about duty-type things. But you know that things in regard to duty are different experiences for me. Of late, I have been busy with procurement and have learned more of French customs and traditions. I will tell you about it when I come home. That will be so great, and it will make our parting easier, especially since I will be home in another 6 weeks. Except for my furlough of 18 days, I will have two weeks with relief troops in Erfurt. Everyone here, regardless of rank, lives for the happiness that comes with being able to go home. Yes, my love, you are to get another letter from me this evening. We will be together. Until then be intimately and tenderly kissed by Your Vagabond and Paulus. Give the children a kiss for me.

Letter no. 165
Officer Training, February 8, 1944,
Soldier Paul Claudius,
Field Post Office no. 56510a

Beloved, Little Wife, My Goldchen!

Well, I can't make any more noise about not getting mail from you. You have seen to that. Thanks – I had just picked up your letter of January 12 (I had merely nibbled on it a little) when the next letter arrived, the one of January 31, 1944. Your letter of the 29th presents a problem for me in terms of how I should answer in accordance with my rank, since I am in the final period of my inspection, and time is more than lean. Today I have barracks duty because of my bad feet. Excessive running has taken its toll. But now to your little letter. (One cannot call it little, since it is a real Goldchen letter.)

I want to thank you for your detailed description of the operation. Apparently some of the letters died in the burning of the railroad station. My Love, I believe you, everything, as always; however, I am ready for the court summons at the end of February. Please make arrangements accordingly, and you will get a tender defendant. I can hardly imagine being able to travel back to Germany and "to be permitted to be home." But the Lieutenant said that the whole matter was "all right." Please don't knock yourself out with grand preparations, especially cleaning. There is no point in that. The keen eye of Lance Corporal and Officer Candidate and Instructor Claudius misses nothing; please don't try. What you wrote about your "trouser bottom" was very funny, but I doubt if it was really that way. Your description of Dr. K.W. is interesting. Why did he have to retire as a Captain, since he had surely been more than a company leader? Well, you will provide me with more detail.

Otherwise, in regard to women he has remained the "Old One," and his love for you still exists. Amazing consequence, ... how it would be to look inside this man. . . . I am afraid to carry these words on, since I too was once so fearful and torn, had I put myself on the same level as Dr. K.W. Does he still love his wife? He made another application with J.G. Farben in Leuna or Bitterfeld? Well, at any rate, I am not all that interested in this guy to the point where I waste my paper or time on W. It must have been a painful situation for you to have run into him again after such a long separation. Inge liked him in her girlish way. That he wants to take her to J.G. (Farben) with him as a secretary is a gross case of impudence.

Well, you probably won't make any excuses for the old fox. At any rate, on February 11, I will really be thinking of you in regard to Dr. K.W.

You seem to be getting together often with Mrs. Mae Lean. She is an interesting, intelligent woman. I haven't heard anything from Jungs since New Years. Kind of slovenly. (lazyness) Writing to you and friends is a privilege. It is a messenger of the thoughts of our times and of the experiences with you and the children.

Your PS matters in regard to Johanna Boeder are shocking and are proof of your warnings to Jo and me in regard to her husband. Jo's life could have been a lot different. Today, deep down, she probably thinks a lot differently than she lets on, outwardly. Back then, when I visited her in Rooitz, (Booitz?) she looked pretty bad, and the conditions were miserable. I just thought I didn't notice it. The two of them were already far apart. My Love, only days separate us. How great things will be then, and we will be able to enjoy each other. This evening I want to answer the letter of January 31st. Be intimately hugged and kissed by your Vagabond and Paulus who loves you.

Letter no.166
Officer Training, February 8, 1944,
Soldier Claudius,
Field Post Office no. 56510a

Sweet Little Herta, You, My Beloved Little Wife!

The jug can only hold so much water – 'til it breaks, and that is the way it is with your little letter of January 31. I fooled around with the envelope and finally tore it open. So I thought to myself "perhaps there is something that I need to know right away?" – yes – And then it happened. My Love, how beautifully you wrote to me again. In a quiet time I must smile about your writing of your concerns. Yes, Dear, I can understand that, since here the "higher ups" (air raids) try to break my desire to write you with interruptions. However, it just makes me more eager to steal a few minutes and grab my pen.

You write that you have sent me money. Hopefully it will arrive in a timely fashion, since I have a few details to take care of in terms of buying butter and bacon. Day before yesterday I procured a lb. of butter from a farmer. Gave it all to the cook. He needed it and traded me other things for it. I am glad the coco and the other nice things arrived in good shape. It would have been a shame if someone else had gotten the fruits of my procurement labors. We shall guzzle. That's it! "Drinking," builds character. During these turbulent times one must celebrate and live as much of life as possible. Please get a good bottle of Pfaelzer or Mosel-Saar-Buwer, since French red wine is not the right thing for you. Yes, my Love, make yourself pretty, since I am starved, no only for you but also for the cleanliness and order. Your complaint about silk sheets (bedding) comes to me at just the right time, and I will try to pick some up. Unfortunately things here are not easy to come by, but I will make an effort.

You shouldn't have written what you did about our marriage bed. My carefully constructed building of control fell apart. But that doesn't matter; it is only a few days. Hopefully Tommy won't visit more often and drop a little present on our roof while we are enjoying ourselves. As to whether or not I will be able to pinpoint the exact time of my arrival is doubtful, since I am to report for inspection immediately, and the time for that is not yet clear, just the date, February 28th. You can get started on the fir. I got it as a present, but there should be enough for the top of a fir hat. You know that I love this hat and that Erika can use it. (Drawing shows how cap should look.)

Enclosed find two stamps for the packages. Please forward these to Mrs. Leichte, since I do not have her address here, and as a soldier, it is very difficult and complicated for me the send away registered letters. On basis of your droll story about Detti's hunger for meat, I have decided to bring a few lbs. of liver (fresh) with me. We can then work it into some sausage. Hope I can carry everything, since I won't be able to bring the big trunk this time.

I have already put two packages aside. I will pack 50 eggs, that is, unless I come up with more in the meantime.

Yesterday I unfortunately had a quarrel with a non-com. I was probably in the right, but that is sometimes another matter when it comes to the military. Often the guys are so young that one can expect some sort of nonsense. Well, with my abilities with the language no one likes to take me on. Today is the ninth of February. A day has passed since the beginning of this letter, since here we always have interruptions such as air raid alarms, building bunkers and fortifications. Slowly the time is coming for an end to the training. A guy can really get lost, and I don't want to do that. Give Mrs. MacLean my very best, and I am happy that she spends a lot of stimulating time with you. What does her husband think of that? My Love, please receive these lines as though they were spoken. . . . You are always in my thoughts; things are looking up. It is such a wonderful thing to be able to be in love with you, and I love you so very, very much. Dear God may we never have to end our relationship.

Intimately, Your Vagabond

Letter no. 167
Officer Training, February 10, 1944,
Soldier Paul Claudius,
Field Post Office no. 56510a

My Passionately Beloved Joy, You My Desire!

It is evening, and all of my buddies sit around the table and write. One writes home, the other to a girl, and I to you, to my sweet little wife.

Well, I want to answer your letter of February 3. I have already written you that I received your long letter. To be sure, some 1,000 letters were lost in Frankfurt, also the package from Inge's country feast. Well – nothing can be done now, . . . it's too late. It's bad that you are having air raid alarms so often, but when one sees what passes over the Channel coast, then I always think to myself "poor Germany," and I think of the poor people who will lose everything, and the children, crying and scared, the evil craft of this frightening world. Do the locals help you when you go into the shelter? What is Mr. Probst doing? Was he home for Christmas? It was very interesting to see that Mr. Baltia is manning flak guns in Bitterfeld. That means he is a real soldier. We in the Army don't recognize the Air Force, since they are more civilian and do not fight at the front. That must be of some comfort to Mrs. Baltia. Unfortunately you forgot to include Mr. Baltia's card with the letter. I could have written him from here and can do it over again. Your fear of my "not coming" is moving and completely understandable. One waits many hours on the most beloved little things on this earth, but oh how the heart sinks in the grip of disappointment when the husband does not come. I will do everything I can not to disappoint you. I have always waited for you, but I always knew that you would come to me, you always came.

I really enjoyed your descriptions of the children. You really have a talent for relating such episodes. So Dettos is learning a thing or two. Erika is lending her ingenious abilities to Mattheu, and Dettos makes prayer with the puppets. Has his stature changed, the sweet little fellow? He must certainly be bigger. Mattheu appears to be like me, the quiet technician with gaming abilities. We will fix the airplane and then shoot it down with Papi's carbine. I'll show him how that is done. "Macho" Dettos will be a smart fellow; I am proud of that. He just looks as though that skull of his is made for soaking up info and thinking things over. (Next to me is a "procured" duck as well as a second, both in line to lose their lives. Yesterday a line of little bunnies got the death sentence. I have ruled out this sort of shopping.)

This afternoon I went with a tank and crew to designated farmers to inform them they would have to evacuate some fortification areas for 3 hours. We did some sharp shooting. It was a maneuver under the direction of General Guderian. I took the opportunity along with Professor Eisenhut (now with armored infantry) to buy some butter and eggs. 3 egg were left for me after dividing them up with the "big" fellows. I baked myself a cake. Recipe: Oatmeal mixed with your sugar and 1 egg (in a deep plate) and stirred into a batter. Melt some butter and stir in. Then put the whole thing on a hot plate for 10 minutes. Tastes great. When I get home, I will bake three pieces for the children. I can bring baking things with me, although these things are seldom used in France because the French don't bake German cakes. Tomorrow will be the eleventh of February, pay day, and I am almost broke. Hopefully your money will come in a timely fashion. Well, my Love, I must close and go to bed. Tomorrow will be another hectic day, and I must be at my post. Sweet dreams and remember that I love you very, very much.

I kiss you intimately,

Your Paulus and Vagabond

Letter no. 168
Officer Training, February 13, 1944,
Soldier Paul Claudius,
Field Post Office no. 56510a

To My Joy, my Heart's Desire!

Today is a Sunday, but for me it was a tough day. The higher authorities again want to live better, and Claudius, Inc. must go procuring along with Dr. Froehlich (we are the best at getting things). So we are again on the run to see what we can buy. Of course a few things have popped up for us, like 3 lbs. of prime bacon and some butter and eggs. However, the greatest portion will again go into the kitchen for meals for the gentlemen. There is a lot I can tell you about such "trips," since we go through the world with open eyes. The distaste for procuring soldiers is extremely high, and it takes a knowledge of the language, persistence and also a certain amount of likeability in order to succeed in getting things. Often we must wait a long time until the women get comfortable enough to come forth with something. It is a travesty to have to make deals of this sort and endure it as a German soldier. Most of the children are sick and weakened, a scruffy little bunch. It often hurts me and pulls on my heart strings when I see a nice, clean child, and I think of home. Yes, my Love, how our Sundays and Sunday evenings used to be. I would scarcely have closed the door when I came home from the office when my life went on then in your beautiful realm, where I felt so at home. And the children also felt that a day was special or a day had only begun when you and I were happy together. You made such wonderful preparations, and everything was so nice. It was such a happy time. Even when we were deep in a war you had so much love and devotion. You put the bright glow of being "carefree" magically into my life, even though you had so many concerns.

I am supposed to somehow come up with 2 kilograms of chocolate in Rennes. I was picked as intermediary in a dispute and I was able to calm down an agitated guy and request that he return the notification with my promise to the regiment. I would then travel with Baeuber (buddy) to Rennes, and we would scare up 2 kilograms of chocolate. I was even able to come up with the chocolate of the same quality and filling. (1 kilogram bar of chocolate with cream filling 25 reichsmarks). In the evening I returned the goods to the man, and he told me again and again how pleased he was with the settlement. Yes, and the Lieutenant was also satisfied. I also bought some chocolate for the children, 3.5 lbs. They can lick it up. Futhermore, I bought 5 meters of elastic, 2.5 kilograms of lump-sugar, 1 carton of fine letter paper and envelopes for you, 4 packages of the finest biscuits and ½ lb. of butter. Everything was well-preserved. 5 bottles of red wine were also ready. Yes, the 36 reichsmarks you sent me really came in handy at the right time. I will use the money that I get for the 10 days to get butter, bacon and coffee. If only I can pack everything. You can see, my Love, that I am already making preparations and want everything paid for. I even got a small broom. I have included a picture of the heavy artillery instruction. I am situated, plain to see, to the right in the standing row. Below me, to the far right, is my buddy Baeuber of the Pioneer Company. "Baeuber", like me, comes from Erfurt. He can remember you when you brought me to the railroad station when I left on the 28th of July. The second picture shows a smaller gun, 8.4 cm, and I am not in this picture. Tomorrow is Sunday, and we must do some work in order to complete our tests. My Love, the day for my departure for home and Germany draws ever closer. Today, during a train ride, I sat in the quiet and went through the trip in spirit (dreamed about it), but I didn't reach the end, since the trip came to an early end. Well, I must put some things in order and then get some well-deserved rest, since I am tired. My Love, intimate kisses and love from Your Paulus. Please tell the 3 urchins about the sweet deals.

Always, Your Paulus

Letter no. 169
Officer Training, February 17, 1944,
Soldier Claudius,
Field Post Office no. 56510a

My Joy, My Sunshine!

Finally, due to special circumstances I have one hour of time and eagerly take pen in hand to write my longing and desires, after two days, to you my happiness. (However there was again an interruption; hopefully I will be back). You may think that your Paulus is always devoid of time. Well, that's true. Unfortunately I have to answer to the document room, so there is very little time left over. (In the meantime I have been interrupted two times.) Yesterday evening I had to make a quick run with the transport truck in order to buy a calf and, at the same time, 2 liters of milk and 3 lbs. of bacon for the Lieutenant and the company. I also picked up some milk for me. At noon I had to make a contract with a French worker for our kitchen, and that had to be written out. Yesterday evening I spent an hour in the officers' mess. I scarcely had time to draw a breath when the Lieutenant came in to talk to someone. A few days ago, all soldiers had to work. He went around with me and brooded over some complicated themes about the post war time. I still had things to do with the books, so we went back into the document room (writing room) and continued to philosophize. Everyone was there, even the dumb sergeant with his eyes glazed over. Today, at breakfast, I discovered that a buddy stole a knife from the officers' mess. I immediately requested that the knife be returned. It would have been just a stupid matter had the guy brought it back an hour later to the company commander. But old Papa Claudius himself went into the lions' den and got the knife. That's the way it goes, day in, day out; and so it will remain.

Hopefully I will be able to lessen my burden of duty to the point it was before. After this training I will no longer be just a common soldier. Then the grind of this training will be over.

But now to your letter of February 6th: My Love, please excuse me if I blurt it out. I can't believe what you wrote about Erika and her class list. It is so wonderful. Erika has her mother's head; that is clear. I am so proud of the child and out of joy have told all of my buddies. You have been able to school Erika so well in my absence to the point that she is almost at the top of a class of 74 children. Please write the parents about that, especially since Erika had connections with Laubegast. I have written father and mother about it, about the good work with calculations. You and Mrs. Blabush make a good team. Concern with good marks makes for good knowledge and good habits. It is clear that I am so happy about that. Good, so . . . my Goldchen . . . . the money arrived yesterday, but I couldn't draw it since I am to get 36 more. That was the result of good relations with the Lieutenant. He gave me money with his eyes closed. Well, now I can make purchases and come home to you like a pack animal (donkey). Your concern about the ownership of "Baron von Distelhof" is really sweet. The four of them should get something to smoke. I will bring tobacco and cigarettes. I plan to buy more. My dealings are not wanting of smoke wares. You will get envelopes. That <u>goes without saying</u>.

Otherwise I would be lost. (In the meantime I had to do some business with a French dealer.) I will get Erika a beautiful pen and some things for her to take to school. I am so pleased with you and the children. My Lieutenant's wife will seek you out at Distelhof this summer. Hopefully you will have the roof fixed. You have had so much snow that traffic is at a standstill, is that true? Well, I am happy to have been able to complete this little letter. Be well my little wife. I am so proud of you, and I love you so much that it really is time to show you how much.

Thinking of you always,

Your Vagabond.

Letter no. 170
Soldier Paul Claudius,
Field Post Office 5651a
Officer Training, February 18, 1944,

My Goldchen, My Joy, You!

I have just returned from Rennes on the matter of my eye glasses. As you may remember, the optician in Erfurt was able to make a new pair of prescription glasses for me in a relatively short period of time. So please take my prescription to the optometrist as soon as possible and ask him to make a second pair of military glasses to be ready for me to pick up at the beginning of March.

Your Papi is sick. He is completely exhausted and wishes that he were dead. My throat is terribly sore, my tonsils are swollen, and thick, itchy socks have altogether put me into a complete state of misery. French cough drops are worthless. Hopefully, I will not get kicked out of camp. That would really screw things up for the future. I plan to be brave and will certainly get better.

But now, to your letter of February 9th which lies before me and brings me so much joy. From it, I note that you have received five letters from me – akin to trench warfare in making their way to you. I need to tell you that your second package, containing the baked goods to die for, has not yet arrived. It's a dammed shame that a poor PFC should have such precious things stolen and eaten, and it is physically painful to me to have something that you made for me with your own hands, end up as lost. The world has become more grim and ugly. Too foul a violation to put into words.

The Lieutenant has already made me a loan of some extra money. I am to repay it directly to his bank in Germany. It is an outstanding thing for him to do this for me, because everything is very expensive, and all food stuffs around here are so scarce that money disappears very quickly. I was on the march again just today to find some fabric for you. With a measure of success, I found some washable silk. Unfortunately, it is laid out and cut into pieces for a dress with only 2.5 meters still intact. I will have to decide whether or not to buy the four meters. You could make a little dress for Erika out of it or maybe something for yourself. I can't get anything from a clothing store without a ticket. I have searched around for undergarments for you. These are unfortunately terribly expensive. A set made out of fine linen costs 35 to 40 reichsmarks. With that, I will not be able to bring enough butter and other things. No matter what, I will bring you a nice pair of panties!!

Well, with that concluded, you can now finish your preparations for my homecoming, and indeed, Frau Claudius, you must surely know that you don't need to get all dressed up for my first evening. I was ever so happy to get a good financial report from you, and I am eager to hear your explanations for it. I got my Wehrmacht Class II license for heavy vehicles today. Interesting in that regard was the fact that two sergeants, along with a few of my buddies, didn't pass the exam.

My throat is really damned sore. What can I do? As of today, I can tell you that our final inspection will be on the 29th of February, 1944. I will therefore leave on the evening of March 1st and arrive in Erfurt on the second or third of March at around 1:30 in the night. Nothing, however, is for certain, and I will write to confirm things for you as soon as I can. The best that I can tell you is that you can plan to be with your "Soldier," hopefully Mr. Corporal, on the second or third of March. (The Corporal with the silver chevron on his left arm and two silver stripes on his shoulder strap.) This week will initiate a final push. We will have to really put out, but the final days will pass.... If only this "passing" would also apply to seeing an end to this war. Today, several of my buddies got the bad news that their apartments were destroyed in the latest attack on Frankfurt. Thank God that I do not have to worry. Dear Lord, may you be spared this horrible and undeserved penalty. My Love, I long so much for you, the children, and my home that my eyes fill with tears. I kiss you in love and longing.

Simply, your Paulus

Letter no. 171
Officer Training,
February 20, 1944,

My Sweet Little Wife, My Goldchen!

I write these lines to you from the watch room of our barracks in this little Breton city. Since we are all required to do certain things before we are finished here, it is important for us to learn how a noncom watch commander must conduct himself, and what his duties are. Toward this end, we officer candidates are required to be on watch from 19:00 hours to 19:00 hours the next day. We have been assigned to night watch and will have command privileges over all of the older soldiers and higher staff recruits. With pistol and steel helmets we sit and record our watch in the watch room. We are responsible for the entire observation – even if commandos, commanders, or any of the generals come before us. All posts must be announced, all clothing must be inspected along with any papers that may be required. I won't go into the details and military refinements that are involved.

Health-wise, I am unfortunately not in tip top shape. My tonsils are even more swollen, and swallowing brings me an extraordinary amount of pain. Last night I had a very high fever and sought to get some sleep and relief from pain by drinking a glass of Calvados, [95] My head ached so badly that I got up in the middle of the night and ended up on the floor, lost consciousness, didn't move, and just remained there. A buddy heard the noise, turned on the light, and got me up. Because of my sore throat, I couldn't speak to answer any of his many questions. Today, I am

---

[95] Calvados – a French brandy made from apples.

on the "Watch Calendar." That's just the way it is with the Prussians. That my watch begins at 19:00 on a Saturday and ends at 19:00 on Sunday is very unfortunate, and since I am now on duty, any time that I may have had to rest and refresh myself has evaporated. I am in no condition for an outdoor assignment, though, and I can't complain about having been given indoor duty. The sentries are checked by the officers and the reports are listed on the military check list.

The coughing fits that come over me are so painful that tears come to my eyes, and although I sit glued to the stove, I am still freezing from head to foot. In order to keep things from getting worse and in any way delay my trip, I will visit the company doctor tomorrow. Thoughts of being with you soon with the order, love, and care that your little hands provide is the anchor that holds me fast in the joy that can be the only assailant against these tough times. How are you, my Goldchen? What are the children doing? In almost ten days, I will see for myself. It has been over four months this time that I have been away from all of you. That's a long time for people who love each other and need each other and desire to "be together" so much. That will be a joy, and oh how much I want to be with you around the home fire.

I understand that you have had an extremely large amount of snow in Thüringen, so much that traffic came to a standstill. Here, we have also had some snow, but it did not stay. (I must now go and wake the cook.) Since as of right now I have no truck at my disposal, I keep worrying about the details of getting packed up. Well, your Vagabond will soon come calling and bring all sorts of cardboard boxes with him. My Love, only a few more days, and the wall that divides us will fall. I have already been on my feet for twenty four hours and have not had even an hour's worth of sleep. So my eyes are very heavy. Goldchen, my Joy, I long so much for you. As your vagabond and husband, I want to be so loving and tender to you.

As always, your Paulus,

Letter no. 172
Soldier P. Claudius
Field Post Office no. 5651a
Officer Training, February 20, 1944,

My Sunday Joy, My One and Only Goldchen, You,

Well, it is already noon, and my stomach is deeply growling for food and drink. I have just sent one of the watch people off to the kitchen with pots and pans to bring some ambrosia back from the kitchen. I have again engaged myself in some deep discussions with my comrades over the status of this war and all of its sufferings. It appears that the soldiers have concluded that the war will not outlast the end of this year, but it is impossible to imagine that we will have a peaceful Germany by the beginning of next year.

As I have already written you, my Love, I steadfastly cling to the private and personal Claudius within me, and am vigorously resisting any urge to be a soldier. Our homeland will be forced to bear the heaviest burden yet, when the soldiers come home like a flood and seek to be reinstated into their old circles of society. The men who have served at the war front for the entire tour of their duty are no longer ordinary human beings. They will no longer find themselves able to take part in everyday life, and they will not be looked upon in quite the same way. It will be very hard for them to reenter everyday life as simple lawful citizens, because they will have to give up the noble image of themselves as heroic soldiers. These are also the thoughts that move the Lieutenant, since the future depends on the economic condition of the world and Germany's roll in it. It is, however, not our concern to find answers. That is a matter for the state. How will the education of our three children fare? In any event, I want to remain as I once was and keep things between you and me and the children the way that they were. Because I love you so much, everything needs to be as it was for us in our happiest of times. Anything else would make me think about deserter prison... oh you – and me.

I sent Mr. Baltus a short letter. Apparently he was able to get you some seedlings for Distelhof. From his writings I could not tell if he has become a soldier or is somehow assigned to the civilian flak guns. Again and again, I keep thinking about the delicate matter with the four Russians, and ask you to please pay attention to being very cautious when you are alone with these people at Distelhof. Let them think that you have a weapon (the small hand gun is on the beam over the door that leads from the living room into the kitchen). I am afraid that these Armenians might get some dumb idea in regard to your girlish figure. Please, be careful and heed my words. If the four Russians want to start at the beginning of March, I will be there and have the time to make an inspection visit. You and I can then look around a bit and do some reminiscing together. I am most anxious to see how things are up there..... if the Virginia Creepers are stronger and if the hedge is still growing and getting thicker. We could have used two or three more trees, but you have probably not had the chance to buy any more. Since you have become the most important working member of our household, especially during the recent frequent air raid alarms, I am curious about your "instructions."

At any rate, I will be released on the second or third of March, and you do not have to be at the railroad station to meet me. I will call you, and you can meet me at the Danziger Freiheit.

My heart beats fast in anticipation, and the ten pfennig piece for the telephone at the station is already in my possession. (21967) will be my first connection to you by wire. Well, I want to send my parents a few lines, and with that my longest watch will end. If all goes well, I will eat at the 'Lion d' Or, and since I am dog-tired, go right on to bed.

Be intimately hugged and kissed by your Paulus. I am always your Vagabond and Paulus. Soon, very soon, my Love, we will love heart to heart and be able to kiss! Oh, may the days fly by.

Give the three urchins, Eki, Matheu and Detti a small kiss from Papi, and save one for yourself.[96]

---

[96] This sentence written upside-down on the top of the letter.

Letter no. 173
Soldier Claudius,
Field Post Office no. 5651a
Officer Training, February 21, 1944,

My Beloved, Ardently Desired Goldchen!
Oh, How I Love You!

One of my buddies was just here and told me that the soldiers have received short wave radio transmission information that the English air fleet has carried out a terror bombing run on Erfurt and that a considerable amount of damage had been done. With a pounding heart, I listened to the latest Wehrmacht report as it related that terror bombers flew nuisance raids over mid Germany and severely damaged the city of Leipzig. Since I have to wait eight days in order to get any communication from you at all, you can imagine my state of mind. Dear God, now the horror has come to our Erfurt, and what has possibly happened to you and the little ones? We are at such a disadvantage here that I must always think that the worst may have happened. I would not be able to endure it. A newspaper will hopefully arrive tomorrow, and I will know something more definite.

For me, as a soldier, it is the uncertainty that is unbearable, and I cling to the thought that we do not live in the middle of the city or near the railroad station and that the Brits hardly ever aim at single housing neighborhoods. Oh, my Love, if I only had a little letter from you telling me that you and the children and Inge are all right, and also our home and Distelhof. Your letter of February 14th lies before me. It arrived yesterday, but I saved it to read today. It is full of happiness, joy, and sunshine with the reality of things being completely different. I was able to get one kilogram of butter from my farmers today. Because of their limited ability with the language, none of my other buddies had any such success. Many of the farmers ask them where the "soldier with the glasses" is. "He should come back because he can explain." "Learned, happy Claudius" has everything under control.

I have just talked to our radio operator, and he told me that the bombers spent the entire day of yesterday over the city of Leipzig, and that the reports agree with the previous broadcasts. That is bad news for you because I know how nerve-racking it is for you to be in the cellar during air raids, especially since you are not feeling all that well. The homeland has become a theater for the war, and all talk of rest and peace has ended. I am doing a little better. Unfortunately, the weather has turned very cold, and because of that, duty has become strictly by the book. I will hopefully be recalled to the Pioneer Company to serve as an instructor. The Lieutenant of the Pioneer Company is busting his buns on my behalf, but the assignment is a matter for the regiment to make. There, at least I would continue to have the opportunity to send you groceries. It is also a lot cleaner at the Pioneer Company.

Oh, my Love, it's hard for me to write a good letter. It is now very comforting to have Distelhof. At least you have a roof over you and are not under direct attack by the enemy. It could be very comfortable if an iron stove could be installed. Hopefully you will be able to laugh at my lines of worry and concern, but, my Love, we see the incoming planes first hand and can count the number of them that fly on to the Reich. We also hear the loud and destructive explosions nearby, but since those are only French houses and people, as soldiers, we simply look the other way. It has taken the play out of life for me, and thoughts that you back at home must now suffer are unbearable. If only an end were in sight for the world and our people to be able to breathe a sigh of relief.

My Love, my reflections of longing and extended love make their way to you with my thoughts. I love you so much. Write as soon as possible.

As always, your Paulus [97]

Letter no. 174
Officer Training, February 23, 1944,

Goldchen, the Joy and Hope of my Life!

Like a rock, amid the turmoil, anger, and intensity of the instruction course, I write a letter to you, my Goldchen. Today was a very big day, and everything here is in a high state of

---

[97] The final sentences and the closing were written on the side of the letter.

agitation, especially with the young people. The high command gave a very special presentation on the concept of being a German soldier. Two decorated generals with iron crosses, many high-ranking officers, and our Lieutenant provided flawless instruction. Most of it, I think, was directly due to our Lieutenant's effort toward becoming a First Lieutenant. He really deserves it. The regular soldiers all had their hearts in their mouths because all of the generals were noteworthy faces. In recent days, the high command has demonstrated how closely they monitor the shaping of their Reserve Officer Candidates and how strongly the entire course of instruction is influenced by the highest breed. This evening a special presenter talked to us about the architecture of the world city of Paris. He talked about Notre Dame, the Cathedral of the Invalides, the Louvre, and Versailles. Slides accompanied his very knowledgeable and well-flowing presentation. The intellectual aspect of our instruction is so good that these lectures, which are never offered to ordinary soldiers, are so lively and easily understood that the officers really appreciate these presentations. I will tell you more of the details in person. It is only eight more days now. February 29th is the big day. It will also be the most physically demanding day for me, because we are to stage a large attack on the maneuver site.

We took the truck into the Foret de Montfort yesterday and "got wood." The saw rang out as we felled trees, then the axes made sure that everything was precisely cut into oven size logs. A couple of days ago, I was out with a sharpshooter troop leader – a noncom (a noncom is to be saluted by every rank) who was accompanied by a heavily armed group of troops. Since the Lieutenant ordered different positions, the practice was a tough one. Time and time again, I had my difficulty and worried about leading my people into the machine gun fire of the defensive sharpshooters. Sweat covered me from head to toe, and I felt thoroughly beaten up but succeeded, at least to a certain extent, in satisfying the Lieutenant. Later, in his critique for the commanders on the hill, he told me that I could have done better.

But enough with the soldier talk; none of it can be of much interest to you. Your dear letter of the 12th lies before me, and I am especially smitten with your final lines. Your writing is so courageous and loving that it makes me feel as though you want to protect me from the battle that the home front endures at the hands of the British and American terror bombing attacks. These lines drop upon my heart like hot blood. You write like the person that I know and love. I wait on mail from you with a wildly beating heart.

An attack on Erfurt took place on the 19th. Today is the 23rd of February, so I won't be able to get any mail from you before the 27th or 28th. I pray that the dear Lord will protect my dearly beloved family. Things here are damned tense. As soldiers, we are required to have our weapons loaded and with us at all times because of the many sniper terror attacks. My throat is better, but the dry cough is as it was. The children await their Papi. Yes, my Love, if only the train were already rolling, and I knew that everything with you was all right. Goldchen, you and I and the children must stay together. Our fortune and bitter struggle in life must, for the children's sake, not be in vain. My Love, I am your Paulus who longs for you and thinks only about you.

Intimately, Your Paulus

Since Soldier Claudius was just days away from making his travels to Erfurt and mail home took from five to seven days to arrive, this was his last letter from France.

CHAPTER THREE

The Notebook

It is a small, three-by-four-inch, brown notebook, a precious relic of World War II. Like a dairy, its pages are by the day, and on them the ink stains laid down in the year 1944 by Hertha Claudius recount her personal thoughts and memories of a time of joy and sorrow amid the turmoil of the second to last year of the war.

The entries begin with the arrival of Paul Claudius in March.

Friday, March 3
Papi arrives loaded down with heavy packages from France for a wonderful and very special 12 day leave. Together with Inge we will take the sled to pick him up.

Tuesday, March 7
With our beloved Papi, all of us travel to Distelhof with the sled. There is much snow. We eat dumplings and pancakes at the "Stätner Wirt" Restaurant.

Wednesday, March 15
The end of the very special vacation. Parting felt so very difficult. All alone, Paulus has gone out into the cold May night on his way to Blau . . .[98]

---

[98] Word here not legible. He was reporting for a new assignment.

Thursday, March 23

The doorbell rings in the middle of the night. Inge wakes up, and even through the commotion I hear that it is my beloved, my Paulus, I spring out of my bed, My joy is so great that I cannot express the whole of it. Our Papi will report as a trainee to the local army base, and gets to sleep here with us until he is deployed to the front.

Sunday, April 9,

Papi has left because he had to deliver laundry for Monday, laundry day. Restful and sunny hours are spent on a beach chair out on the balcony.

Friday, April 28

A farewell celebration.

Sunday, April 30

The beginning of the last furlough before being assigned to the front.

Friday, May 5

Grandma and grandpa come from Dresden to see their youngest son once more.

Sunday, May 7

We go to Distelhof with our Papi and his parents.

Wednesday, May 10

The departure of the parents with a last farewell for their son.

Thursday, May 11

Sunny days at Distelhof with our beloved Papi.

Friday, May 12

An especially beautiful, quiet and sunny day with my vagabond, Paulus.

Saturday, May 13
The roof of the cabin is repaired, and my dear Paulus, the builder of Distelhof, is very happy about it.

Monday, May 15
We leave Distelhof. In the evening Paulus picks me up from the concert.

Tuesday, May 16
We buy 32 tomato plants, and Papi plants them with help from the girl. It is our last time at our beloved Distelhof.

Wednesday, May 17
With my dear Paulus, we visit . . . [99] near Chemnitz. We again overnight at the Ilsinger Hof.

Thursday, May 18
For our official last evening meal together I made yeast dumplings immediately after our return. Papa ate fourteen, and I was afraid that he would have a stomach ache – but by the next day his appetite for dumplings has returned (with tomato puree and a goose.)

Friday, May 19
The last official vacation day for our beloved Paulus.

Sunday, May 21, Mothers Day
One last Sunday with my beloved husband, Paulus.
My Paulus decorates the table with flowers and a chocolate torte that he himself has prepared. In the morning, he and the children surprise me with a beautiful poem from him. Erika even recites a special poem for me.

My way was long
My way was a heavy burden.
It is not comprehensible
for me to know

---

[99] Name of town or village here not legible.

where I will find the strength
or how I can complete him.[100]

A May 24, entry in Paul Claudius's Military Pass book
indicates that he reported to the Military doctor for a medical
check up before being transferred to active duty at war front.

Thursday, May 25
A last parting for me from my endangered, youthful life
partner. (Our 9th wedding anniversary Day.)
The listing in his War pass book for that day states that he was
being deployed to serve with a Panzer Division (tank unit) at the
Eastern war front in Lemberg, Poland, now part of the Ukraine. [101]

Sunday, May 28, Pentecost Sunday
Lonely holidays.

Sunday, June 4,
Matthias gets sick with scarlet fever.

Letter no. 175
The East, June 6, 1944

My Passionately Loved Girl, My Heart's Desire, You!

You will think , . . . here comes another little letter, and so
much yearning for home, for rest and peace.   Yes, my dear

---

[100] This poem is strikingly similar to a poem entitled "Gretchen am Spinnrad" or
"Gretchen at the Spinning Wheel." It appears in Goethe's literary classic
"Faust." Gretchen's world has been turned upside-down, and she sits at the
spinning wheel and voices the destabilization of her life with the poetic words:
*Meine Ruhe ist hin, Mein Herz ist schwer, Ich finde sie nimmer und nimmer
mehr. My peace is gone, my heart is heavy, I will never, never find them again.*
She will never find peace after her encounter with Doctor Faust.
[101] Lemberg, later known as Lviv was the second largest city in Poland and is
located approximately seventy kilometers from the Polish border and about 160
kilometers from the Easter Carpathian mountains. Lviv and its population
suffered greatly as the result of World War I and World War II and the invading
armies of that period. Lviv celebrated its 750th anniversary in September 2006.

Goldchen, I am over it for just a moment. I am so thankful when the sun shines upon me, as it did on our wonderful hours together at Distelhof, . . . and as it will on the tomatoes, pickles and berries. Dear, did you go up there on Pentecost? I have so many plans for us up there. We should build a temporary home up there with a size of 20 square meters. We must get all that approved, the building, that is, and also build a terrace. And we need a nice, deep cellar. Then we'll have some 50 square meters of living space. But those are the types of plans that we should make together. How are things with you, my Goldchen, and the three rascals? They are probably celebrating Pentecost vacation. Yes, how often I look at those pictures of all of you. It calms me. You mean so much to me, especially out here. One is so alone, especially as an educated person. Well, my Dear, I kiss you on your lovely mouth and dream of coming home and being happy. Give the little ones all my love.

Kisses from your Paulus.

Saturday, June 10
All of us must to go to the hospital with scarlet fever.

Letter no. 176
Noncom Claudius
37207
In the East, June 19

Goldchen, Beloved Little Mother!

I just looked out across the stacked row of sandbags to get a lay of the land; something flew overhead, and the letter that I had just finished fell from my hands. Yes, the beautiful sun stands high, and my duty for the day is to prepare for the demolition of another bridge. I have thirteen men and two Pioneer tanks to command. The third Pioneer vehicle has not yet arrived and is either lost or has broken down. I have the apprehension that "Ivan"[102] is

---

[102] Ivan – German soldiers often referred to the Russians as "Ivan."

planning a counter attack for us in the next few days. As far as I can tell, we find ourselves boxed into a position that he wants to close up. Troop morale has been good since the invasion; also, we get schnapps on a daily basis, 96%! As a result, the guys are a dangerous group of fighting men. Stola is also here – another hand from the homeland, and I am really happy about having him here.

That you long for mail from me fills my heart with a glow. I will try to write you more frequently in the future but don't know where I can get any of the letters mailed out. You can't in your wildest dreams imagine the conditions here. There are tons of bed bugs. So far I have been able to keep the infestation at bay.

My Love, the time lost between us has made a different Paulus of me. Dear God, let me come home alive – and yet, I am apprehensive about your demeanor. How will you receive me? Maybe I should remain here in the filth, where I can write to you and you can write to me and give me strength. – It is all over and done with. My parents know nothing about the child.

Please tell Mattheu that war here is real and that here, his paper helmet and toy gun are useless. I have seen steel helmets with holes in them that are as big as a fist. Your birthday falls on a Sunday. Is it true that you must remain in the hospital for six weeks?[103] Who brought this sickness home? (It must be in the air, all kinds of things are in the air here.) Eki will have to return to school for more of her diligent learning, and Mattheu will need to get ready for his first school year. I hope to be home with all of you by then.

Well, it's time for me to get ready. I am so happy to have been able to complete two more letters. I hope that you will also be happy about that. I will write home and hope that the letters will get there. I know where you and the little ones are, and I am with you in spirit. My love for you is unending.

Your Paulus, Father and Husband.

Friday, June 30
I leave the hospital and take personal responsibility for the children.

---

[103] Reference here to Scarlet Fever.

Sunday, July 2
Mutti spends a lonely birthday – but aunt Manus brings 50 reichsmarks for birthday flowers from our dear Papi.

Monday, July 3
My Paulus writes an oh, so loving letter from the front. It is the last one that I have received from him.

Tuesday, July 11
My beloved Paulus writes one last letter, in this life, to me from the front.[104]

Thursday, July 13
Our dear Papi sends his Frontkampferpäckchen (war front package of provisions) to his three darlings and writes them his last notes.

Friday, July 14
The battle in Lemberg begins.

Sunday, July 16 (This entry must have been made posthumously.)
The death of my above everything else beloved husband and father of my children.

Paul Claudius's Wehrpass, his military pass book, would be sent to his wife, along with his personal belongings on September 5th. Under the heading of "Active Duty," and a subheading of "War related illnesses or injury" It states: Died, "Für die Richtigkeit ."
Block G, Grave Nr. 36

---

[104] Hertha Claudius received two final letters from her husband. They were dated July 7th and July 11th. These letters, however, were not included in the collection that Erika found. Erika believes these were such keepsakes that her mother kept them to herself, never permitting anyone to read them, and not including them with the letter collection.

Tuesday, July 18
The mail man brings me the last letter of my beloved husband.
(7-11-44)

Wednesday, July 19
We move to stay at Distelhof. I work very hard in the garden
with the hope that my Paulus will soon return.

Thursday, July 20
A bombing raid on Erfurt that we felt, even at Distelhof.

Friday, July 21
Liselotte (our children's helper) brings one – last – and very
late arriving letter from my beloved husband, Paulus, to me at
Diestelhof. (7-3-44)

Saturday, July 22
Worries over my Paulus will not let me rest or come to peace.
We have a severe thunderstorm in the evening.

Sunday, July 23
The weather has turned bad but worse is the fear that my
beloved husband will not come home again.

Tuesday, July 25
Mrs. Stoll has invited me and the children to a birthday event.
Both of us are waiting for news.

Wednesday, July 26
News from Mrs. Stoll about the difficult circumstances of my
dear Paulus.
Thursday, July 27
The terrible time of waiting begins.

Monday, July 31
Bishleben the . . . [105]

---

[105] Entry here not legible.

Tuesday, August 1
All of August is spent in waiting and is filled with agony.

Hertha Claudius sent the following letter to Dr. Todoroff on September 3, 1944:

I am in an extreme state of worry over my husband because I have had no reports or news about him for over eight weeks. He reported to the front on May 25th as an officer in training in order to complete his assignment there. I heard from one of his comrades that he was severely wounded seven and a half weeks ago, in the East. Since then, all inquires about him have failed to turn up any news. I don't know where he is or if he is alive. This not knowing is a frightening thing. For many, many weeks I have awaited the daily mail but always without results. May God protect him. He asked about you in his last letter of July 11.

Monday, September 4
News reaches me about the hero's death of my one and only beloved husband, Paulus.

Tuesday, September 5
Through his Company leader, the Government Party delivers the official notice of his death.

It reads:
True to his oath to the flag, giving up his life in the battle for the freedom of Greater Germany. Noncommissioned Officer, Paul Claudius, 10th Pioneer, Tank Grenadier, Regiment 113, A Hero's death for Führer, Folk and Fatherland.

July 16, 1944
stamped with government seal
Signed by: the the 10th Genadier Regiment, 113, Hashke

On the 16th of July 1944
The following document with original documentation is hereby submitted on the 12th of September, 1944.
His death certificate reads:

Resident of: Erfurt
Number 3230/1944.
The engineer, last promoted to noncommissioned officer, Paul Matthias Claudius, Lutheran

Last known address: in Erfurt – Hochheim, Wachsenbergweg 7
died: on the battlefield near Lemberg / Brzezany, on July 16, 1944
the deceased was born on : August 26, 1912, in Chemnitz, Germany

Office of record: Chemnitz II, Number 284/1912
Father: Lead Engineer, Ludwig Peter Martin Claudius
Residence: in Dresden
Mother: Wilhelmine Auguste Claudius, born Qumard
Residence: in Dresden
The deceased was married to: Hertha Julia Gabriele Claudius, born, de Veer
Residence: in Erfurt-Hochheim

It is dated:
November 9, 1944, and is signed by the official in charge of the Office of the Registry

There are no further entries in this small, light brown, little day book.

CHAPTER FOUR

Postscripts

God, Nature and Fatherland

One hundred and forty-three years before Paul Claudius enlisted in the German Wehrmacht, a *school* of writers was putting its stamp on the German psyche, a stamp born of the Thirty Years War, the French Revolution and the War of Liberation from Napoleon's rule. The spirit of this movement would gain an eternal life in the history of a nation that would fight a second Thirty Years War from 1914 to 1945.

This school of writers sought to re-evaluate the achievements of the German past in literature, art, philosophy, politics and society. *Die Romantische Schule,* the Romantic School of writers glorified German nationalism and sought to inspire contemporaries with a new love for the timeless qualities of German thought, life and culture.

One of the members of the Heidelberg branch of this movement, a typical example of the Romantic philosophy, was Joseph von Eichendorf. As a member of the Free Corps of Major von Lützow, von Eichendorf took part in the war against Napoleon. His prose and poetry focused on God, nature, folk and fatherland. He continually glorified the changing moods of nature and painted a poetic analysis of the human heart with its unending cravings and yearnings. *Fernweh*, an unending craving, *Heimweh*, home sickness, and *Wanderlust*, the desire to roam and be free, were the subjects of his focus. Romantic authors viewed human love as both sweet and sad. All striving, according to von Eichendorf, was an unquenchable quest for our eternal home, and everything transitory a symbol of eternity. Man must often pay a price for his unquenchable desires.

The letters of Paul Claudius reflect all aspects of von Eichendorf's writings and the *Romantic Movement*. God, nature, folk and fatherland were the guiding principles in the life of Paul Claudius. He admired the French and continually wrote about nature, the preservation of his family and the Reich.

In his admiration of what he considered the carefree life of the Frenchman, he echoed a facet of Romantic philosophy portrayed by von Eichendorf and other Romantic authors, the concept of being free to live as one wants. In Paul Claudius's mind, however, he was bound to do his duty to the Reich to gain the ability to live as he wished, to return home to his beloved Distelhof, his wife, his children and his garden. And he truly paid the price for his "unquenchable desires."

Blood and Paper.

On March 25, 1919, twenty-four years before Paul Claudius enlisted in the Wehrmacht, Prime Minister David Lloyd George issued his Fountainbleu Memorandum in an attempt to "tempter" the Treaty of Versailles, which he viewed as filled with arrogance and injustice in regard to Germany. The Fountainbleu Memorandum became one of the most prophetic documents in history. Lloyd George described the German people as a "people who have certainly proved themselves one of the most vigorous and powerful races in the world."

The Treaty of Versailles took away German World War I victory in the East, a victory that had settled border disputes with Poland and Czechoslovakia. Germany had won the war in the East. German soldiers had given their lives to restore eastern boundaries in what had been Prussia, part of the original German Empire. Now a piece of paper, a treaty, was washing away the spilled blood of German soldiers.

"The proposal of the Polish Commission," Lloyd George wrote, "that we should place 2,100,000 Germans under the control of a people which is of a different religion and which has never proved its capacity for stable self-government throughout its history must, in my judgment, lead sooner or later to a new war in the East of Europe."

When Lloyd George's famous Memorandum was leaked on April 8, 1919, the uproar against his attempt to "water down" the Versailles Treaty caused him to back down, and those seeking to exact harsh reprisals on Germany had their way. The Kaiser was forced to abdicate, creating a political vacuum in one of Europe's wounded, but potentially most powerful countries.

Twenty-one years later, a resurgent Germany would seek to redraw the map of eastern Europe, and Paul Claudius would go from winding motors and "working" as an engineer for the Siemens Company to "serving" as an engineer, first in France, then on the Eastern Front.[106]

---

[106] World War II began in 1939 in Poland. As predicted by Lloyd George, the Polish government's attempt to govern the 2,100,000 Germans who found themselves within its borders was a failure. Germans under Polish rule in cities like Danzig felt oppressed. Poland was sitting on the Germans in a conglomerated cultural "mess" in what was once Prussia, bolstering its legitimacy to do so via the Versailles Treaty and assurances from France and Britain to come to its rescue in the event that Germany would decide to reestablish old borders in the East.

It is ironic in the 21st Century that Poland has agreed to the placement of US missiles on its soil as a supposed deterrent to rogue states in the Middle East. Russia views the missiles as a provocation. Russian leaders see the missile installations as a threat, not to far-away rogue states in the Middle East, but rather to Russia. To Russian leaders, this represents part of a master plan by the US and NATO to "surround" Russia. The placement of missiles, along with written protective agreements between the US, Poland and the Czeck Republic, where the US plans to install radar stations to compliment the Polish missiles, could, as per the words in Lloyd Georges' 1919 Memorandum, "lead sooner or later to a new war in the East of Europe," . . . . and beyond.

of a people which is of a different religion and which has never proved its capacity for stable self-government throughout its history must, in my judgment, lead sooner or later to a new war in the East of Europe."

When Lloyd George's famous Memorandum was leaked on April 8, 1919, the uproar against his attempt to "water down" the Versailles Treaty caused him to back down, and those seeking to exact harsh reprisals on Germany had their way. The Kaiser was forced to abdicate, creating a political vacuum in one of Europe's wounded, but potentially most powerful countries.

Twenty-one years later, a resurgent Germany would seek to redraw the map of eastern Europe, and Paul Claudius would go from winding motors and "working" as an engineer for the Siemens Company to "serving" as an engineer, first in France, then on the Eastern Front.[106]

---

[106] World War II began in 1939 in Poland. As predicted by Lloyd George, the Polish government's attempt to govern the 2,100,000 Germans who found themselves within its borders was a failure. Germans under Polish rule in cities like Danzig felt oppressed. Poland was sitting on the Germans in a conglomerated cultural "mess" in what was once Prussia, bolstering its legitimacy to do so via the Versailles Treaty and assurances from France and Britain to come to its rescue in the event that Germany would decide to reestablish old borders in the East.

It is ironic in the 21st Century that Poland has agreed to the placement of US missiles on its soil as a supposed deterrent to rogue states in the Middle East. Russia views the missiles as a provocation. Russian leaders see the missile installations as a threat, not to far-away rogue states in the Middle East, but rather to Russia. To Russian leaders, this represents part of a master plan by the US and NATO to "surround" Russia. The placement of missiles, along with written protective agreements between the US, Poland and the Czeck Republic, where the US plans to install radar stations to compliment the Polish missiles, could, as per the words in Lloyd Georges' 1919 Memorandum, "lead sooner or later to a new war in the East of Europe," .... and beyond.

love as both sweet and sad. All striving, according to von Eichendorf, was an unquenchable quest for our eternal home, and everything transitory a symbol of eternity. Man must often pay a price for his unquenchable desires.

The letters of Paul Claudius reflect all aspects of von Eichendorf's writings and the *Romantic Movement*. God, nature, folk and fatherland were the guiding principles in the life of Paul Claudius. He admired the French and continually wrote about nature, the preservation of his family and the Reich.

In his admiration of what he considered the carefree life of the Frenchman, he echoed a facet of Romantic philosophy portrayed by von Eichendorf and other Romantic authors, the concept of being free to live as one wants. In Paul Claudius's mind, however, he was bound to do his duty to the Reich to gain the ability to live as he wished, to return home to his beloved Distelhof, his wife, his children and his garden. And he truly paid the price for his "unquenchable desires."

Blood and Paper.

On March 25, 1919, twenty-four years before Paul Claudius enlisted in the Wehrmacht, Prime Minister David Lloyd George issued his Fountainbleu Memorandum in an attempt to "tempter" the Treaty of Versailles, which he viewed as filled with arrogance and injustice in regard to Germany. The Fountainbleu Memorandum became one of the most prophetic documents in history. Lloyd George described the German people as a "people who have certainly proved themselves one of the most vigorous and powerful races in the world."

The Treaty of Versailles took away German World War I victory in the East, a victory that had settled border disputes with Poland and Czechoslovakia. Germany had won the war in the East. German soldiers had given their lives to restore eastern boundaries in what had been Prussia, part of the original German Empire. Now a piece of paper, a treaty, was washing away the spilled blood of German soldiers.

"The proposal of the Polish Commission," Lloyd George wrote, "that we should place 2,100,000 Germans under the control

Author Credits

Prologue.............................Jack R. Meister
Poetry & My Family Research..... Erika Wolfe
Translations..........................Jack R. Meister
Notebook Intro......................Erika Wolfe
Footnotes & Research...............Jack R. Meister
Erika Wolfe

Postscripts &
Historical Perspectives..............Jack R. Meister

LaVergne, TN USA
22 October 2009

161766LV00002B/2/P